PRACTICAL JUNG

Nuts and Bolts of Jungian Psychotherapy

Harry A. Wilmer, M.D., Ph.D.

Chiron Publications
Wilmette, Illinois

Printed in the United States of America

Second Printing

Edited by Priscilla Coit Murphy and Ann Taylor
Book design by Kirk George Panikis

Library of Congress Cataloging-in-Publication Data

Wilmer, Harry A., 1917–
Practical Jung.
Bibliography: p.
Includes index.
1. Psychotherapy. 2. Jung, C. G. (Carl Gustav), 1875–1961. I. Title.
RC480.5.W49 1988 150.19'54 87-18233
ISBN 0-933029-24-1
ISBN 0-933029-16-0 (pbk.)

With love to Jane Harris Wilmer,
my wife and companion for over forty years

Also by the author

HUBER THE TUBER: THE LIVES AND LOVES OF A TUBERCLE BACILLUS
CORKY THE KILLER: A STORY OF SYPHILIS
THIS IS YOUR WORLD
SOCIAL PSYCHIATRY IN ACTION
THE MIND—FIRST STEPS
VIETNAM IN REMISSION

I am, more specifically, simply a psychiatrist, for my essential problem, to which all my efforts are directed, is psychic disturbance: its phenomenology, aetiology, and teleology. Everything else is secondary for me. I do not feel called upon to found a religion, nor to proclaim my belief in one. I am not engaged in philosophy, but merely thinking within the framework of a special task laid upon me: to be a proper psychiatrist, a healer of the soul. That is what I have discovered myself to be and this is how I function as a member of society.

Jung, *Collected Letters*, Vol. 2, pp. 70–71

Jung listening, around 1942.

The round table in the garden, at which the speakers and others at the conference met daily for meals. When Jung saw this picture, he remarked to the Iranologist Henry Corbin, *"L'image est parfaite. Ils sont tous là."*

Acknowledgments

I am grateful to Louise Mahdi who, upon seeing the Jung syllabus I prepared for students at the University of Texas Health Science Center at San Antonio, persuaded me to write this book and encouraged me at every step.

I am grateful to James S. Waldron, Director of Educational Resources at the above university, who sat in on my Jung seminars in a program to help professors with their instructional work and material. He not only gave good advice on the seminar but led me to write the syllabus. Betty Sue Flowers, Associate Professor of English, University of Texas at Austin, read my manuscript and syllabus and gave me many helpful suggestions. My editors Priscilla Coit Murphy and Ann Taylor were of great help, as was Kirk Panikis with the book design.

I am grateful to Joseph Wheelwright for introducing me to Jungian psychology and working with me on my teaching unit at the University of California in San Francisco. I appreciate the help and wisdom of C. A. Meier in Zurich. Finally, Joseph Henderson, who wrote the preface for this book, has always been an inspiration to me as both sage and practical Jungian analyst, who knew Jung and worked with him, and whom I count as a friend.

Contents

Foreword

Dr. Harry Wilmer is a man of many talents, one of which is his ability to discuss the data of psychotherapy in a refreshingly unconventional manner. His discussion of Jungian psychology does justice to its subject leaving out no essential part of Jung's theoretical contribution, yet remains true to those principles of treatment that are to be found in any authentic form of depth analysis. No wonder his nuts-and-bolts approach found approval with his psychiatry and psychology students as he tells us in his very explicit introduction that follows. Although he refers to himself as an *eclectic Jungian,* I think he deserves a legitimate place in the hierarchy of those whose training was acquired in the mainline tradition of the Freudian practitioners who became Jungian in an evolutionary process similar to that in which Jung found himself by separating from Freud's early influence and founding his own school of thought.

There are two ways of teaching that are well represented by Dr. Wilmer. One is cognitive and the other is conative; the first relies upon the function of thinking and the second, upon the function of feeling. Both, according to Jung, are rational functions understandable to any mature person, but their expression widely differs. Cognitive psychology relies upon logic and intellectual discrimination, whereas conative psychology has to do with values other than ideas and is best expressed by imagery of all kinds all the way from great works of art with their universal meaning to the personal idiosyncracies of human body language, so well shown in Dr. Wilmer's photographs, cartoons, and diagrams.

But this book is not only a form of teaching; it provides a good outline of Jung's psychology for the general reader. Most previous outlines of this kind have been concerned with theory more than practice, and where they have used visual imagery it is chiefly in the form of illustrations by artists other than the author. I am thinking of Jung's picture book, *Man and His Symbols,* and Esther Harding's exposition of analytical psychology in *The I and the Not-I.* Good as they are, they lack something we find here. Harry Wilmer's innovative personality is comfortable in producing both literary and artistic forms of his own and creations liberally embellished with relevant quotations and images from widely different sources. This allows him to present his material clearly and with a view that communicates very well in a general way yet remains his very own.

Joseph L. Henderson, M.D.

Introduction

The psychology of C.G. Jung has attracted increasing numbers of people because of its helpful, hopeful, and unique ways of experiencing the human psyche. With due consideration of religion and the spirit of individuals, it also embraces the collective history of humanity. With its emphasis on individuation, wholeness, and centering, there is consequently a focus on the healthy elements of the human mind and soul and a quest for balance. It is unusual to think of presenting Jungian psychology as *practical* since so many people are caught up in its complexities, its depth, and concern with far-out things. But *practical Jung* is the viewpoint of this book, because it is my viewpoint.

The spiritual and archetypal world, alchemy, typology, complexes, the esoteric and the occult, mythology, and mythologems tend to put people off, not because they are uninteresting, but because they seem useless to practical-minded American psychotherapists and individuals working with the human psyche in all kinds of healing relationships. Indeed, Jung's writing is often obscure and difficult to read and understand—without studying it carefully and taking pains to read it thoughtfully.

This is a how-to book. It is a distillation of my forty years of experience in psychiatry and medicine as therapist and patient, analyst and analysand, teacher and pupil, and supervisor and student. In this book I try to offer thoughtful and intuitive ways to integrate and implement both my own psychology and that of C.G. Jung.

For fourteen years I have taught a seminar in Jungian psychology at the University of Texas Health Science Center in San Antonio, which is a requirement for psychiatric residents. I have taught two elective seminars in analytical psychology: "Nuts and Bolts of the Practice of Psychotherapy" and "Dreams." A printed syllabus for students contains diagrams I made to illustrate my points, and these are the basis for the drawings in this book.

I have been pleasantly surprised when my students showed a keen interest in these Jungian seminars because hardly any of them have had personal experience in the analysis of their own archetypal world or in personal psychoanalysis. Although Freudian analysis is the basis of most of their training in psychodynamics, they were refreshingly open-minded about an alternative approach. Possibly they were intrigued by the way these ideas were conveyed as well.

Basically this book is a nuts-and-bolts application of Carl Gustav Jung's psychology in the light of the actual interactions between therapists and their patients. Students and beginning psychotherapists are often perplexed by new experiences and encounters which might never have even crossed their minds. They are often mired down with dogmatic theories, rote techniques, or worse, the habit of playing psychotherapist by the seat of their pants. People tend to cling to single explanations when there are multiple hypotheses to explain or interpret whatever happens between individuals. The nuts-and-bolts approach of practical Jung offers insight into multiple working hypotheses and alternate ways of understanding the psyche.

Psychotherapy opens up wounds that, if mishandled, may become worse or may not heal. It almost goes without saying that any method of treatment can be misused. The intimacy of psychotherapy and the power projected upon the therapist make that potential misuse especially dangerous. This book highlights ways for both patient and therapist to recognize when the wrong direction has been taken and alerts them to positive ways of coping with such problems, ways in which what might have gone wrong is turned into what can be most helpful in psychological growth.

The focus of this book is not traditional psychopathology, reductive analysis, or big interpretations. It is about what is and what facilitates an I-Thou relationship. It is about ordinary courtesy and human concern without sentimental shibboleths. It takes the therapist down a peg or two and puts the relationship of patient and therapist up a couple of pegs.

I have generally used the generic term *he* for the doctor, resident, and patient. I use the term *patient* because it comes naturally to me, and I find that *patient* carries a certain dignity. You can substitute *client, person, she,* or whatever seems right for you.

The philosophy of my approach is influenced by my early Freudian training and my later, extensive Jungian training. You might say I am an eclectic Jungian. While this book is titled *Practical Jung,* the practice of Jungian psychotherapy is no trick and cannot be done with the simplistic use of profound writings, or by rote and clever techniques. Rather, it is done with disciplined hard work in reflecting in a creative spirit of sophisticated play.

I sometimes wonder what C.G. Jung might have thought about my nuts-and-bolts approach. I do know that he was always interested in what works; and for me and my students, this works. A how-to book on depth psychology is a paradox, but it expresses the subtle, dynamic, illogical, non-mechanical, and irrational psyche with all its power for healing, as well as destruction. I am not foolish enough to think that my *Rules of Thumb* are any more than my truth. Every teacher conveys rules of thumb, labeled or intimated. At best they are wise aphorisms, at worst, psychic flimflam. In my book they are manifestations of grappling with the inordinate amount of garbage which characterizes many psychological formulations.

On June 4, 1907, Jung wrote Freud, "I'd like to make an amusing picture-book in this style, to be enjoyed only by those who have eaten of the tree of knowledge. The rest would go away empty-handed." (McGuire, *Freud/Jung Letters,* p. 57). Two days later Freud answered.

> A picture-book such as the one you are thinking of would be highly instructive. Above all, it would provide a general view of the architectonics of the cases. I have several times attempted something of the sort, but I was always too ambitious. To be sure of making everything absolutely clear, I tried to show all the complications and consequently got stuck every time. But why shouldn't you attempt such a project in earnest? (*ibid.,* p. 59)

I have tried to avoid the two pitfalls which blocked these giants—creating something to be enjoyed only by those who have eaten of the tree of knowledge and being too ambitious.

Harry A. Wilmer
Salado, Texas

PART

I

Nuts and Bolts

Charlie Chaplin in Modern Times

We are always at risk of taking ourselves too seriously and taking those we care for too lightly. Both theory and clinical exposition become ponderous, and we need some knack of looking anew at the old, to reexamine ways of helping others, and in the process to reexamine ourselves. To simplify this with rules of thumb is one way to get things straight. When the *thing* at issue is the human mind, we need any help we can get. "The human mind, in its never-ending changes, is like the flowing water of a river or the burning flame of a candle; like an ape, it is forever jumping about not ceasing for a moment."

(*The Teaching of Buddha*, p. 94)

In this spirit let us begin.

Rules of Thumb

Rules of thumb, not absolute rules but guiding rules, we invoke for the:

impasse,
predicament,
pickle, plight,
or dilemma,

and if that's not enough, try:

quagmire, tight spot,
kettle of fish, muddle,
cul-de-sac,
or Sisyphean task.

RULE OF THUMB:
Too much is too much.
Keep it simple.

RULE OF THUMB: The Beginning
No problem where to begin.
"Wherever you are is the entry point."
(The Bijak of Kabir, *Parabola*, pp. 95–96)

But the great thing is here and now, this is the eternal moment, and if you do not realize it, you have missed the best part of your life; you will have missed the realization that you are the carrier of a life contained between the poles of an unimaginable future and an unimaginably remote past. Millions of years and untold millions of ancestors have worked up to this moment. Anything that is past is no longer reality, anything that is ahead is not yet reality, reality is now. . . . Therefore in our psychology, in the life of the individual, it is of the greatest importance that we never think of the situation as merely now, with the hope of something coming in the future. You may be sure it will never come if you think like that. You must live life in such a spirit that you make in every moment the best of the possibilities.

(Jung, *Interpretation of Visions*, vol. 6, pp. 103–104)

RULE OF THUMB: Don't Point

I call this phenomenon the *First Finger Singular*.
People point the first finger.
It is a favorite pose of pedants on camera,
of politicians and news-making authorities.
We see it in the media all the time—
—people stabbing away to make a point.

Vice President George Bush

Australian Prime Minister Bob Hawke

Annie Oakley

"Mark my word," the father said, pointing
his index finger.
Sonny boy went through life
always looking for a daddy to point the way
or a mamma whose pointer carried a big charge.

Beware of pointing your real or psychological finger
at your patient. You may create a sensation, but
you will never make your point that way,
jab as you may.
Each one of us has to find our inner compass arrow
to point direction. We need to point ourselves,
if you get the point.

Watch out for subtle, sub rosa pointers.
They get under your skin before you know it.
How do you discern the phantom pointers?
By putting your finger on your hunch:
thus finding the meaning of the First Finger Singular,
wherever it may roam.

Remember the metaphor of the dancing finger:
trembling, fumbling, tyrannical, blaming,
authoritarian, absolute, assuming, accusing.
Heed the metaphors of the finger pose
and note it in your *Mental Catalogue of Finger Registers*.
Or just

Don't point!

Israeli Cabinet Member Ezer Weizman and Egyptian President Hosni Mubarak

More Pointers on First Fingers

The exact tilt of the raised
finger is a matter that only
connoisseurs of indignation,
righteousness and *upfingermanship*
can savor.

The rest of us, pointed at, over,
down, up, to, and into, know that
the need to jab points across
reveals a lot about both the
jabbers and the jabbees.
It is not for no reason that
there is a nail in the end of the finger.

Rod Steiger as W. C. Fields

First Finger Signals

Jung in conversation with Sir Herbert Read
makes his point toward the sky.
A judicious use of pointing helps us get around,
find the right thing, the right person, or object.
Freud would have had a simple displacement theory
for the phallic finger and would have made his point
pointedly. Jung seems to be hovering over a mandala.
A finger is a finger most all of the time.

First Finger may not be Singular, but the point of
a graceful ballet of the hand
indicates more or less what we don't know.

The first finger may point with an open hand in an open gesture. The upside-down point is in this instance a beautiful human gesture.

Zeus Himself Fears Wrath of Weinberger

A banner headline in the *New York Times*: the gods and secular power? Is this a joke?

Secretary Caspar Weinberger

The archetypal nature of Caspar Weinberger's rage was
that of the greatest of the gods.
The collective nature of power is caught in the article:
"Weinberger has managed to transmogrify himself into something closely resembling a touchy foreign power." ("Senate Appropriation Committee Meeting," *New York Times*, 26 July 1984)
First finger singular grasps the lightning bolts of two pencils
and with a chin-down scowl, he holds the enemy at bay.
Power—Oh my God—Power.
Finger the enemy and you have spotted evil with the right trigger finger.

Soviet Foreign Minister Andrei Gromyko

Power is a kind of aphrodisiac.

First Finger may not be the *Singular* finger
I have been talking about, not always;
but it is a gesture of potency.

If you like to lecture to your patients,
try to keep your first finger down
and open your hands.

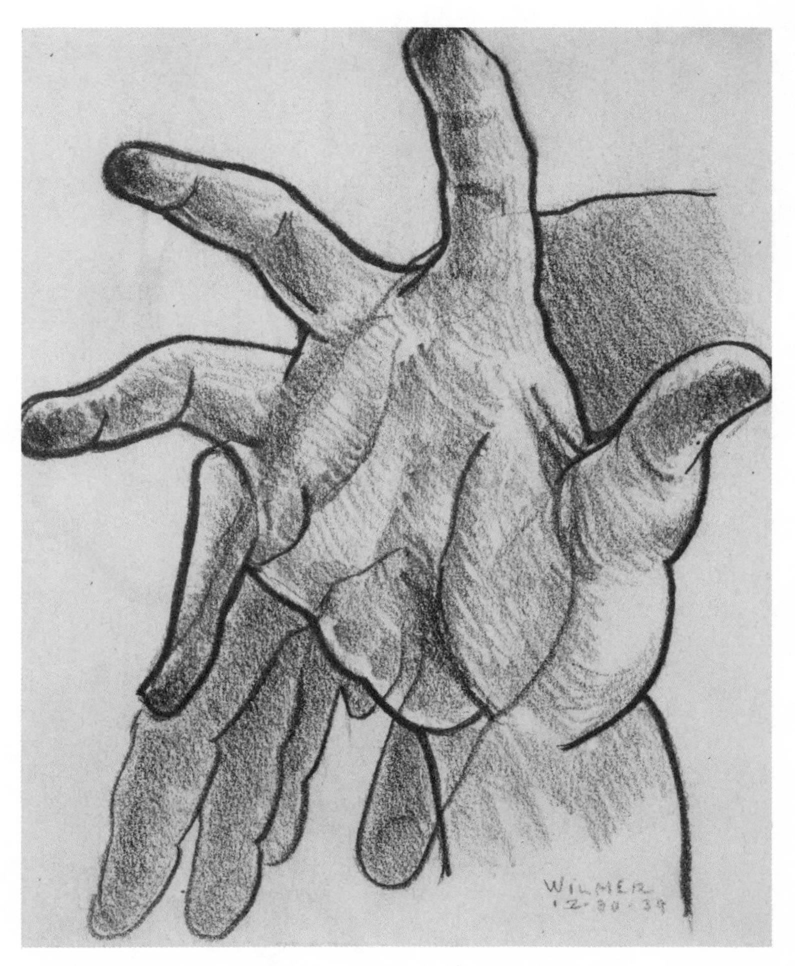

Two hands holding between them a connecting space;
the first finger is no longer singular even on one hand.

La Malinche between Cortes and the Indians, in Florentine Codex, *XII*
(Biblioteca Laurentiana, Florence)

First Finger Singular is nothing new.

The Political Persona:
There is nothing new under the sun.

The professor is always in a good spot to point the finger to his heavenly authority, and it is no wonder he gets god-like omnipotent projections when he himself would not raise a finger to refute the divinely pleasant positive transference. He has to hold on for dear life with his other unseen hand to keep one hand from knowing what the other is doing. This is called trying to get a hold on yourself, while you make your point.

The ultimate index finger symbol: Model of Saturn rocket fastened to the tower of the cathedral in Utrecht to mark a space exhibit in the city. The dark sky is a kind of celestial commentary.

A Little Story of Hands

The little boy was walking across the lawn
followed by his mother.
She made her points explicit by touching
the tips of the first three fingers of one hand
with the index finger of the other.
"Make up your mind!" she said.
"What do you want for dinner: hamburger, chili, or stew?"
One, two, three.
"Fish," the little boy replied.
"I don't have time for that. Make up your mind:
hamburger, chili, or stew?"

Well, he had made up his mind, hadn't he?
It was her mind that was not made up.

A Memory

When my own children were small,
I took the five of them to an ice cream store.
"What flavor do you want?" I asked generously.
All hell broke loose.
Assorted choices and changing of minds rang out.
I got angry.
So I said, "I'll get a chocolate ice cream cone
for everyone who wants an ice cream cone."
Just one flavor: no choice.
"If you don't like it, then no ice cream cone."
When their hurt looks simmered to resignation
and I held up old index finger in my mind,
they all had chocolate ice cream cones and were happy.

Touching is Another Matter

The touching business worries the students:
Fond of? Scared of embracing?
Warmth? Intimacy? Kindness? Affection?
Or seduction—more or less?
When is a hug a hug?
Who makes the first move?

Of course, you can always shake hands.
Not a bad idea if you are unsure of your motives,
like the hunter who brought two monkeys to the taxidermist.
"Do you want them mounted?" he asked.
"No. Just shaking hands."

Holding hands may be all right on some occasions.
Rarely.
The students and I agree that hugging some patients
at the end of an hour may be in order:
a grieving patient, for example,
and some others who are tense, lonely, or frightened,
always provided that
common sense takes precedence.

RULE OF THUMB:
Don't hug patients for kicks.

You don't hug patients as a part of therapy:
It is a part of human contact, of being human-to-human.
Then it's I-Thou, and how.

RULE OF THUMB: Hugging, i
You need not be afraid to hug a patient provided
you don't need to hug him or her
or touch or put your arm around the other one.
If you are a laid-back person—don't lean over.
If you're a laid-forward person—use restraint.
If you are naturally a reaching-out extravert,
touching, hugging are OK provided
your secret thoughts are not seductive, then you had better shake hands.
Wave if you must.

If a problem is sexuality, don't hug.
You may raise more dust than you can settle.
A hug in the middle of an hour may be suspect;
a hug at the door may be fine.
On the other hand, a choreographed ballet at the door,
a *pas de deux*, needs to be looked at and talked about.
Next hour, please!

At the door, a patient who is leaving the session
suddenly embraces and kisses you.
Then what?
Relax: there's a *Rule of Thumb:*

RULE OF THUMB: Hugging, ii
Stand your ground.
Don't push the other away rudely and say,
"The feeling is not reciprocated."
Just disentangle yourself. That's the rule.
Remember there is probably an element of
real love and affection,
and you have a hook to hang the transference on.

Hugging a Child Patient is Another Thing

Why?
If you stand healthy *in situ parenti,*
an embrace, a pat on the shoulder,
an arm around the child may be
just the warmth the child needs.
But some children who fear being touched
must wait until their antipathy to closeness is less,
or you arouse fear and suspicion,
for which they have good reasons that are bad enough.

For some children, like some adults,
any touching is akin to invasion.
You will know that, if you know your patient.
For them not touching is touching.
The only real touch may be
after a very long time,
maybe not until the last hour of the last day of therapy.

All Alone by the Telephone

Nuts-and-bolts: all variety of telephone calls can be anticipated. Ding-a-ling!

"Hello, this is Tom Jones. I'm a lawyer representing your patient Edgar Lewison. I wonder if you could tell me. . . ."

"Sorry. I can't talk about any patients over the phone. I have no idea who you are. . . ."

"I'm Tom Jones, a. . . ."

"Yes, so you say. I never say anything to anyone over the telephone about whether someone is or is not my patient. I suggest you write me a letter stating what you want and enclose a signed release—original signature—from your client. Good-bye."

"Hello. This is Eric Smith from Dun and Downstreet. We are bringing our records up to date on doctor's offices in this area, and want to ask you a few questions. . . .

"Sorry. Good-bye."

"Hello. This is the Forever Insurance Company. I'm calling about Lou Mary White, a patient of yours. I need some information on a medical charge. . . ."

"Sorry, I never talk over the telephone about such matters. I am astonished you would call and ask. Is this your company policy? Write and send consent forms. Good-bye."

"It is just a matter of. . . ."

"Let me talk to your manager. Hello? Hello?"

"Hello. I'm a friend of your patient Edgar Lewison. I want to tell you something very important about him that you should know. You're going to see him this morning, aren't you?"

"Sorry. I can't listen to your comments. It is my policy never to discuss my patients, or even to acknowledge the identity of any of my patients in any way over the telephone."

"Hello. This is Fred Gunderson of the FBI I want. . . ."
Ditto

"Hello. I am the mother of your patient. . . ."

"Hello. I'm the uncle of your patient. . . ."

"Hello. I'm the employer of your patient. . . ."

"Hello. I'm . . . I'm . . . I'm . . . I'm . . . [ad infinitum].
Ditto

"I don't want you to tell your patient that I called. It is important that I speak to you about. . . ."

"Sorry." Same thing.

RULE OF THUMB: The Telephone, i
Avoid answering the telephone
when you are with a patient.
If you expect an important telephone call that you must answer,
tell your patient ahead of time.
If you have a secretary or answering service,
have them screen your calls,
or plug in your answering device.
Don't get involved in any long-winded phone conversations
with anyone
when you are with a patient.
If you take many calls while you are with your patient,
you can be sure you will turn him off.
The least you can give to your patient
is your undivided attention.

If you must answer the telephone,
give your patient an opportunity to discuss feelings.
If you make a habit of repeatedly answering the telephone
when you are with a patient,
then you are doing too much,
you are being too important,
you are a scatterbrained shrink.

RULE OF THUMB: The Telephone, ii
Obiter dictum:
Never answer the telephone when
you are with a paranoid patient.
Never.
You'll be sorry.
You never know who might be calling, and
more often than you would like—
chance and fate being what they are—
the call will relate to the paranoid patient.
Even if the call doesn't concern him, the patient has suspicions
and projects onto the unknown and uncertain.
It doesn't make any difference if the call is from someone
really connected with the patient
or connected by paranoid projections.
It's the same kettle of fish.

Your not answering the phone
when you are with a seriously paranoid patient
is an excellent model of healthy behavior—
ignoring intrusive thoughts, disturbing voices,
and diversions.
Who's hearing voices anyway?

RULE OF THUMB: The Telephone, iii
A patient asks you if she or
he can call you at home
or at the office before
the next regular appointment.
Rule of Thumb: Use Your Head: Is the patient
(check one) ☐ depressed
☐ suicidal
☐ disturbed
☐ panicky
☐ anxious
☐ a clinger

Let wisdom, experience, discretion, and temperament take over.

You may either invite special trouble, double trouble,
with a resented intrusion into your personal life,
or you may offer a potent psychological elixir
by being available in times of desperation and panic,
a solace and a hope, a symbol and a person.

I rarely discourage patients from calling me
if they feel an overwhelming need.
I do not encourage them to do so, either.
But I give a suicidal patient my home number,
even though it is listed in the telephone book.
In this case I say, call me if need be.
Few people ever abuse the offer.
However, some neurotic patients do call excessively,
and then I listen to them patiently,
do not say much on the phone,
and deal with it at the next visit.

For patients whom I have seen over a long period
who have moved to distant places and
do not want to start over again with someone new,
I sometimes set aside regular appointments
to talk over the telephone.
There was a time when I thought that telephone psychotherapy
was for the birds and the exploiters,
but no more.
I have known it to work in wonderful ways.

RULE OF THUMB: The Telephone, iv
Discourage relatives of patients
from calling you on the telephone.
When you actually know the husband, wife, mother, father, child, or person,
you may opt to listen briefly.
Tell them to tell your patient of the telephone call.
You tell your patient also,
then you don't get enmeshed in a devious or conspiring
maneuver, or fantasies within fantasies.
If you do get involved in unconscious collusion, you will live (hopefully)
to regret it.
If the call is from someone who claims some relationship,
don't accept the call or the message.
If you get caught before you realize what is happening,
then follow this

RULE OF THUMB: The Telephone, v
Get off the connection as gracefully and expeditiously
as possible and do not, repeat, do not,
say anything of any substance.
Say nothing at all.

If annoying calls persist,
tell the caller you cannot accept any more calls.
Unambiguously say no.
It is rarely necessary and usually unadvised
to hang up on anyone.
I guess I've done it a few times.

RULE OF THUMB: The Telephone, vi
Patients make their own appointments.
"Hello. This is Mrs. G. Wiz Johnson. I am
calling to make an appointment for my husband,
Jim, and he is at the office now and asked me
if I would call for him. His problem. . . ."
"Ask him to call me himself, and I will see
what we can arrange."

"Whatever the spirit that calls a kindred spirit will answer." (Novalis)

Remember this wise aphorism.
It will come in handy many times.
It says something profound.

Gifts and Giving

She wanted to give me a very old and valuable carving.
She said it was a precious artifact she had treasured.
It was early in therapy, and I did not want to accept it
because it seemed to me that it was a subtle gesture
creating a surreptitious bond, whose real value I did not know.
I did not want not to take it
or to refuse her gift that was a real token
of gratitude and esteem.
Although she paid my professional fees regularly,
she said that money did not express what she owed me.
Raising the fee would have been falling into a different trap.
She had a powerful need to make a symbolic offering,
and it seemed the wiser course for me to take it.
I told her, "I will keep it for both of us,
as a gift between us now, because
someday you might want it back, or
I might want you to have it again."

I thought that in time she would see her
customary, over-giving generosity as partly beguiling and enchanting,
partly bribing and mesmerizing,
as well as an expression of her truly giving, caring self.
It was important for her to give me something symbolic other than money.
It is important for me to remember to give it back someday.

Giving for some people is buying power over people.
It disguises an inner shadow of dark and ominous images of worthlessness
and low esteem.
It may be both escape from, and entrapment in bondage.
The inner treasures need not and cannot be given away.
When my patient learns to value the material world less
and to feel the radiance of her inner treasure and her spirit more,
her substance that casts the shadow will be revealed.
Then she can have her gift and join the human comedy
of the ordinary world.

Another Clinical Story

A woman patient left a beautiful picture book of the Swiss Alps
on my desk inscribed, "In appreciation."
I wrote her a short note
expressing my surprise at finding the book
and thanking her for the gift of the images
that we both loved.
When I saw her at the next session,
she told me that she had tormented herself over whether
or not to leave the book on my desk
and felt strangely freed by my letter.
Her anguish was over giving me something she could not
bring herself to hand me,
for fear that I would refuse it or analyze it
into nothingness.

She was afraid I would make her feel guilty,
so she left the Alps on my desk.
Freely given. Freely taken. Free of guilt.
No big deal.
Thank you very much.
"Was it appropriate?" she wondered to herself.
Was it appropriate for me to write her a thank-you note?
Yes.
Yes.

The Other Side of the Coin

It was a different story
when a near-destitute man brought me a valuable gift.
As a matter of fact, his deplorable financial situation
resulted from his cavalier extravagance.
He managed always just to squeak by. Always.
I said I would keep the gift until we had a chance
to talk about it.
When he found out the meaning of his giving,
I did my giving
back.

The Umbrella

Once upon a time, a woman patient left an umbrella
in my waiting room on the last day of her analysis.
She moved far away.
Three years later she came back
to pay me a visit and tell me
how positive her life had been since
she had completed her analysis.
She had just one question,
could she have her umbrella back?
Did I have it?
Yes.

I had had a hunch when I saw that she had left the umbrella
that she would someday come to retrieve it, and so
I had kept it in the closet.
She was pleasantly surprised when I produced it
without explanation. Just gave it back.
She was grateful because now she could leave
knowing I had remembered her
and her symbolic gift.
After all, it might have rained.

More of the Gifts of the Gifted

At the end of an initial interview with a new patient,
I ask a question, more or less like this:

If I were smart enough or clever enough,
what question might I ask you, or what might
you have told me about yourself, that would
be of vital importance to understand you?
Anything whatsoever.

It is amazing the things I find out that way.

What are the Gifts of a Naturally Gifted Therapist?

Talent and skill,
saying the right thing at the right moment.
This would be a golden rule if it could be reduced to a rule.
A klutz, on the other hand, has the gift of glib gab.
Giving freely is the only way to give appropriately.
Taking without hidden strings and without greed
is the way to take.
Charity begins at home—with yourself.
Be charitable, so you can be charitable
to others.
Here, here!

The gifted therapist,
at least in my eyes,
has a natural openness, an inherent anti-unctuousness,
an inherent self-respect nurtured by life experiences,
successes and failures,
and a capacity to overcome "the noble temptation
to see too much in everything." (G. K. Chesterton)

The gifted therapist does not say "when all things
are going badly that all is well." (Voltaire)

He or she has a capacity to sense that "nature has given to men
one tongue but two ears, that we may hear
from others twice as much as we speak." (Epictetus)

and the ability "to watch out wh'n you er gittin'
all you want. Fattenin' hogs ain't in luck." (Joel Chandler Harris)

The gifted therapist realizes that "if we want light
we must conquer darkness." (J. T. Fields)

"Judge every word and deed which are according to nature to be fit for thee;
and be not diverted by the blame which follows from any people, nor
by their words, but if a thing is good to be done and said, do not consider it
unworthy of thee. For those persons have their peculiar leading principle
and follow their peculiar movement; which things do not thou regard, but
go straight on, following thy own nature and the common nature; and the
way of both is one." (Marcus Aurelius)

RULE OF THUMB: Don't Bemoan Your Fate as Being Unappreciated
It might be negative transference.
On the other hand, it might be right.
There is an Irish saying:
"People who complain they don't get all they deserve
should congratulate themselves."

Plato was imprisoned by the tyrant Dionysius
and sold as a slave;
he was finally ransomed by one of his academicians.
Aristotle was put in prison as an atheist.
Ovid was exiled.
Luigi Galvani was crowned with a clown's cap,
laughed at, and dubbed the dancing master of frogs.
The physicist du Moncel demonstrated Edison's phonograph
at the French Academy of Sciences on March 11, 1878.
When the machine suddenly began to talk
and repeated faithfully the words that
du Moncel had recorded a few moments previously,
Jean Bouillard, a famous physician, 83 years old,
rushed to his feet, grabbed the platform, and roared,
"You wretch! How dare you deceive us
with this ridiculous trick of a ventriloquist?"
Six months later Bouillard spoke to the academy,
still maintaining that the phonograph
was a ventriloquist's trick.
This is an example of a sane man hearing voices.
(Tabori, *Natural History of Stupidity*, p. 154)

Sir Walter Raleigh spent 13 years imprisoned
in the Tower of London.
He began an eight volume history of the world,
and got as far as 130 B.C.
(*ibid.*, p. 165)

Voltaire was twice in the Bastille and then exiled.
Cyrano de Bergerac is remembered through Rostand's play,
but he was a forgotten persecuted genius.
Twelve editions of his books were destroyed
by a mysterious brotherhood that persecuted
anti-religious, anti-government literature.
When he was dying someone stole his last manuscript,
"The History of the Spark."
(*ibid.*, p. 164)

RULE OF THUMB: Rude Humor
Avoid joining in your patient's delusions.
Avoid flippant, rude humor,
because you will sound crazier and funnier than he does.
For example,
I placed a patient in a mental hospital 35 years ago.
He was in an acute manic phase of a manic-depressive disorder.

There were no effective antipsychotic drugs in those days.
When I came to see him the second morning,
he was in a large tub of very warm, running water
with a canvas cover laced over him.
He was in high spirits in the tub,
jovial and raucous, singing sailor chanteys.
I approached the tub and said with a smile,
"What is the name of your ship?"
He stopped singing, looked sternly at me,
and replied, "I'm in a tub, you boob."
I never forgot that lesson.

In the Navy

A psychiatrist friend of mine was making rounds one morning.
He stood in the doorway of a seclusion room
looking at a psychotic patient crouching in the corner.
The "crazy" patient shouted an order:
"Let me out of here, I'm an admiral!"
The psychiatrist stood at attention, and said,
"Aye aye, sir."
Before he could utter another word,
the crouching sailor sprang at him,
and decked him.

Rules of Thumb as General Lessons

Six Lessons in Search of Therapists

(lettre d'envoi—letter of advice)

1. There is a difference between pinball, bean-ball, and on-the-ball psychotherapy. (Better to be with it than in it, or out of it, or without it).
2. Only with caution lift the lid of the id of the kid (or anyone else for that matter).
3. Never raise more dust that you can settle. (This doesn't mean you have to keep it clean.)
4. Never cut when you can untie. (It is simpler, better, and less bloody.)
5. Avoid techniques of desperation. (If you are lost, forget it, keep quiet, or admit it. Don't run either way. Heroism is the shortest career there is and often fatal.)
6. *Non nocere primum*. (If you can't do good, don't do harm.)

RULE OF THUMB: Be clear!

Muddiness is not merely a disturber of prose, it is also a destroyer of life, of hope: death on the highway caused by a badly worded road sign; heart-break among lovers caused by a misplaced phrase in a well-intentioned letter. . . . Usually we think only of the ludicrous aspects of ambiguity. But think of the tragedies that are rooted in ambiguity; think of that side, and be clear! When you say something, make sure you have said it. The chances of your having said it are only fair.

(Strunk and White, pp. 79–80)

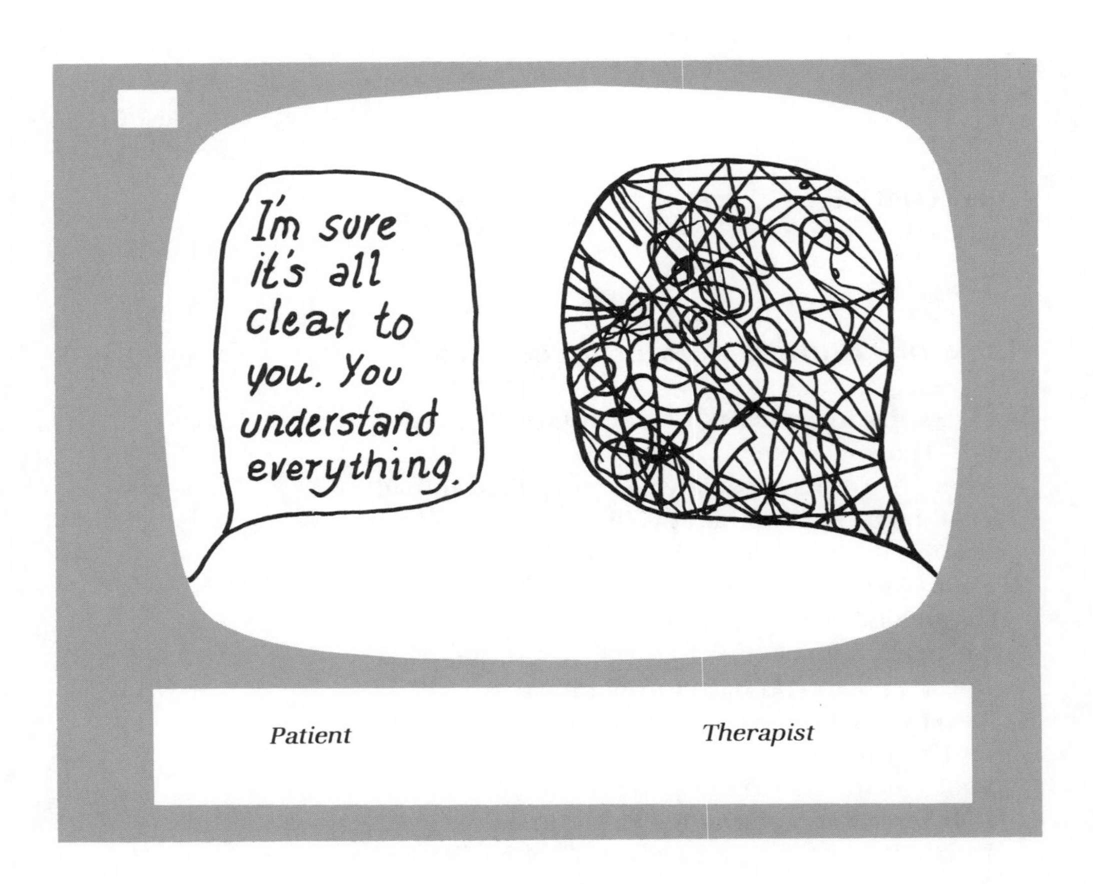

All beginnings are small. Therefore we must not mind doing tedious but conscientious work on obscure individuals, even though the goal towards which we strive seems unattainably far off. But one goal we can attain, and that is to develop and bring to maturity individual personalities. And inasmuch as we are convinced that the individual is the carrier of life, we have served life's purpose if one tree at least succeeds in bearing fruit, though a thousand others remain barren. Anyone who proposed to bring all growing things to the highest pitch of luxuriance would soon find the weeds—those hardiest of perennials—waving above his head. I therefore consider it the prime task of psychotherapy today to pursue with singleness of purpose the goal of individual development. So doing, our efforts will follow nature's own striving to bring life to the fullest possible fruition in each individual, for only in the individual can life fulfil its meaning—not in the bird that sits in a gilded cage.

(Jung, CW 16:229)

Psychopathology means. . . .

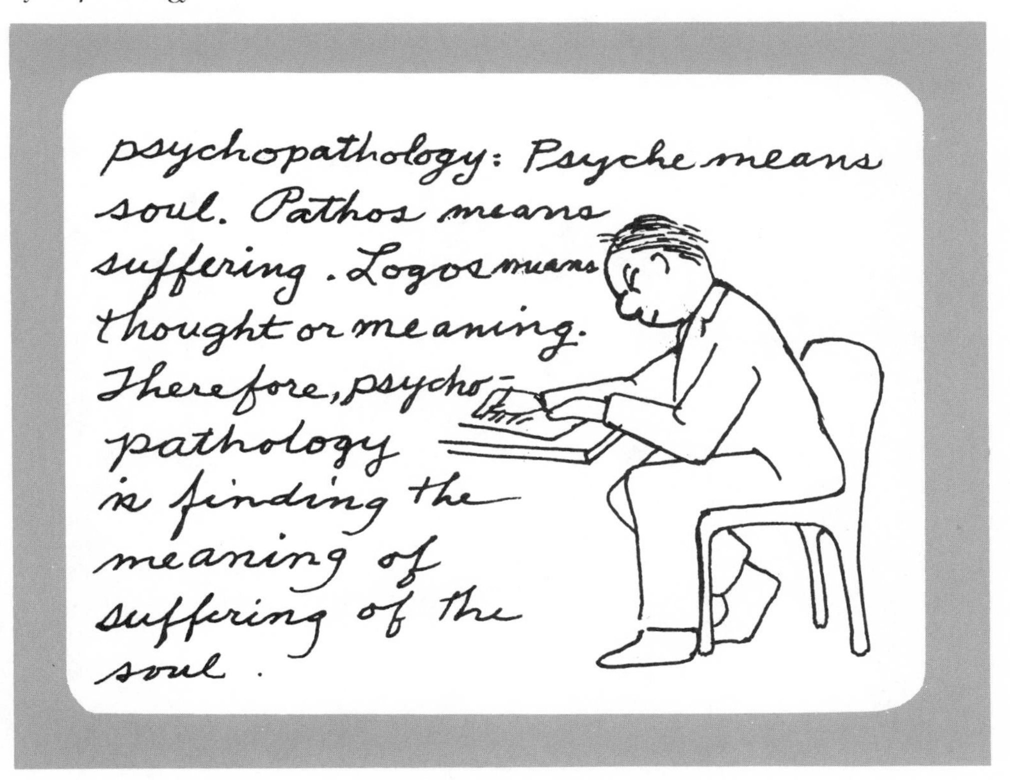

PART

II

Transference and Countertransference

Transference-Countertransference

Every therapist experiences love in the transference;
it's a kind of inevitable *rondo unconscioso* that is
projected by the patient onto the therapist.
We don't know how it happens or why it really happens,
therefore it is irrational.
What lies deeply buried in the psyche beyond
conscious comprehension is experienced outside in someone else.
There is always a reality basis,
some hook on which to hang the projection,
something that is actually lovable or hateable.
Hate in the transference is the same phenomenon.
The problem comes when the therapist takes it too personally.
The patient has to cope with something on top of the transference—
the countertransference.
The patient evokes love or hate in the therapist.
The big problem comes when the therapist is unconscious
of countertransference.

Sounds complicated?
It is. But it is a key to human relationships.

Both transference and countertransference
have their roots in childhood,
in the repressed memories, feelings, and images from
parental figures or others who were very close
to the child.
These powerful feelings also have their source
in the actual relationship of patient and therapist.
It is important always to remember
the unconscious is unconscious until we are conscious of it,
even then it only comes to us in glimpses.

There are transference and countertransference feelings
that do not come from our repressed personal life memories
but from the collective unconscious,
the deepest realm of the unconscious which is
our inherited psyche.

Every therapist encounters transference.
Every therapist experiences countertransference,
irrational thoughts and feelings about the patient,
not all face transference and countertransference.
Many about-face.

Countertransference implies that the therapist's transference
is evoked by the patient's transference.

That is not always the case.
It can be there on its own,
just like the patient's transference.

Often in subtle or not so subtle ways, the therapist
is caught in the web of transference-countertransference.
In every case it is the therapist's responsibility
not to be blind
and to create a safe, caring space,
in which the patient can face these projections,
and come to understand them without the danger
of being either the victim or the victimizer
of strong unconscious forces.

RULE OF THUMB: A Blank Screen
The therapist is more than a blank screen,
more than an anonymous figure behind a couch.
The therapist is real enough
and no more than enough.

The therapist also gets shadow projections
of badness, evil, hatred, jealousy, rage, and anger
and of Olympian, omnipotent, godlike, and priestly powers.
Savior and guru: oh, it's so tempting to believe.
In the love-hate diathesis, the patient and therapist
are carried by powerful forces
between Charybdis and Scylla.

RULE OF THUMB: Love in the Transference, i
A nuts-and-bolts approach acknowledges first
that there is a reality to the love transference.
It is precarious to explain to a patient
that his or her love transference is a neurosis
caused by the treatment or that it is
unreal and different than real love,
because all falling in love is a kind of transference.
Everyone knows that people in love are not rational.
They are in another world caught together.

RULE OF THUMB: Love in the Transference, ii
Avoid immediate reductive interpretations of
the love transference.
Repeat: avoid analysis of the love in terms of
omnipotent, infantile parental projections.
The first rule is to honor and respect
the dignity of love.

Acknowledge some reality basis inherent in the relationship.
This is good for the patient and the therapist.
It is ego. But it is not enough.
The problem is to resolve these illogical feelings
so that neither positive nor negative transference
dominates therapy and holds it stagnant and in turmoil.

RULE OF THUMB: Love in the Transference, iii
Do not, repeat, do not return the love confession,
"I love you," even if you think you do.
The therapist must have an inner love
that transcends physical love.

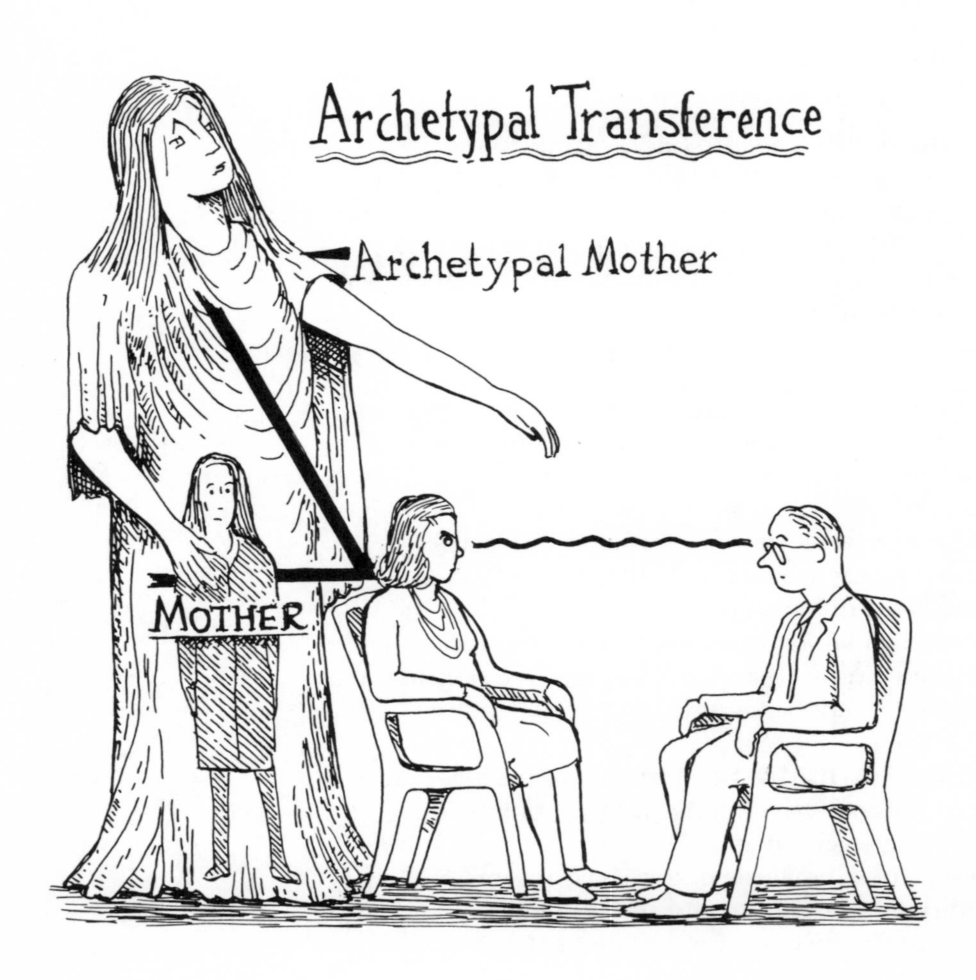

Not returning the love that is offered
is the greater love.
Disciplined therapists are professional
in the highest sense of the word.
Amateur therapists fly by the seat of their pants.
Better scratch *pants* and replace it with *emotion*.
If you are a true-blue professional, you will say *affect*.

More about sex later.
For now let us look more closely at
Transference-Countertransference from the point of view
of practical Jung. Take mother projections for example.

When the patient says *mother*, thinks *mother*, or
is unconsciously *mother*, the therapist
is in an interesting place.
He will see first his patient,
then her mother, and if he has 20/20 psychological vision
he will see her mother archetype.
Indeed, he will hear the archetype talking through his patient
and exerting a power on him as well.

In the collective unconscious we are in
the archetypal world of humanity.
It is like finding ourselves in a living myth.
The archetypes appear in symbolic expression.
The presence of the archetype is known by powerful feeling.
We are all born of mothers.
Our real mother embodies transpersonal images and powers.

Guess which one is behind you at this instant:

☐ the great mother
☐ the tragic mother
☐ the terrible mother
☐ the devouring mother
☐ the cruel mother
☐ the tyrannical mother
☐ the wise old woman
☐ none of the above

Think about these figures,
but use them in therapy sparingly and well.
Nothing is worse than glib archetype talk,
or in psychotherapy, glib talk of any kind.

Think of transference-countertransference
as a two way street.
In any kind of deep psychotherapy, transference is an issue.
In Jungian terms a positive transference is the psychic soup
in which rapport and learning go on.
Jung often used the metaphor of the cauldron
as the container for the interaction of opposites,
and of the interaction of real and symbolic people.
Psychic soup is less grand, less melodramatic,
and more in keeping with down-to-earth
psychotherapy. Earth Mother prepares the psychic soup
for the doctor and patient to brew and cook,
out of which comes a new concoction for both.
The metaphor implies what is in the cauldron.
The soup is, unfortunately, often a fog.

Negative Countertransference

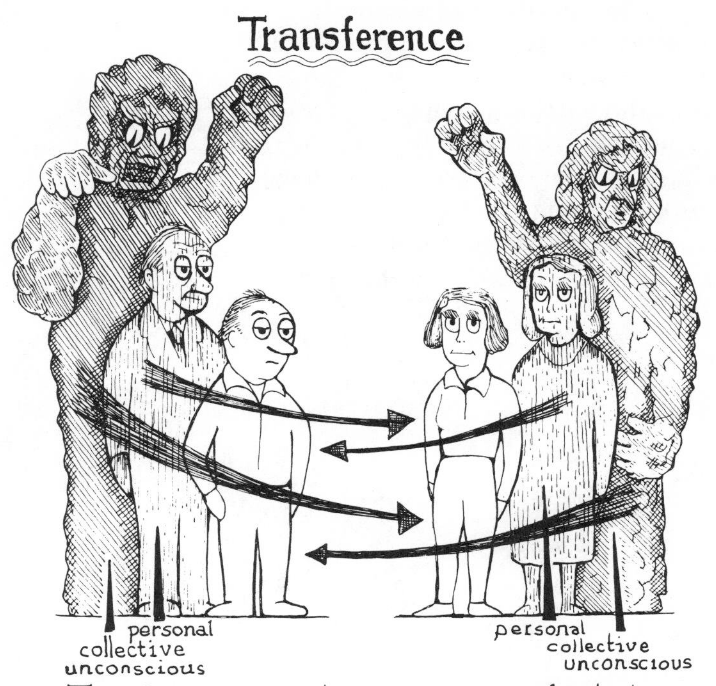

- Transference is positive, negative, or ambivalent
- It is an unconscious projection of the repressed personal and collective images
- Transference can apply to people, things, ideas, etc.

A positive transference is the desirable state in which analysis flourishes.
But it is not a steady state. It fluctuates.
Whenever two people are in close relationshlip,
transference is there.
It is, first of all, personal, a reflection of real people,
and then it is nonpersonal, a representation of inner objects,
which are not a part of our subjective life and
come from the collective bin of humankind.
These images still live in mythology, fairy tales, legends,
and heroic fantasies and in the inner world of good and evil.
They are there all right—
these archaic inner forces.
In the above drawing only figures of the same sex
are seen as projections.
They can be persons of the opposite sex
of no sex, or of androgynous sex, or nonhuman
beings or objects from nature or fantasy.

In the pressure cooker of psychotherapy,
it is a marvel that we can keep any of this straight.
But we must try because
in therapy extraordinary things happen to ordinary people.
Trying to keep perspective and be nonjudgmental
is aided by being aware of the archetypal images.
It helps us to stop blaming real people
in our lives for our own psychic problems.

Let us look at the origins of transference again.
Transference begins with infantile relationships
Take mother.

MY MOTHER in capital letters
is red-white-and-blue, the Fourth of July,
strawberry shortcake, and motherhood.
Oh, don't forget Mother's Day.
The stores will be unhappy
and mummy will be hurt.

On the other hand,
your real mother is unique in the world of mothers.
It is not *your* mother when someone says, "Take *that mother* out of here!"

Why do we need to talk about mother archetype? why not just variations of fantasies of real mother?
Because the personal mother's influence comes from archetypal projections on her. Both mothers are real!

Mothers of the world and the underworld unite!

These are diverse archetypal mother symbols:
the dark cave, milk, nurse, fruitful earth,
the muse of creativity, Mother Earth,
Nature, the Mistress of the elements,
Sovereign of all things spiritual,
Origin of life, Moon goddess,
perpetual renewal,
creator and destroyer.

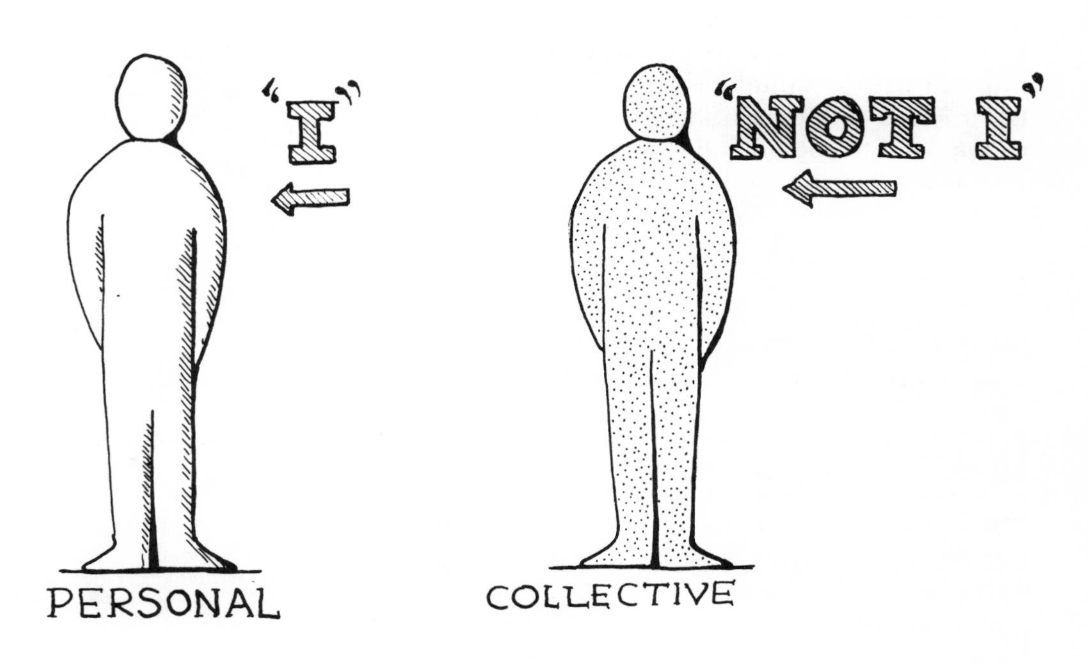

RULE OF THUMB: the I and the not-I
There are two worlds, the world of the I
and the world of the not-I. Don't mix them up.
The personal psyche is the I. It is ego,
and all the dimensions of ego, superego, and id.
You can understand that domain by understanding
the patient's real world.

We are conscious of the enclosing world around us.
We sense and imagine it as an endless sphere.
Part of the great world where I live
is this inner and outer personal world of the I.
We perceive it according to our moods, attitudes, and typology,
as well as our culture, reason and experience.
We can see the same old world in diametrically different ways.
In becoming really conscious and looking within
to find out who is in there and
who we are in both worlds,
we begin to differentiate the I from the not-I.
When the child first says *mine, I,*
wisdom and trouble begin.
The deeper self of the not-I
is the symbolic center of life and our world.
The *Self* with a capital *S* is
the inner, all-encompassing archetype,
as opposed to *self* meaning just our personal self.
This is the essence of the not-I.

The Not-I world of archetypes presents in its cast of thousands, the following dramatis personae:

- anima
- animus
- shadow
- good mother
- bad mother
- good father
- bad father
- wise old man
- wise old woman
- Satan
- redeemer
- savior
- *bête noire*
- demons
- daimons
- monsters
- king
- queen
- night sea journey
- floods
- storms
- *puer aeternus*
- *puella aeterna*
- trickster

And a Supporting Cast of Thousands

- gods and goddesses
- images of God
- serpents
- Antichrist
- tree of knowledge
- tree of life
- sun
- moon
- fish
- tornado
- hurricane
- earthquake
- sacred mountain
- acausal orderedness
- child
- mandala
- Trinity

Maja, the all-mother

Davy Dolldrum dream'd he drove a Dragon:
Did Davy Dolldrum dream he drove a Dragon?
If Davy Dolldrum dream'd he drove a Dragon,
Where's the Dragon Davy Dolldrum
dream'd he drove?

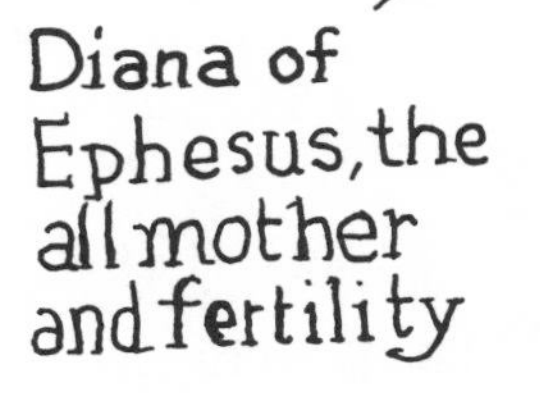

Diana of Ephesus, the all mother and fertility

- quaternity
- hieros gamos
- imago Dei
- Christ
- soul
- persona
- rebirth
- spirit
- ad infinitum

Question: Why are there so many forms in which archetypes appear?
Answer: Because archetypes are expressed in an infinite variety of symbols.

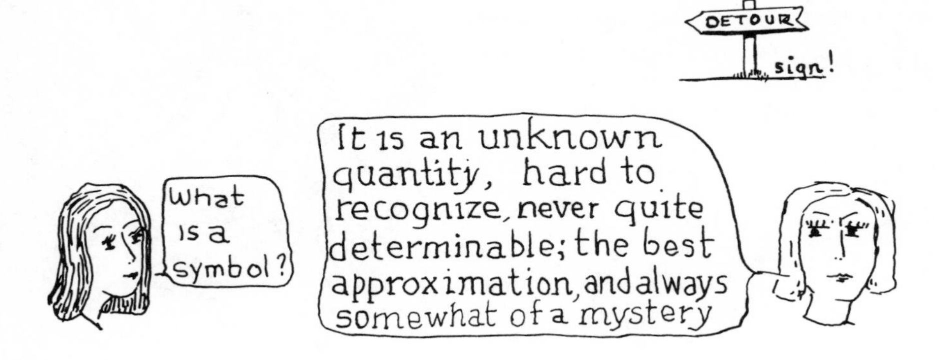

Enough of mothers.
Let us turn to fathers: our Father and all fathers.
Father is said to represent the world of
moral commandments and prohibitions.
The heroic ego is invested in the father.
Our outer world is short of heroic figures,
so we think, but in truth
it teems with heroes. Then why
are there no universal heroic figures that we venerate
in the here and now?

Question: Where did they all go?
Answer: They went inside waiting to be discovered or projected.
Each one of us carries our heroic personalities,
male or female, father or mother, brother or sister.
Question: How do we know that they are *inside*?
Answer: By looking at our dreams and fantasies.
The inner world is not short of heroes,
neither are literature, film, and the creative arts.
But some heroes are shadow heroes, and
we must be aware always that there are two sides of archetypes.
The hero is immortal.
If killed the hero returns reborn or resurrected.
If he is divided or torn apart, he is once more whole.
The heroic spirit is everywhere
at the service of good and bad.

The father is said to personify the intellect
and the Holy Spirit.
Our archetypes are figments of our imagination.
Imagination is another reality.
Three cheers for imagination:
Our Father who art in heaven,
Our Mother who art in heaven.

More on the I and the Not-I

Yes, the not-I is an archetypal phenomenon.
Take the mother and father once more.

The more remote and unreal the personal mother is, the more deeply will the son's yearning for her clutch at his soul, awakening that primordial and eternal image of the mother for whose sake everything that embraces, protects, nourishes, and helps assumes maternal form, from the Alma Mater of the university to the personification of cities, countries, sciences, and ideals.

(Jung, CW 13:147)

The Pietá

The father represents the world of moral commandments and prohibitions, although, for lack of information about conditions in prehistoric times, it remains an open question how far the first moral laws arose from dire necessity rather than from the family preoccupations of the tribal father. . . . The father is the representative of the spirit, whose function it is to oppose pure instinctuality. That is his archetypal role, which falls to him regardless of his personal qualities; hence he is very often an object of neurotic fears for the son. Accordingly, the monster to be overcome by the son frequently appears as a giant who guards the treasure.

(Jung, CW 5:396)

On Loving

A patient's erotic transference coupled
with a therapist's erotic countertransference
is a lusty, potent aphrodisiac.
For the therapist to take advantage of this
is to embezzle love.
You might call it incest.

Falling in love is both natural and magical.
Unfortunately, falling in love is also being mad.
It is not by chance that we speak of
falling under the spell of love.
Falling out of love is another matter.
But there are other ways than falling out.

RULE OF THUMB: Love Nitty Gritty

What do you say when a patient says:
"I love you."
"I dreamed I was sleeping with you."
"What would you say if I told you, I love you?"
"Why do you blush? I know! You love me."
"Why are you hiding your desire behind jargon?"
"Can we meet for dinner or drinks?"
"Let's get together and talk outside your office. OK?"

Not so fast. One at a time.

What do you say when a patient says, "I love you?"
You do not say, "What kind of stupid question are you asking me"?
Do you have cookbook answers up your sleeve?
Answers come in many languages and in countless volumes;
answers come from art, music, drama, and stories
and from prehistoric times.

Try again.
What do you say when a patient says "I love you?"
I say yes in my own idiom, which means
message received, message accepted as your truth.
These feelings of love are feelings that naturally evolve in such a
relationship as this. The message is honored and
received empathically.
You can remind yourself that
overt sexual behavior between therapist and patient
butchers psychotherapy.
Above all, after getting the message straight,
Don't intellectualize!
That's a cop-out for either of you.

Therapist or vice versa *Patient or vice versa*

RULE OF THUMB: Sex

No.

Some psychotherapists have said that
there is nothing wrong with having sex with a patient.
Would you believe it? You would? Oh!
Who's to blame for the consequences?
What? You don't assign blame if you're a psychotherapist? Ha!
Slick trick. That is prestidigitation.

The ultimate pay-off for the nonblaming therapist
is the mystique of nonblaming oneself.
We are all children of sham.
That is the painful truth.
It is our unending labor to rise above sham.

RULE OF THUMB: Using a Couch in Therapy

I gave my psychoanalytic couch away twenty years ago.
Some therapists like to use the couch:
It fosters regression which might be useful.
It might even be used by some therapists
to avoid a human relationship.
It matters that you remain conscious
of your sexual and power fantasies.

For some the couch is an icon.
For some it is handy, and for others, dandy
because it takes the patient out of eye contact.
Personally that is not a problem for me.
If it were, I would use the couch
because the fewer problems I have,
the more we can deal with the problems
that the patient has.

Suppose a patient says to you:
"What would you say if someone said they love you"?

Play it again, Sam. It's a sensitive, subtle question.
Almost any question that any patient may ask can be managed by
reflecting on its seriously and in plain English.
If someone asked me:
"What would you say if someone said they love you?"
That person wants the other to say,
"I love you."
It's called seduction.

Sex again? Sex with a patient?
Sex with a patient is not possible.
Sex is not possible with a patient, because
sex always transforms a relationship into something else.
Sex is not therapy.
It is the end of therapy.
Sex in psychotherapy is exploitative and destructive.
Sex with a patient?
Not a patient and a therapist but an *it* and an *it*.

No doubt therapists and patients fall in love,
and once in a while they get married.
That is unfortunate but not necessarily
the end of anything but the therapy.

When there is love in the transference
that is the time, above all, to be empathic

to retain your distance, your cool, and your equanimity.
Your aplomb too, if you think you might lose it.
That is the time for reason to prevail over feeling.
If managed properly nothing is lost and much is gained, and
psychotherapy becomes ever more interesting
and ever more likely to help.
But if mismanaged the therapy is shipwrecked.

RULE OF THUMB: Taking
You don't have to take everything that is offered.
As a matter of fact, you had better not.
The touchy-feely era of psychotherapy was a passing phase.

RULE OF THUMB: Sticky Fingers
Always keep your sticky fingers off sticky situations.

Projection of the eternal woman and falling in love.
"Appeared a lady under a green mantle
vested in color of the living flame."
(Purgatory XXX)

Falling in Love

Every man carries within him the eternal image of woman, not the image of this or that particular woman, but a definite feminine image. This image is fundamentally unconscious, an hereditary factor of primordial origin engraved in the living organic system of the man, an imprint or "archetype" of all the ancestral experiences of the female, a deposit, as it were, of all the impressions ever made by woman—in short an inherited system of psychic adaptation. . . . The same is true of the woman: she too has her inborn image of man.

(Jung, CW 17:338)

Love develops naturally
in the intimate relationship of psychotherapy.
The love may range from caring to passion.
It is a model which helps us to understand love in the world.
Falling in love is the unreal idealization of the other,
a marvelous enchantment, a spellbinding fascination
with the image of the other.
Falling in love is conceptualized as reciprocal anima-animus projections.
It is this which draws people into relationship
by creating a fantasy relatedness.

WITHDRAWAL OF PROJECTION
PERMITS RELATIONSHIP

The inner image carried by the psyche is
projected onto a real other person and never quite fits.
But it is a good approximation.
As time goes on and the glorious idealization
begins to be seen in the light of the real other person,
the projections are withdrawn.
Some people pretend this doesn't happen,
and a sham love relationship results,
but for others the withdrawal of projections
is the beginning of a real relationship—
affinity instead of infatuation,
deep caring instead of blind adoration.
This is the beginning of individuation and growth
in the relationship.
It is the same thing in psychotherapy.

RULE OF THUMB: What to Say
You can say almost anything to a patient
if you are not caught in countertransference love or hate.
If you are not covertly hostile or seductive,
you will be astonished at the direct, candid,
and sham-free things you can say.
There is no more significant Rule of Thumb.
Eros always wounds but in wounding heals.

Yes, I do love my patient but in a different way.
No, I do not love my patient, but I care and try to understand.
If I neither care nor love and am only in there
pitching, I might as well become a stockbroker.
In the end there is nothing extraordinary about therapy.
When the pupil is ready the teacher will appear.
Once a loving child said to me,
"You're not an ordinary MD. You're a D.U."
Thinking, *duodenal ulcer*, I asked "What is D.U.?"
"Oh, don't you know? That's Doctor of Understanding.
Like my best teacher."
If you don't take hostile bait,
you can be straight as an arrow.

A middle-aged man was telling me of a hassle
over making his adolescent son's lunch.
I asked him why he didn't let his son make his own lunch.
He turned on me with condescending hostility:
"And when did you start making your own lunch?"
"Not soon enough." The words had instantly come to me

as if from someone else.
There was a momentary double take,
then a smile crept over his face,
"I get it," he said.

Therapists wear an invisible toga
when they put on their helping persona.
This toga is preferable to putting on the dog,
but the hidden message symbolized
by the healing toga is that
we will not fail our patients,
we will not desert them, and
we will stay near them.
We will do our best to help them
because in the end, we will both have grown
and both become healthier.
We will have tolerated the kind of healthy hostility
that is lauded in the rotunda of the Jefferson Memorial
in Washington, D.C.:

> *I have sworn upon the altar of God*
> *eternal hostility against every form of tyranny*
> *over the mind of man.*

Why Would Anyone Want to be a Psychotherapist of Any Kind?

My grandfather used to answer questions of this kind
by saying, "Reminds me of the farmer that kissed his cow.
It's all a matter of taste."

Some people become psychotherapists because

- They want protection against looking inside themselves.
- They have psychological problems they want to solve.
- They are driven by an inner muse or daimonion.
- They are intensely curious about the mind.
- They are philosophical at heart.
- They have seen mental illness and want to be a healer.
- They want power over other people.
- They idealize some therapist or analyst.
- They are intrigued by mind-body relationships.
- Because like the mountain, it is there.

On the Choice of a Vocation

Ad infinitum. Or like the psychoanalyst said, "Yes, but what are the real reasons?"
Ad nauseam.

THE GREAT MASTERS: A Matter of Awareness and Projection
Jung is, unfortunately, a stranger
to most psychiatrists, psychologists, and psychotherapists.
Often just his name conjures up, yes, conjures up:

the occult,
alchemy,
esoterica,
mysticism,
soul,
unfathomable archetypes,
religion,
mandalas,
Freudian antipathy, and
darkness.

He is often written off as wooly-minded and exotic.
On the contrary there was and is a very practical Jung
who can help us understand dimensions that are
otherwise obscure.

Deification of the great masters, Freud or Jung or whomever,
stops thinking and begins prayer and worship.
Then come cults, followed by doctrine and dogma.
What were once radical, revolutionary, and new discoveries
become status quo and are held inviolate along
conservative, orthodox, and classical party lines.
The true believers rally round the flag,
saluting and genuflecting at the same time, and
brand less bound thinkers as muddled dissidents
and deviants. Yes, literally deviants.
To many Freudians, Jung is actually odious
for having broken with the master
and created his own school of analytical psychology.
It is a pity we must call ourselves by the names of masters:

- "I am a Jungian."
- "I am a Freudian."
- "I am an Adlerian."
- "I am a Kleinian."
- "I am a So-and-Soian."

There are relatively just as many strange Jungians as there are strange Freudians.

The point is, *what can we learn from those pioneers who began to search the unconscious that can help us help people?*

We are a long ways from a science of psychotherapy.
We are approaching a scientific neuroscience.
Biological psychiatry flourishes.
New, effective drugs help patients—
lithium, antidepressants, antipsychotics, anxiolytics.
PET and CAT scans, and the marvelous nuclear magnetic resonators
don't touch the soul.
No antipsychotic drug has ever cured schizophrenia.
Antidepressant drugs control symptoms.
The psyche heals itself. Psychotherapy helps.
Practical Jung opens the door to
different ways of looking at psychological facts.

The Method of Multiple Working Hypotheses

One can practice psychotherapy with a ruling theory
to which one is wedded.
One can also have an alternate hypothesis to prove
one idea wrong and provide another.
Or one can have multiple working hypotheses.

Multiple working hypotheses diminish the danger
of parental affection for our favorite theory offspring.
This method suggests variable lines of inquiry
that might otherwise be overlooked.
A geologist, T.C. Chamberlin, first proposed the idea in 1890;
his paper ("Multiple Hypotheses," 1890) is required reading for my students.
It contains the essence of the danger of belief.
Armed with multiple working hypotheses,
one is more likely to see the true nature
and significance of phenomena.
Biases are diminished
and what is happening
is not clouded by presumptions.

There are many ways to skin a mule.
There are many ways to help the psyche heal.
Not all of them work.
Some of them don't work at all
for some people.

The diversity of methods, schools, and ways of psychotherapy
attest to the plurality,
multiplicity, and complexity of the psyche.

RULE OF THUMB: Separation Anxiety

Patient: But to whom will I talk when I am no longer seeing you? Whom will I talk to when you are away?

Doctor: Your self.

Patient: My self?

Doctor: Yourself

Your Self.
You already talk with me between sessions in your head.
I suppose it is like leaving home again.
You can always talk to the me inside you. It will be
talking to your inner self in the most sane way conceivable.

"Mr. Prentice is not your father. Alex Binster is not your brother. The anxiety you feel is not genuine. Dr. Froelich will return from vacation September 15th. Hang on."

When Things Go Consistently Wrong

Psychoanalysts speak of a
"negative therapeutic reaction." (Fenichel, *Psychoanalytic Theory of Neurosis*, pp. 298 and 501)
They mean that a case develops to the point
where the patient reacts to analysis by getting worse
and by increasing resistances
that are thought to be rooted in the patient's character.
The psychoanalysts conclude that the problem is the patient,
not the analyst, not the analysis.

Another way of looking at it is that analytic treatment
is the wrong medicine.
To blame the patient for a
"negative therapeutic reaction" may lead to a great deal
of futile, costly, painful, and destructive treatment.

In such cases there may be a monumental negative transference
to the psychiatrist who becomes an impotent, hated object.
But the analyst may hang in there and treat the patient
as though the patient is afraid to face the insights that the analyst sees.
In short, the patient may be accused of cowardice.
There are nicer ways of putting it.
There are no rules of thumb for the psychiatrist
handling this kind of situation, except to admit
that the treatment has failed because
of the treatment, or because the psychiatrist-patient is wrong.
But I want to say something to patients on this score.

RULE OF THUMB: Escape

When your therapy is getting nowhere and even worse,
you are convinced that your therapist is not able
to treat you, and you dislike him or her
and can't accept transference explanations,
then quit.

Seek a therapist whom you like and want to work with.
If there is no such person,
then you'll have to pull yourself up by your own bootstraps
or take the battering fate gives you
and in the end hope to come out the better for it.
Hope.

There is no handy way to quit.
How to Abandon Ship is a wartime book
published in 1942 to aid people in getting off
sinking ships and reaching eventual safety in the
best condition possible.
The book begins,

> The time has passed when you can indulge in boat-drill lethargy, when you can fiddle with a rope or two, while you "let George do it." When the torpedo hits, "George" may prove to be even more panicked and less skilled in launching a lifeboat than you. (Richards and Banigan, p. 3)

Rule of Thumb About Rules of Thumb

The *First Finger Singular* was one finger
called the *First Finger* but it is only the first finger
after the thumb. So if we have five fingers then
the first finger is the second finger.
On the other hand the thumb and first finger
are handy indicators.
Taken together, index finger to thumb, we have grasped
the essence of the rule of finger-thumb business:
the prehensile quality of being able to hold onto things,
either like the monkey's tail or the grasp of the hand
or the tool in the hand.
Rule of Thumb about Rules of Thumb: Get Hold of Live Metaphors!
A metaphor leads us to symbolic thought and
one imagination playing on another to give us new insights:

> *In a world of fugitives*
> *The person taking the opposite direction*
> *Will appear to be running away.*
>
> (T. S. Eliot, *The Family Reunion*)

> A more adequate and workable way of understanding metaphor must be sought, and of course it will not be anything as simple and rule-of-thumb as the grammarian's distinction . . . . What really matters in a metaphor is the psychic depth at which the things in the world, whether actual or fancied, are transmuted by the cool heat of the imagination.
>
> (Wheelwright, *Metaphor and Reality*, p. 71)

PART

III

Archetypes

Nike celebrates the Victory of Samothrace in 306 B.C.

The Archetypes

The world of the archetypes
is the invisible world that we have never seen;
it is hypothesized to be the deepest realm of the psyche,
which has the potential to evoke images
of a more or less predictable nature. It is these that we see.
They keep recurring worldwide in all people's psyche,
and they have been reappearing from time immemorial.
We know them through myths,
fairy tales, sagas, legends, and stories told the world over.

Images and events which are foreign
and antithetical to science
are at home in the soul—
the quest for the treasure
in a place hard to find that is
guarded by powerful, mysterious forces
capable of casting spells,
superhuman, supernatural beings,
gods and goddesses,
heroes and prophets.

The psychic land where these potential forms
exist is the collective unconscious.
From it arise our inner objective experiences,
our wisdom and our folly,
which are *objective* because they are not *subjective*,
not of our own lives.
It is the realm of inherited psychic instincts
and behavioral patterns.
This is another reality.
This is a separate but interpenetrating reality.

The outer world and its repressed elements
are known to us as the *I*.
We know from within, the inner world of *not-I*
that is the collective unconscious.
The not-I transcends our personal being.
The archetype is experienced in projections,
powerful affect images,
symbols, moods, and behavior patterns such as
rituals, ceremonials, and love.

Jung compared the archetype (the preformed tendency
to create images) to a dry river bed.
Rain gives form and direction to the flow.
We name the river,

but it is never a thing located any place;
it is a form but it is never the same;
it is always changing. But it is a river,
and we know that rivers ultimately flow into oceans
which are symbolic of the unconscious.

On another occasion Jung compared the archetype
to a supersaturated solution which,
at a given point and time, forms specific crystals
around a nidus, the symbolic breeding point of formations
that are characteristic of that kind of
supersaturated liquid and no other.
For example, a supersaturated solution of ordinary salt
will precipitate out only the square-faced crystals
which are characteristic of salt, NaCl.
The cubes come in different sizes and sometimes
are engraphed onto other cubes in odd building block shapes
but they are only cubes.
You might imagine that sodium chloride is the archetype of a
reactionary, superconservative psyche.

One could compare such an archetype to
the mythical King Midas
and speak of the Nidus of Midas.

The nidus does not exist as a thing but as a powerful
potential, a representative *in posse* of the archetype.

A *complex*, according to Jung, is the sum of all
the associated ideas and feelings that are attracted
to an archetype; the complex
gives the archetype a form of expression.
The complex is powered by affect.
It is feeling this affect which tells us
we are experiencing an archetype.
Trumpets, enter the King! Thunder and lightning!

- Archetypal images are among the highest values of the human psyche, and the treasures of the motifs of mythology.
- Symbols are infinitely variable expressions of underlying archetypes.
- Archetypes (collective) endow the individual (personal) with strong affect.

The archetype is a tendency to form motifs.
It is the lightning which draws our attention.
Archetypes *are not* inherited images;
they are forms to which our culture and
life experience give substance.
Mother—momma—mom—mummy—ma—mammy;
Father—papa—dad—daddy—pa—pop;
archetypes of ancestry.

Archetypes are a priori patterns for universal symbols
that are characteristic of eternal human nature.

The archetypal content of powerful language is metaphor.
The metaphor, like the archetype, is an organizing principle
that facilitates depth of meaning.

Once again, the form in which an archetype appears
is a projection. It is clothed and formed
according to one's personal life experiences that are
drawn from conscious and repressed unconscious elements.
Repeat: Archetypes are psychic instincts
of characteristic inborn behavior patterns and potential images.

The parable of the cave illustrates the archetype.

In the 7th book of Republic *Plato tells his famous parable of the cave as an illustration of his theory of eternal Ideas or Forms: man is compared to a creature living in a cave, bound immovably hand and foot. At his back is the entrance to the cave, and all he can see are the shadows of the forms passing outside thrown on the wall in front of him . . . , mistakenly he believes the shadows to be the real things.*

(Jung *Collected Letters*, Vol. 2, p. 372n.)

Jung had his own nuts-and-bolts philosophy of practical use of the archetypes in therapy.

It is quite obvious that it is not at all necessary to uncover the archetypes in every treatment of neurosis. One can get along successfully with far less, but it is equally true that it is sometimes not at all in your hand to decide whether you will go into archetypes or not, since they turn up all by themselves, sometimes with a vehemence you wouldn't like. I never look for archetypes and don't try to find them; enough when they come all by themselves. This is almost regularly the case when an analysis lasts a bit long or when it is a matter of a person with a somewhat vivacious mind.

1. There is no point in trying to make a patient understand archetypal material as long as he has not yet gained some insight into his personal complexes, and particularly into the nature of his shadow.

2. The patient may be practically cured without ever having heard of an archetype.

(Jung *Collected Letters*, Vol. 2, pp.160-161)

My apologies to all the archetypes I have slighted,
to any gods and goddesses,
especially Artemis and Wotan,
to the serpent and the sacred mountain, and
to Atman and Philemon.
Just to be on the safe side, knock on wood.

On Being in the Clutches of an Archetype

Jungians speak of being possessed by an archetype.
In ancient times people spoke of being possessed by demons.
Now we make DSM III* psychiatric diagnoses,
but to the patient psychosis or severe neurosis still seems like
being possessed by a mysterious, invading power.

You want to know what it is like
to be possessed by an archetype, to be in its negative power?
Imagine you are an inquisitor.
Imagine you are a Shiite Moslem terrorist.
Imagine you are a Nazi in Germany in 1941.
Imagine you are schizophrenic.
Imagine you are an Aztec sacrificer of human beings.
Imagine you are the sheriff at the lynching of a black man.

---

*DSM III : acronym for Diagnostic Statistical Manual of the American Psychiatric Association (third version) published in 1980. Diagnoses are given numbers. Neuroses no longer exist officially as a diagnosis but exist under 300.0; 300.1; 300.2 all the way to 300.9.

And what is it like to be in the positive power
of an archetype?
Imagine you are Dante seeing Beatrice.
Imagine when you first fell in love.
Imagine you are Mozart hearing in
your head the Concerto in D minor.
Imagine you are in your most wonderful dream
or your most heroic fantasy.

The Archetype = an affect image
the concept of the archetype is derived from
repeated observations of universal myths and fairy tales

Outer world images from
repressed personal life contents
AFFECT
IMAGE
Archetypal reality: psychic images
from the inner world

"The patient said he was possessed by demonic thoughts,"
the resident said in presenting the case to me;
and he found the word *possessed* abhorrent,
preferring the word *obsessed*.

For him it was too close to superstition
to be respectable.
Change a *po* here
to an *ob* there
and you're in like Flynn.

Trying to explain what an archetype is
is like trying to tell someone
what a ghost is, a ghost in Plato's cave.
Coleridge, when asked if he believed in ghosts,
said no, he'd known too many of them.
Repeat: An archetype is known to us by the company it keeps,
projected onto outer objects, persons, or events.

The inner world has two realms:
the personal (subjective) unconscious,
which is what Freud called the unconscious,
and the collective (objective) unconscious,
which Jung discovered.
The personal unconscious is inhabited by images,
memories, feelings, and ideas which were once conscious,
but are now repressed.
Repressed means that they are not directly accessible to consciousness.
The unconscious contains the whole range of our experiences
from our noblest to our darkest.

The unconscious is not a demoniacal monster, but a natural entity which, as far as moral sense, aesthetic taste, and intellectual judgment go, is completely neutral. It only becomes dangerous when our conscious attitude to it is hopelessly wrong. To the degree that we repress it, its danger increases.
(Jung, CW 16:329)

The collective unconscious
can be thought of as being inhabited by motifs, images, ideas,
personalities, moods, places, visions, and spirits we have
never known in day-to-day life.
We are born with our collective unconscious;
we psychologically create our personal unconscious
after birth.
We are not born with a mind that is a *tabula rasa,*
a clean slate.

Psychological Growth

- Expansion of consciousness by outer world experiences - outer object relations

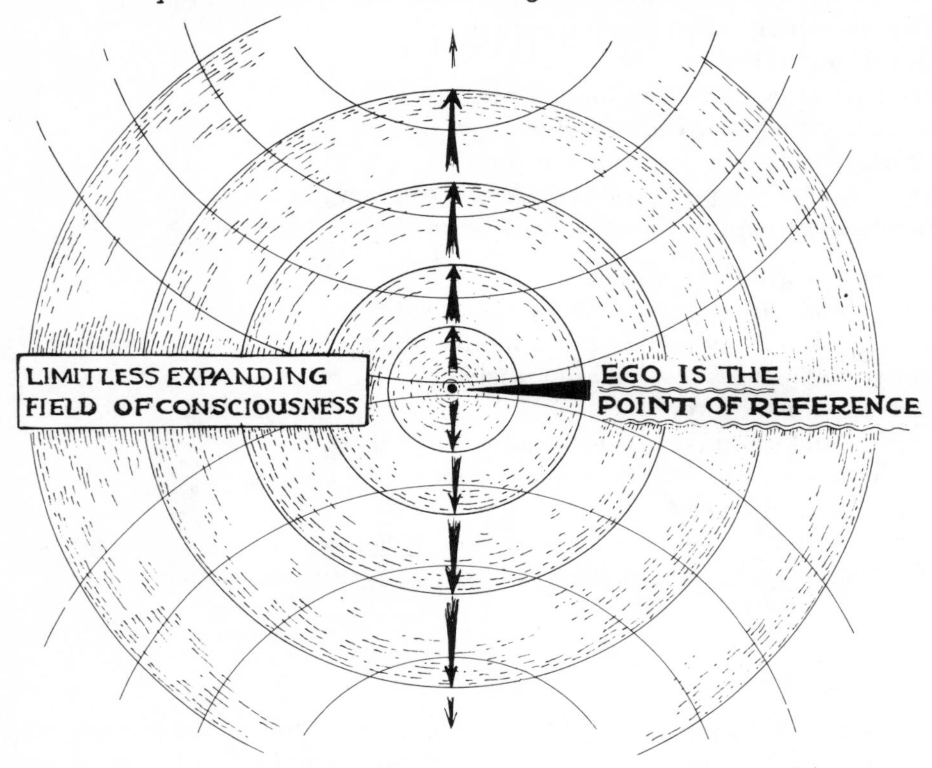

- Expansion of consciousness by inner world experiences - inner object relations by the personal and the collective unconscious

Just as the biological nature of a person comes ready-made
so does the psyche.
At the interface between personal and collective psyche
is the reflection of the archaic world still within us.
At the interface between consciousness and the personal unconscious
is the shadowy realm of preconsciousness
wherein flows the river of the unconscious,

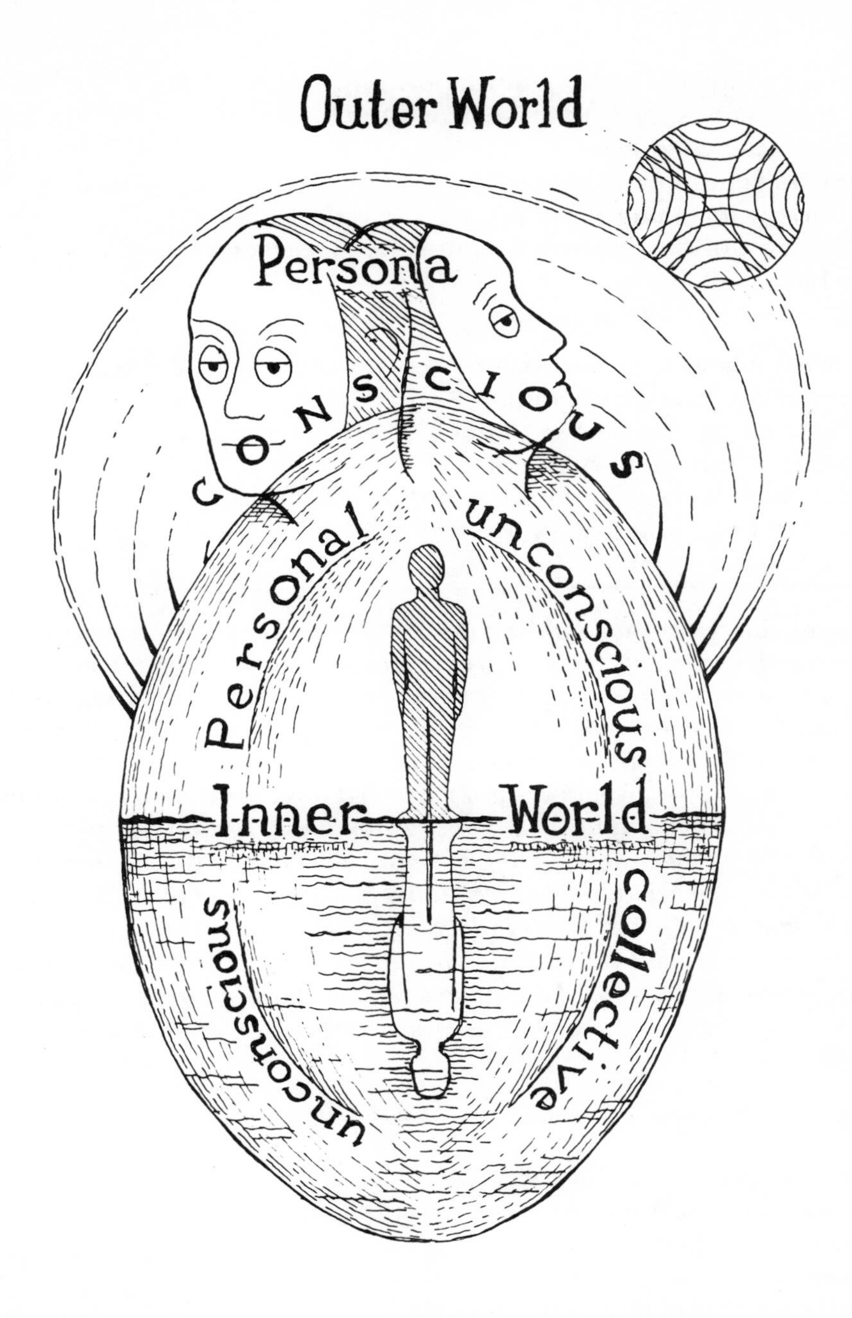

the formless dreams that float through our minds
when we are awake and when we are asleep.
This twilight zone beckons with unbidden inspirations.
We can dip into it through meditation, deep thought,
and effortless reflection.
Between consciousness and the outer world we interpose our persona.

Our lives are directed by the motive powers
of the unconscious more than we like to think,
even more than we dream.
People who are not conscious of the unconscious
scorn or deny its manifestations.
In America we pride ourselves on our good sense and reason
and on being self-made.
We believe we control our destiny.

When my wife and I first moved to Texas, we admired a
huge, dried fish head that a rancher
had placed on a fence post in front of his driveway.
My wife asked him good-naturedly,
"Did you put that there for luck to ward off evil spirits?"
"No, lady, in Texas you make your own luck," he replied.

The irrationality of events is shown in what we call chance, which we are obviously compelled to deny, because we cannot in principle think of any process that is not causal and necessary, whence it follows that it cannot happen by chance. In practice, however, chance reigns everywhere, and so obtrusively that we might as well put our causal philosophy in our pocket. The plenitude of life is governed by law and yet not governed by law, rational and yet irrational. Hence reason and the will that is grounded in reason are valid only up to a point. The further we go in the direction selected by reason, the surer we may be that we are excluding the irrational possibilities of life which have just as much right to be lived. It was indeed highly expedient for man to become somewhat more capable of directing his life. It may justly be maintained that the acquisition of reason is the greatest achievement of humanity; but that is not to say that things must or will always continue in that direction.

(Jung, CW 7:72)

The clearest example of the collective unconscious
can be seen in the symptoms of acute schizophrenia.
Fortunately, or unfortunately,
such patients are drugged so quickly that
we hardly see the unconscious
before blotting it out.
But in such split personalities, the split is
evidence of the unconscious invading the boundaries
of consciousness. Schizophrenics live in their dream world
and see and talk with demons and devils,
God and gods, Satan and monsters, and

they tell us of the horrendous battle
between good and evil.
The I is overwhelmed by the not-I.

There is a great deal of common sense
and wisdom in the schizophrenic's talk.
Jung was one of the first psychiatrists really to
listen to them and to try to understand what they were saying.
When I ran a psychiatric ward,
I had a sign on my door
which read, "Please knock."
Every time one of the schizophrenic patients walked by
he knocked.
Finally I understood
and took the sign down.

The Persona

In Greek drama actors wore masks
that turned them into the *dramatis personae*.
By wearing the mask, the actor *becomes* the person impersonated.
The persona is the guise and manifestation of the role
which disguises the personality of the actor.

The persona is an archetype; it is a functional complex that is
necessary for adaptation to interpersonal relations.
The persona is a show to show others
the role we impersonate.
It is a compromise between what we wish to be
and what the surrounding world will allow us to be.
The persona is a manifestation of interactional demands.

The persona may be a dazzling manifestation of
a charismatic person or a wimp.
The persona is a sort of announcement:

- I am the boss!
- I am the doctor.
- I am in charge here.
- I am tough.
- Who the hell do you think you are?
- I am no threat to you.
- I am beautiful, and I know it.
- I am a scholar and an intellectual.
- I am a real man.
- I am an elegant lady.
- I am a tough lady.

But what is it like at the interface of the person and the mask?

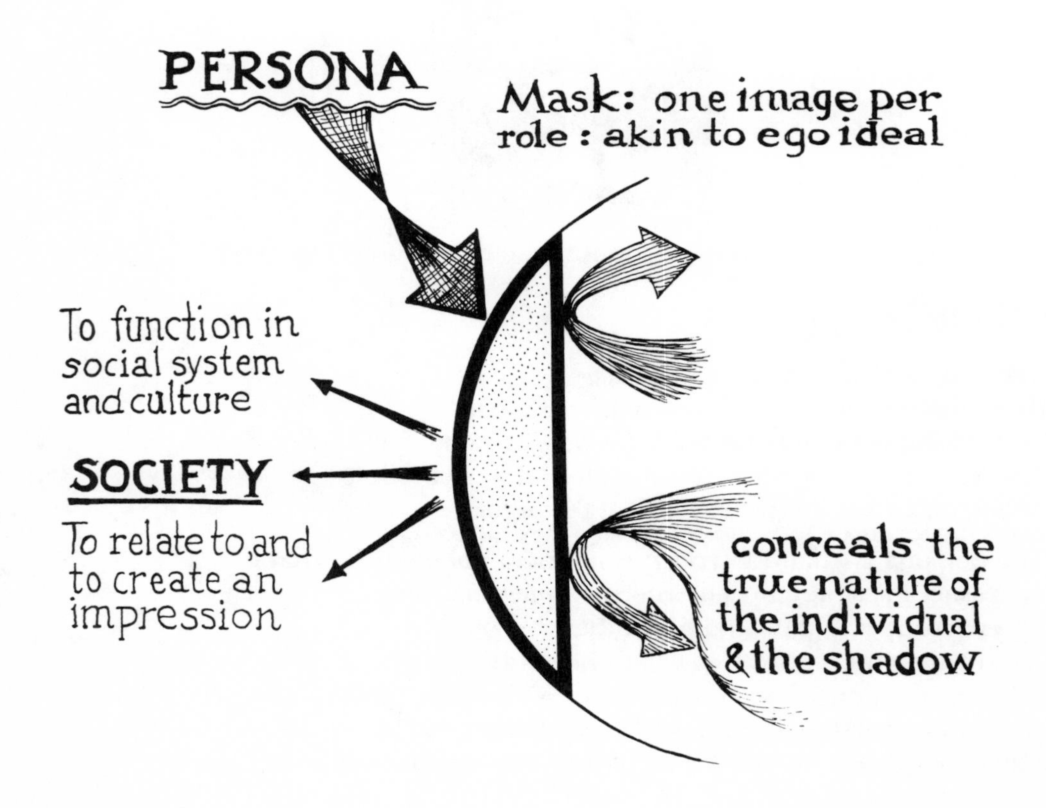
PERSONA
Mask: one image per role : akin to ego ideal
To function in social system and culture
SOCIETY
To relate to, and to create an impression
conceals the true nature of the individual & the shadow

The persona conceals our true nature and
disguises both our shadow and our finest ideals,
yet it tries to approximate our ego ideal,
so it is like putting on a face.
The automobile salesman may personify the salesman persona.
The preacher may have one persona in the pulpit
and another at home with his wife and children.
The businesswoman may have one persona at the office
and another one in bed.
The way we dress, move, talk, stand,
the way we outwardly do everything is our persona.

To think that the persona is superfluous one must be identified with the persona and not know one's true self.

Yes, and to think it is unnecessary one has to be unconscious of the true nature of other people.

It is preferable to have only a few personae
at our beck and call.
Two conspicuous ones are optimal,
one for work and one for home.

If one has too many personae,
people will not know how to identify the one behind the mask.

- Dilettante
- Genius
- Con artist
- Chameleon
- Multiple personalities

As people become more specialized,
and it is no trick for technology to put
an encyclopedia on the head of a pin,
it is no longer possible for an individual
to be a Renaissance person.
We have more pinhole people in pigeonholes.
The odd ones and the misfits
who in their uniqueness transform society
are cast aside.

In Jungian psychology self-realization and
becoming who it is in you to become
have a high priority.
We are running the risk of becoming a society
whittled down to mediocrity,
honed to conformity, and valued in statistical averages.
We are becoming computerized, monopolized,
bureaucratized; we are becoming hero worshipers at the Temple of Sham.

Persona of the politician: Vice President Hubert H. Humphrey.
Oratory demands an impressive presence.

Since it was man's unfitness—his being an outcast and an outsider on this planet—which started him on his unique course, it should not seem anomalous that misfits and outsiders are often in the forefront of human endeavor and the first to grapple with the unknown. The impulse to escape an untenable situation often prompts human beings not to shrink back but to plunge ahead. Moreover, it is in accord with the uniqueness of the human pattern that the misfits of the species should try to fit in not by changing themselves but by changing the world. . . . It is the unique glory of the human species that its rejected do not fall by the wayside but become the building stones of the new, and that those who cannot fit into the present should become the shapers of the future.

(Hoffer, *Ordeal of Change*, p.126)

Anima and Animus

Within the unconscious of men,
there is an opposite or feminine psyche, the anima.
The contrasexual archetype is universal.
Within the unconscious of women,
there is an opposite or masculine psyche, the animus.

These archetypes appear in dreams, fantasies, visions,
creative thoughts, and imagination,
"that inward eye which is the bliss of solitude." (Wordsworth)
The conscious masculine principle is defined as Logos,
which represents the discriminating and cognitive quality
of the thinking mind.
The conscious feminine principle is defined as Eros,
which represents the connecting and relating quality of
the feeling mind.

Jung called Eros the great binder and deliverer,
and he anticipated a growing awareness
of the androgynous aspect of our personalities.
Each one of us, to some degree, is both male and female.
The unisex movement is an extreme denial of
the macho and the belle and a blurring of the
contrasexual being as well.

The homosexual personality
often infuriates individuals who would deny like crazy
anything but their conscious heterosexual life.
They hate and despise being reminded
that within them is the personality of
the opposite sex.
Man is not all man.
Woman is not all woman.

Jung's concept of anima and animus
gives us a psychological understanding of the women's movement
and sexist attitudes.
This formulation breaks with Freud's
patriarchial concept of women
as flawed, castrated males
having the ubiquitous unction of penis envy.

There is contemporary criticism of the anima-animus hypothesis
as sexist and chauvinistic.
Nonetheless, practical Jung makes use of these archetypes.
The idea that a woman's conscious personality is
characterized by Eros
and her unconscious personality is
characterized by Logos
and a man's conscious personality is
characterized by Logos
and his unconscious personality is
characterized by Eros
now seems only partly to be the case.

A man with dominant feeling function can be consciously Eros,
and a woman with dominant thinking function can be consciously Logos.

An extreme feminist who projects negative animus
onto the hated male seems to be the
mirror image of the sexist male who projects negative anima
onto the dangerous female.
The misogynist male sees the hated female as his projection.
There is always a hook on which to hang a projection, but
in essence it is a case of hating oneself,
the projection of one's own contrasexual being.
In love we love that part of ourselves
which fits the other
until we see where it does not fit.

Note: The contrasexual sides are not
male and female but
masculine and feminine principles.
There is no disentangling oneself from words.
Substitute another set of words, and
we have another set of problems.

Where love reigns, there is no will to power; and where the will to power is paramount, love is lacking. The one is but the shadow of the other. . . .

(Jung, CW 7:78)

The masculinity of the woman and the femininity of the man *are* inferior, and it is regrettable that the full value of their personalities should be contaminated by something that is less valuable. On the other hand, the shadow belongs to the wholeness of the personality: the strong man must somewhere be weak, somewhere the clever man must be stupid, otherwise he is too good to be true and falls back on pose and bluff. Is it not an old truth that woman loves the weakness of the strong man more than his strength, and the stupidity of the clever man more than his cleverness?

(Jung, CW 10:261)

The anima and the animus both contain positive and negative sides.

ANIMA-ANIMUS/CAT-AND-DOG FIGHT

And How Do You Score?

The *positive animus* qualities of woman are

- ☐ assertiveness
- ☐ control
- ☐ thoughtful, rational
- ☐ strong and compassionate

The *negative animus* qualities of woman are

- ☐ opinionated
- ☐ always gets the last word
- ☐ ruthless
- ☐ destructive

The *positive anima* qualities of man are

- ☐ tenderness
- ☐ patience
- ☐ consideration
- ☐ kindness and compassion

The *negative anima* qualities of man are

- ☐ vanity
- ☐ moodiness
- ☐ bitchiness
- ☐ easily hurt feelings

Recent thinking has changed the way we look at Jung's original ideas:
The Eros-Logos and Logos-Eros qualities
do not always strictly distinguish the sexes.
Jung never really said they did,
but that is the way the word came down.
Nevertheless,
The anima-animus squabbles and fights
are well known to almost everyone
by the cat-and-dog arguments of
men and woman.
The hostility and brutality between the sexes
can be understood as
outrageous outbursts of our odious opprobrium,
in other words, our shitty side.
It starts with a simple argument.
"All I said, dear, was . . . ."

In the abstract, anima and animus resemble their origins:
Eros is the Greek god of Love, son of Aphrodite, and
Logos is Greek for speech, word, or reason.
In the beginning there was the word.
The word was God.
God is Love.
Love is caring.

Ms. Animus and Mr. Anima speak their own rhetoric,
whose metaphors are the symbols of the archetypes.
The negative animus rhetoric
is sweeping generalizations, pontificated,
eternal truths, and unassailable opinions.
It is brilliant illogic.
While the rhetoric of the negative anima
is "*na*gative," accusatory, authoritarian,
boastful, vain, and power-wielding,
in an anima-animus fight
the woman wins
with an unanswerable parting shot.

"Says who?" is right on the button
because *he* is not speaking.
It is the archetype's voice of animosity.
There are no answers to an eternal truth.
I call these kinds of unanswerable questions
the *beautiful questions*.

One characteristic of an anima-animus fight
is that the combatants don't really know
what they are arguing about and slide from one issue to another.
After it is over no one can exactly remember
what they were *really*
fighting about.
Sez who? Oh.
The anima provokes the animus. The animus provokes the anima.
The anima is resentful. The animus is angry.
Nothing makes sense.

If the man does not take up the gauntlet
thrown by the animus, she doesn't know what to do,
and the battle ends.

If the woman does not react to the bitchy, moody anima,
he gets no mileage out of it and sobers up.
It is not themselves having this fight
but ogres that live within them.
They talk like ventriloquists.

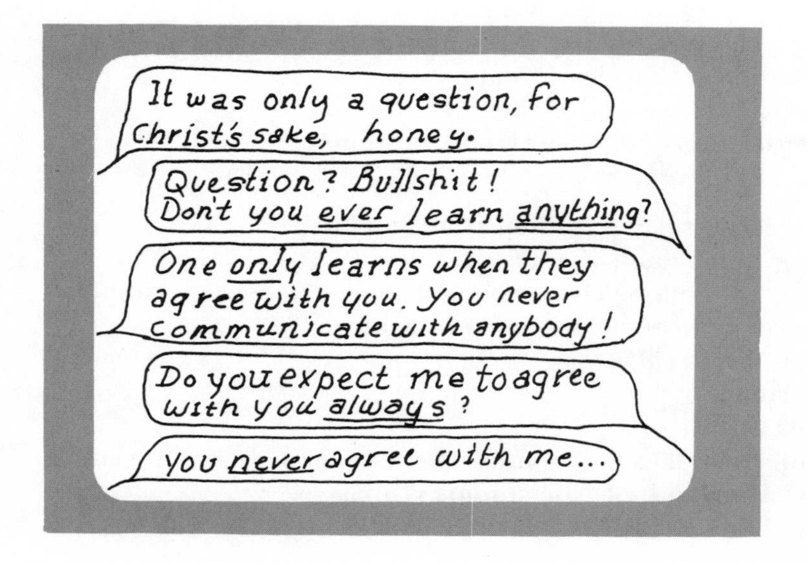

When anima and animus go at it,
People talk words in balloons without people.
Hostile antagonizing questions demand answers—
answers to unanswerable questions.

Reason replies, "Of course not."
Provocation says, "You're damned right I don't."
When a psychotherapist sees
a man and woman in conjoint therapy,
it may be astonishing
to realize that these are archetypes talking to archetypes.
The real people are seething, passive victims.

No man can argue with a negative animus for more than 5 minutes without becoming the victim of his own anima. He is unaware that the banal, exciting argument would become unexciting if he were to quit. The anima and animus are unconscious so that the man and woman tend to be almost totally unaware that they are not relating but their archetypes are having a go at it.

JUNG

Now Let Us Try to Clarify the Impasse of Anima-Animus Encounters

Write your own script from a recent fight.

Woman	Man
I said________________	I said________________
He said________________	She said________________
Then I said________________	Then she said________________

Woman: I was thinking, "How can I talk to such a person? He doesn't understand common sense. He doesn't see how things really are. Bullheaded! Now I suppose he'll kick the door or the dog. He'll sulk, yell at the kids, walk away. He thinks he's always right about everything, Mr. Know-it-all. Well, let me tell you a thing or two. . . ."

____

Man: I was thinking, "How can I talk to such a person? She just wants everything her way. Now I suppose she'll start the crying act again. And start nagging all over again. Nag, nag, nag. She always wants the last word. There is no way I can win. What a bitch. She thinks she's always right about everything. Ms. Know-it-all. Well, let me tell you a thing or two. . . ."

____

Have a nice day.

Repeat to Clarify If Possible

1. The conscious personality of women is predominantly Eros but the unconscious is Logos.
2. The conscious personality of men is predominantly Logos but the unconscious is Eros.
3. This state of affairs compensates each so that together they represent a balance.
4. Conflict and tension occur by an unconscious clash.

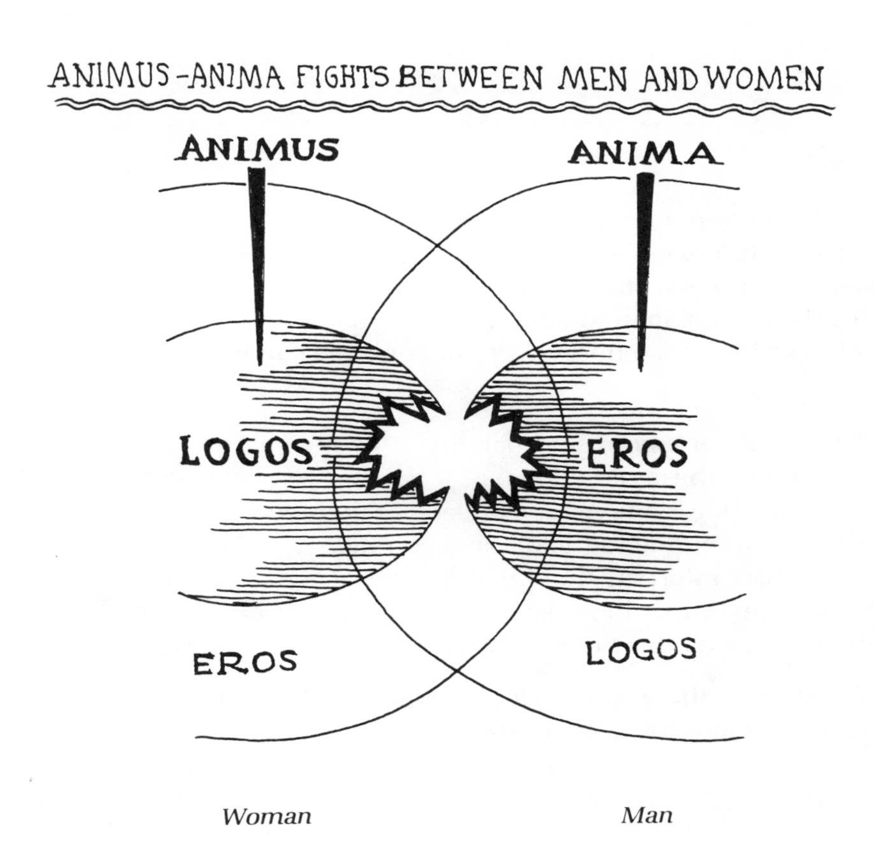

Woman *Man*

Diagrammatic image of interface of different perspectives; this can reveal positive or negative relationships.

MAN—WOMAN

TRANSFERENCE RELATIONSHIPS

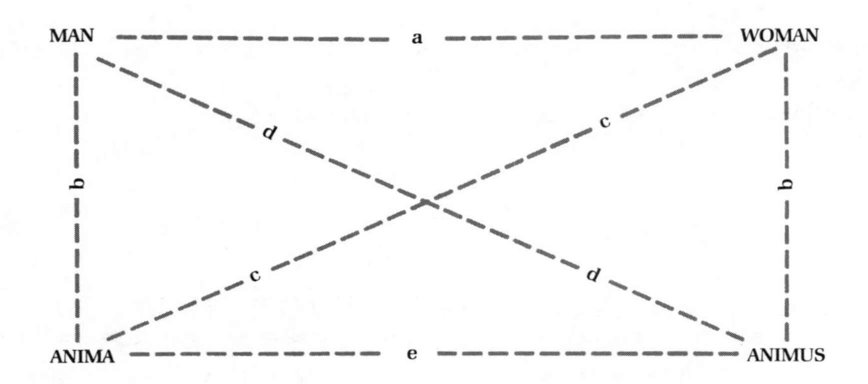

a = Relationship person to person.
b = Relationship of person to that person's archetype.
c = Relationship of woman to anima archetype.
d = Relationship of man to animus archetype.
e = Relationship of unconscious to unconscious archetypes.

The relationship of therapist to patient
may be in any of these directions;
it is a paradigm for relationships outside of therapy.
The relationship of one to the other is contingent
upon a complex interplay that includes
the relationship of the therapist to his or her own unconscious, and
the unconscious connections between her or his archetypes.

Consciousness is the beginning of the way out of the predicament.
Dreams are a major insight into this area.

Anima and Animus • Contrasexual Archetypes

WOMAN

Conscious:
EROS - the connecting quality of relatedness

Unconscious of woman is ANIMUS - or LOGOS, or the masculine principle

MAN

Conscious:
LOGOS - the discriminating cognitive quality of thinking

Unconscious of man is ANIMA or EROS, or the feminine principle

The Self: Central Archetype of Wholeness and Totality

The word *Self* does not refer to the individual self,
but the whole of the personality—
ego, consciousness, personal and collective unconscious.
Its numinous power is centering.

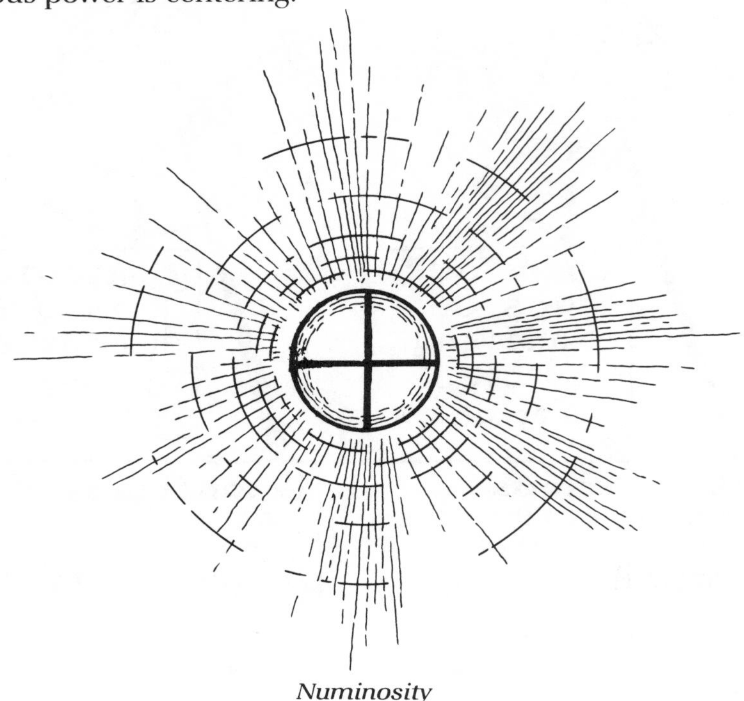

Numinosity

Jung wrote to a distressed woman patient:

Yes, your trouble has very much to do with the dissolution of the ego. It is the ego that doubts, hesitates, lingers, has emotions of all sorts, etc. In your patientia *you have your Self. You have missed nothing and have failed nowhere, you simply suffer from things that happen to you. No matter how you interpret them. The ego wants explanations always in order to assert its existence. Try to live without the ego. Whatever must come to you, will come. Don't worry! Your mood on dawn (April 7th) tells you everything. Don't allow yourself to be led astray by the ravings of the animus. He will try every stunt to get you out of the realization of stillness, which is truly the Self.*

Jung, *Collected Letters*, Vol. 1, p. 427

The Self appears in dream, myths, and fairy tales
as the king, the hero, the prophet, the saviour.
It appears as the magic circle, the square, and
the cross; it is the total union of opposites.
The Self is a united duality as Tao and yang and yin.
It appears as the mandala.

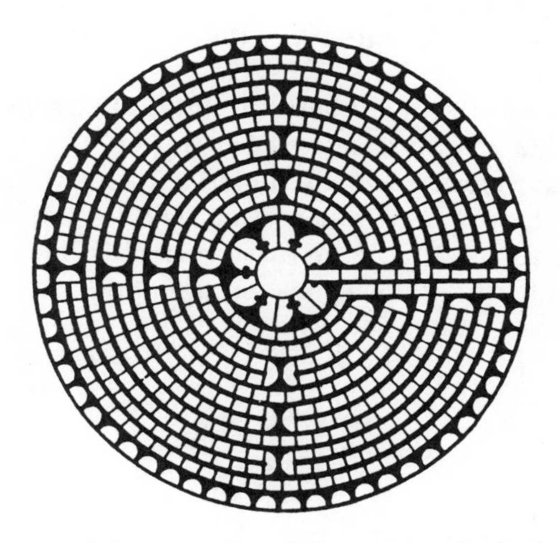

Mandala Maze from Chartres Cathedral

The Archetype of the Self Appears as *Imago Dei*

The image of God is equated with
the totality of Self which is supraordinate
to all other elements of the psyche.
The image of God is universally expressed,
and the power of this creation is within the Self.

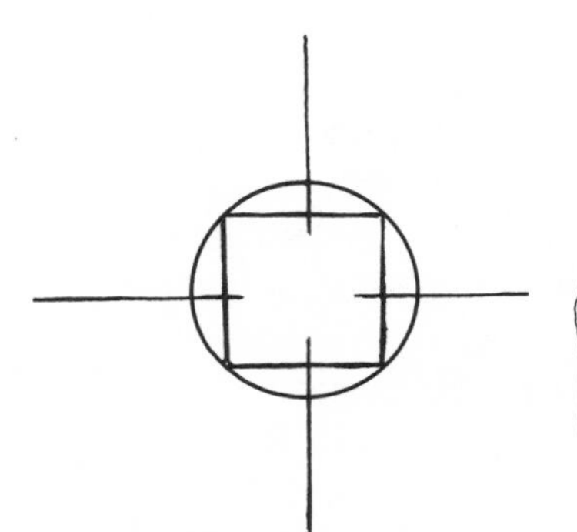

the square in the circle or the circle in the
square is an age old symbol - back to pre-history.
It is found all over the earth and it
expresses either the deity or the self.
These two terms are psychologically very
much related - which doesn't mean that I
believe that God is the self or the self is God.
I simply state that there is a psychological
relation between them

JUNG

Even if God has been pronounced dead, the psychological God lives
and is equated with supreme power and supreme being.
God can be worshipped in many guises:
machines, computers, material possessions,
states, nations, money, idols, icons,
woman, man, child, animal, and even as atheism.
All substitute and stand in for *imago Dei*.
Supernatural powers are attributed to whatever carries
the image of the Self.
Whatever we are committed to, in awe, in blind allegiance,
or devoutly in faith, is an expression of *imago Dei*.
Abstractions such as Science may be reified versions of God.
The psychology of the unconscious archetype does not
say anything about the reality of the existence of God
but only of the psychic manifestations experienced
by individuals.

- The Self may appear in many images such as a child, as Christ, numinous visions, a mandala, quaternity (or symbols of four), wholeness & totality.
- The Self is the uniting symbol which epitomizes the total union of opposites in the form of a cross, circle or sphere.

Mandala, Shri-Vantra. Cosmic Diagram. Hindu-Vedic.

In a letter to a professor of philosophy and
comparative religions in Switzerland, Jung wrote:

When I say "God" this is a psychic image. *Equally, the self is a psychic image of the transcendent, because indescribable and inapprehensible, wholeness of man. Both are expressed empirically by the same symbols, or symbols so similar that they cannot be distinguished from one another. Psychology is concerned simply and solely with experienceable images whose nature and biological behavior it investigates with the help of the comparative method. This has nothing whatever to do with God* per se.

(Jung, *Collected Letters*, Vol. 1, p. 487)

We are now like primitive societies that have lost numinosity, lost raison d'etre and then decayed. Society now strips mystery and numinosity of all things so that nothing is holy.

The number *four* symbolizes wholeness or totality.
It is, therefore, also a symbol of the Self.
The four is also the square and the quaternity.
Four is an archetype of universal occurrence.
If you want to describe the horizon as a whole,
you name the four quarters of the heaven.

The circle and the sphere are natural symbols of completeness;
their natural minimum division is a quaternity.
Jung loved the word quaternity.
It's not a bad word.

We talk of the whole person
almost to the point of cliché.
but there seems no doubt that such completeness
or wholeness is an elemental force in life élan vital.

The Sun-Cross— among the most ancient of all symbols.

The Dalai Lama names four human qualities:
love
compassion
tolerance
and will.
(in *Parabola* 1985)

That's not exactly hard science,
but it is enlightening.

Is not the result of adequate psychotherapy
enlightenment and dispelling darkness?
Dispelling.
Enlightening others lightens our own burdens and
inevitably involves the human spirit
and the religious attitude.
In Jungian psychology religion is not an illusion
and neither can it be reduced to analysis of infancy,
rather it is a central pillar of life and death.

Academic psychiatry's main thrust is science
and the rational world of medicine,
steering clear of whatever seems irrational and illogical,
thus keeping a cool status with colleagues.
This is appropriate, but
in the process some important things can be ignored
or lost.

I didn't realize this until one day
Joseph Henderson asked me, "Don't you see the obstacles
you face trying to teach Jungian psychology in a medical school?
They have no way to take in such concepts as the Self.
How can you expect them to see archetypes
when they've not dealt with their own archetypes?"

I understood, but in the next seminar series I talked
about the quest for the Holy Grail
and found, to my surprise and delight, that the students
understood the myth of the quest for the treasure that is hard to find.
Maybe, Joe, there is space for the Self here.

In my training I was taught by teachers
who did not see medicine as a trade or a business
but as a vocation.
There were the oaths of Hippocrates and Maimonides to swear to.
"Thy Eternal Providence" was not the insurance company,

the malpractice lawyers, nor the front office.
It was a manifestation of the power of the Self.

> *Thy eternal providence has appointed me to watch over the life and death of thy creatures. May the love for my art actuate me at all times; may neither avarice, nor miserliness, nor the thirst for glory or for great reputation engage my mind. . . . May I never forget that the patient is a fellow creature in pain. . . . I have been sanctioned to care for the life and health of mankind.*
> (Oath of Maimonides [1135–1204], court physician to Saladin)

When I graduated from medical school in 1940
we still repeated the Hippocratic Oath, which
physicians have taken for twenty centuries:

> *I swear by Apollo Physician and Asclepius and Hygeia and Panacea and all the gods and goddesses, making them my witnesses, that I will fulfill according to my ability and judgment this oath and covenant.*

This is strong archetypal stuff.
The mythological basis of medicine is not far removed,
nor are the priestly projections of the healing physician.
The Oath contains ancient admonitions no longer relevant
to modern medicine but it concludes with these words:

> *Whatever houses I may visit, I will come for the benefit of the sick, remaining free of all intentional injustice, of all mischief and in particular sexual relations with both female and male persons.*
>
> *What I may see or hear in the course of treatment or even outside of the treatment in regard to the life of men, which on no account one must spread abroad, I will keep to myself holding such things shameful to be spoken about.*
>
> *If I fulfill this oath and do not violate it, may it be granted to me to enjoy life and art, being honored with fame among all men for all time to come. If I trangress it and swear falsely, may the opposite be my lot.*

Does it seem quaint to reflect on such ancient ceremonials?
What with the DRGs, third party payments,
HMOs, PPOs and all the clever ways to advertise,
with malpractice suits proliferating and awards soaring to
astronomical amounts,
with a new cynicism and devotion to technology,
where will the humanity of medicine and therapy go?
I swear by Apollo Physician and Asclepius and Hygeia . . . .
Perhaps it is time to remind the healing profession
of its roots in antiquity
if it is to survive as more than a trade.

Mandala Forms in Nature

The latter phase of a splash; the crater has subsided, a columnar jet has risen, and the jet is divided into droplets.

Hippocrates (577–460 B.C.) was *the* great
Greek physician.
He did not treat the illness but the patient.
He helped nature heal.
In his time temples were erected to Asclepius,
god of medicine, at Cos, Athens, Epidaurus, and Pergamum.

"To those who came to his temple in search of a cure.
the god, once a physician himself, gave, in a trance,
instructions which did not differ from those
of a contemporary physician." (Acknerknecht, *The World of Asclepios,* p.24)

Asclepius

Hippocrates was the father of medicine,
Asclepius, the god of medicine.
The physician still uses a mythological symbol,
the caduceus.
The appropriate symbol of the physician
is the staff of Asclepius
with one serpent around it.

The two serpents entwined around a staff,
which are often seen on insignia and prescriptions,
are the symbol of Hermes who was the god of science
but also the god of thievery, commerce, and eloquence, and a messenger of the gods.
He was symbol of moral equilibrium and good conduct,
a master of getting himself out of tight spots by telling a story.
He was the god of money, boundaries, and exchanges and
guided souls to the underworld.
Hermes wore a winged hat and sandals
and carried the caduceus.
He had unlimited powers of transformation,
which is symbolic of the process of individuation.

Christ as hero and God-man may signify also
the psychological archetype of the Self.
Imago Dei is both God and shadow,
good and evil, deity and devil.

Hermes—Guide to the Soul

The archetypes are always the opposites
unified in the Self into wholeness.

In the quest for unity,
in our striving for integrity,
we yearn for paradise,
the numen of where we were.
Ah, *numinous temenos* of the Self,
a poetic foreign phrase
that means a desire to hit the bull's-eye on life's target.

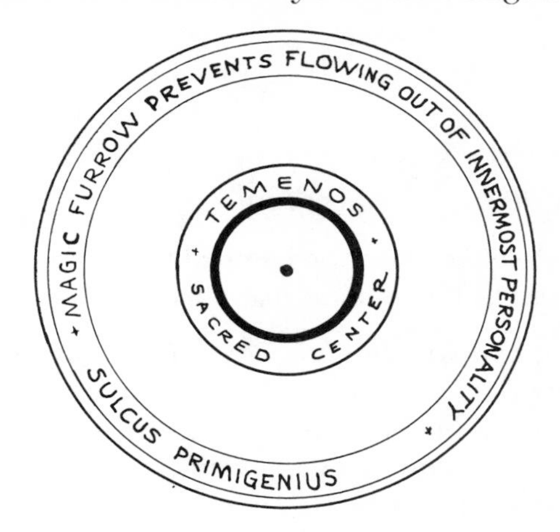

Temenos? Why the devil does Jung use such words?
Temenos is Greek for a piece of land cut off as a sacred domain,
a sacred precinct, or temple enclosure,
a grove set off and dedicated to a god,
or the spellbinding center of a circle.
It is a protected space set off as holy and inviolate,
your center.
In founding a city an original furrow or *sulcus primigenius*
was dug to create the protected *temenos*.

Age-old magical effects lie hidden in this symbol, for it is derived from the "protective circle" or "charmed circle," whose magic has been preserved in countless folk customs. It has the obvious purpose of drawing a sulcus primigenius, *a magical furrow around the center, the temple or the* temenos *(sacred precinct), of the innermost personality, in order to prevent an "out-flowing" or to guard by apotropaic means (to ward-off evil) against any disturbing influence from outside.*

(Jung, *CW* 13:36)

Thomas More's island of *Utopia* is a cut-off piece of land
that is seen as paradise.
It was originally a peninsula.

The search for paradise and the nostalgia for home, utopia,
or Erehwon (*nowhere* spelled backwards) is the symbolic
quest for the Self symbolized as *temenos*.
Other symbols are the Garden of Eden, Shangri-La, and the City of God,
the enchantment of an earlier time and a place that is
hard to find.

The perils of the soul:

Dream: *The dreamer is surrounded by a throng of vague female forms. A voice within him says, "First I must get away from Father."*

Visual Impression: *A snake describes a circle round the dreamer, who stands rooted to the ground like a tree.*

The drawing of a spellbinding circle is an ancient magical device used by everyone who has a special or secret purpose in mind. He thereby protects himself from the "perils of the soul" that threaten him from without and that attack anyone who is isolated by a secret. The same procedure has also been used since olden times to set a place apart as holy and inviolable; in founding a city, for instance, they first drew the sulcus primigenius *or original furrow. The fact that the dreamer stands rooted to the center is a compensation for his almost insuperable desire to run away from the unconscious. He experienced an agreeable feeling of relief after this vision—and rightly, since he had succeeded in establishing a protected* temenos, *a taboo area where he will be able to meet the unconscious. His isolation, so uncanny before, is now exalted into an aim, endowed with meaning and purpose, and thus robbed of its terrors.*

(Jung, CW 12:58, 62–63)

Take the mandala, for example, as an image of
the archetype of the soul.
Mandalas are used ritually
as objects of contemplation or meditation.
The mandalas of Tibetan Buddhism are particularly beautiful.
They draw our eyes and mind to the center and then
to the four gates or portals, a cross.

The Island of Utopia by Sir Thomas More. Originally King Utopus had 15 miles of the peninsula excavated to make Utopia an island. There were fifty cities on the island and the Anyder (waterless) River arises at the left.

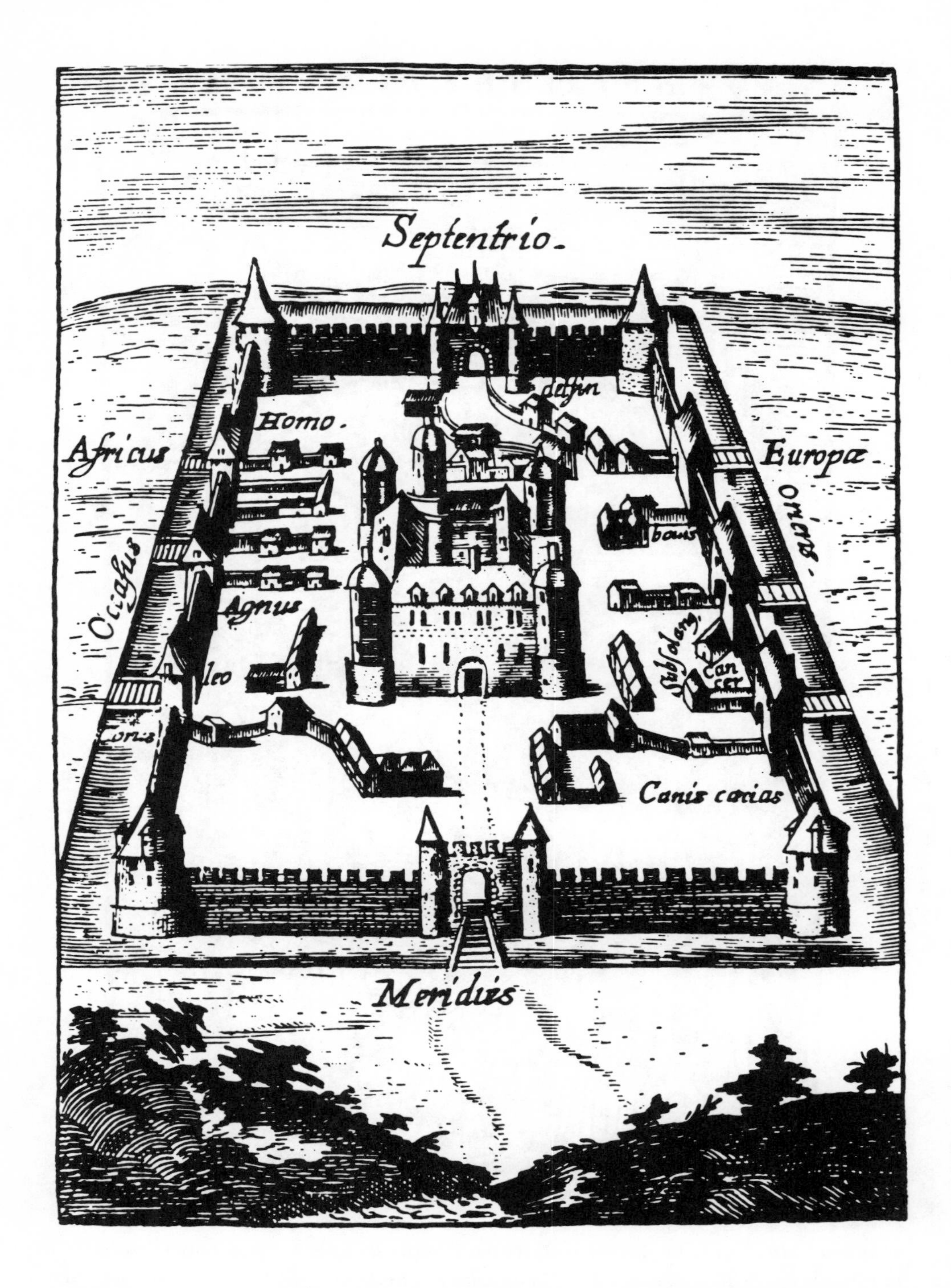

The symbolic city as centre of the earth, its four protecting walls laid out in a square: a typical temenos.*—Maier,* Viatorium *(1651) (from Jung, CW 12:82)*

Once Upon an Archetype

Libretto
[*recitativo*]:

Patient: Doctor, how am I doing?"
Am I getting anywhere? Tell me, Doctor,
that no matter what I think, you will love me.
Tell me, Doctor, what should I do?

Doctor: I cannot tell you what to do,
but it seems to me that you are doing very well.

Patient: Well? . . . Well? . . . Well?
What do you mean, Doctor, how am I doing well?
Tell me, Doctor, how am I doing?
Am I getting anywhere? Tell me, Doctor, tell me
that no matter what you think you will not leave me.
Tell me, Doctor, what shall I do?

Doctor: Speaking from my Olympian perspective
here in Delphi, in my Platonic best, I would say
that you are doing very well.

Patient: Oh, thank you, Doctor. Thank you, Doctor.
But, will I continue to get better?
Tell me, Doctor, what I should remember that you said.
Tell me, Doctor, how am I doing?
Will I be all right? How long will it take?

Doctor: You will be all right after you are born.
From the Temple of Apollo at Delphi
I can see that you are still unconscious.
When you are born psychologically,
you will see the light and you will be all right.

Patient: What light?

Chorus: Before enlightenment
there was drawing water and carrying wood.
After enlightenment
there was drawing water and carrying wood.

Before enlightenment the mountain was a mountain,
then the mountain is not a mountain.
After enlightment the mountain is a mountain.

Patient: Zapped with Zen.
But what do those words mean? What do those words mean?

Doctor: There is no more critical point in life than when
you have achieved your goal.
Your situation is not that critical.

Patient: Oh, thank you, doctor, thank you. Tell me what to do
to reach that point.

Chorus: In walking just walk.
In sitting just sit.
Above all don't wobble.

Patient: More Zen zap.
Tell me Doctor about the Self; how I can learn
to live and understand the collective unconscious?
How can I use these ideas? Tell me, Doctor!

Doctor: We could begin by looking at one of your dreams.

Patient: I don't remember any dreams. I told you that!
How can I remember dreams?

Doctor: They will remember themselves when you are ready for them.
We do not need dreams for therapy.
Not always.
What about your daily life and each day's bread?

Patient: I don't know what to say.

Chorus: Tell me, Doctor, how am I doing?
Am I getting anywhere. Tell me, Doctor,
that no matter what, you will love me.
And tell me, am I getting well?
Tell me, Doctor, what shall I do?

Doctor: I could say that, if not actually disgruntled,
you are "very far from being gruntled." (P.G. Wodehouse)

"Once Upon an Archetype" is a story about the projection
of the Self upon the doctor.
He is invested with godlike powers and omniscience.
If the therapist identifies with this projection, she or
he is in bad trouble.
Inflation and hubris,
God-almighty personhood
is wicked business.

If power symptoms creep into the work that is done round y
minish your own power and let others have more responsibility.
you a very sound lesson. They will learn that more power and mc
bring more suffering, as you yourself are learning under the present conditions.

One should not assert one's power as long as the situation is not so dangerous that it needs violence. Power that is constantly asserted works against itself, and it is asserted when one is afraid of losing it. One should not be afraid of losing it. One gains more peace through losing power.

(Jung, *Collected Letters*, Vol. 2, p. 463)

All Kinds of Doctors and Healers Get Projections

When you finish your training
and are a full-fledged whatever-you-are practitioner
your labors will become weary, and at times
you will be downcast and disheartened.
If your heart is too much in it
and your life is too much against you,
you will be in dark despair.
Your patients will expect not just miracles
but will ask for more of you
than there is,
let alone what there *is* to give.

I wrote these lines to help myself handle my own feelings about a patient:

> Anxiety cries for answers.
> He who gives the asker answers
> ties the asker.
> But he who makes the asker answer
> makes the asker answer-master.

It was good medicine for me.

The Shadow Archetype

Wherever good is, is evil.
Wherever shadow is, is light and substance.
Shadow is the name of the archetype of the alter ego.
The shadow is more or less synonymous with what Freud called "the unconscious."
But it is more than that
because it is both personal and nonpersonal,
both I and not-I.
For the purposes of practical Jung, we first know the shadow
as the personal unconscious,
all we abhor, deny, and repress:

power,
greed,
cruel and murderous thoughts,
unacceptable impulses,
morally and ethically wrong actions.

All the demonic things by which human beings
betray their inhumanity to other beings is shadow.
Shadow is unconscious, therefore, we encounter our shadow
in other people, things, and places where we project it.

Shadow projections have a fateful attraction to us.
It seems that we have discovered where the bad stuff really is:
It is outside, in him, in her, in that place, there! *There it is!*
We have found the bête noire at last,
succubus and incubus in the collective unconscious.

In the still depth of the collective unconscious
dwells absolute evil.
Its model is hell and purgatory.
It is manifest in cruel torture, fiendish torment, and terrorism,
in deeds so dark we know they are malevolent,
heartless, diabolical.

Evil flourishes in mobs, in soccer games gone murderous.
Evil lacerates atrocities and wars.
The perverse chimerical power of torture is pain.
Not the word *pain*, but PAIN! RAW PAIN!
What we see on television is violence.
We could not bear to see raw pain.
Shot, brutally wounded, killed, but there is no real pain.
Where has all the pain gone?
We talk of war, we see wars and battles fought all over the world
and acts of terrorism, but the pain, where is the pain?

Soldiers march. Soldiers shoot. Rebels and guerrillas shoot.
Soldiers and guerrillas are wounded and killed.
Where is the pain?
Politicians speak calm, soft words about hard evil things.
Reason pretends to prevail, while passions are concealed.
Pow! Pain, excruciating pain, unremitting pain.

A soldier in Vietnam is shot. His hideous head wound
is bleeding. All night he screams and cries.
His buddies wait helplessly for the medivac chopper.
In the morning, thank God, the screaming man is gone.
They don't forget those sounds. That is the sound of raw pain.
Back home it is chalked up somewhere as one more wounded soldier.

Bad as this is, it is not as bad as the pain of torture
inflicted continuously and intermittently unto death.
Pain! Do you ever stop to feel the pain?
Of course not.
Turn to the sports section. Or "Peanuts."
Switch on "Dallas," or "MASH."

Terrorism and torture
are justified by claims of "cause," "belief," and "right."
Extermination, holocaust, lynching, mutilation,
the collective shadow bursts like
napalm in your face.

Good and evil are a pair of opposites.
Where one is, there is the other.
Hitler was the necessary evil that summoned
the heroic Churchill,
whose personal power and magnetism thrived on the evil it opposed.
When the evil had been destroyed
and Hitler was dead,
Churchill's mission was fulfilled and
the people voted him out of a job.

The really dangerous ones are the harmless dreamers who don't know that they want to perish gloriously yet again through their accursed playing the savior. One time they strike their fellow men dead in order to convert them to the new religion of Naziism; the next time they preach disarmament in order to hand over their country to Russian tyranny. . . . [The Russians] are universal saviors who want to cure the whole world with their own disease, just as the Nazis did.

(Jung, *Collected Letters*, Vol. 2, p. 11)

Jung saw the Nazi holocaust as epidemic insanity,
the eruption of collective evil
into a deceptively ordered world.
The Jews were the German shadow
and became its scapegoats.
This evil shadow still lurks in contemporary humanity.
We are all capable of such regression.

When evil breaks at any point in the order of things, our whole circle of psychic protection is disrupted. Action inevitably calls up reaction, and, in the matter of destructiveness, this turns out to be just as bad as the crime, and possibly even worse, because the evil must be exterminated root and branch. In order to escape the contaminating touch of evil we need a proper rite de sortie, *a solemn admission of guilt by judge, hangman, and public, followed by expiation.*

The terrible things that have happened in Germany, and the moral downfall of a "nation of eighty millions," are a blow aimed at all Europeans. . . .

It has filled us with horror to realize all that man is capable of, and of which, therefore, we too are capable. Since then a terrible doubt about humanity, and about ourselves, gnaws at our hearts.

(Jung, CW 10:411 and 412)

Almost everyone has at least one particularly hated person.
This hated one is a remarkable clue to
the most unpleasant parts of the hating one.
Try that one on for size:
That's your dark twin.

Remember that you have a shadow. When a patient
thinks you are a stupid, greedy, self-centered, power-driven
quack, or thinks you are a god who knows everything,
he's put his finger on the healer's shadow.
By the same token the patient has the shadow
of the sick one: helplessness, weakness, and infantile insatiability.

The shadow is inexhaustible.
It is advisable to be able to eat your own shadow.
This metaphor always seems odd.
But there is something to it;
if you can stomach your own shadow
you can take on almost any old thing.

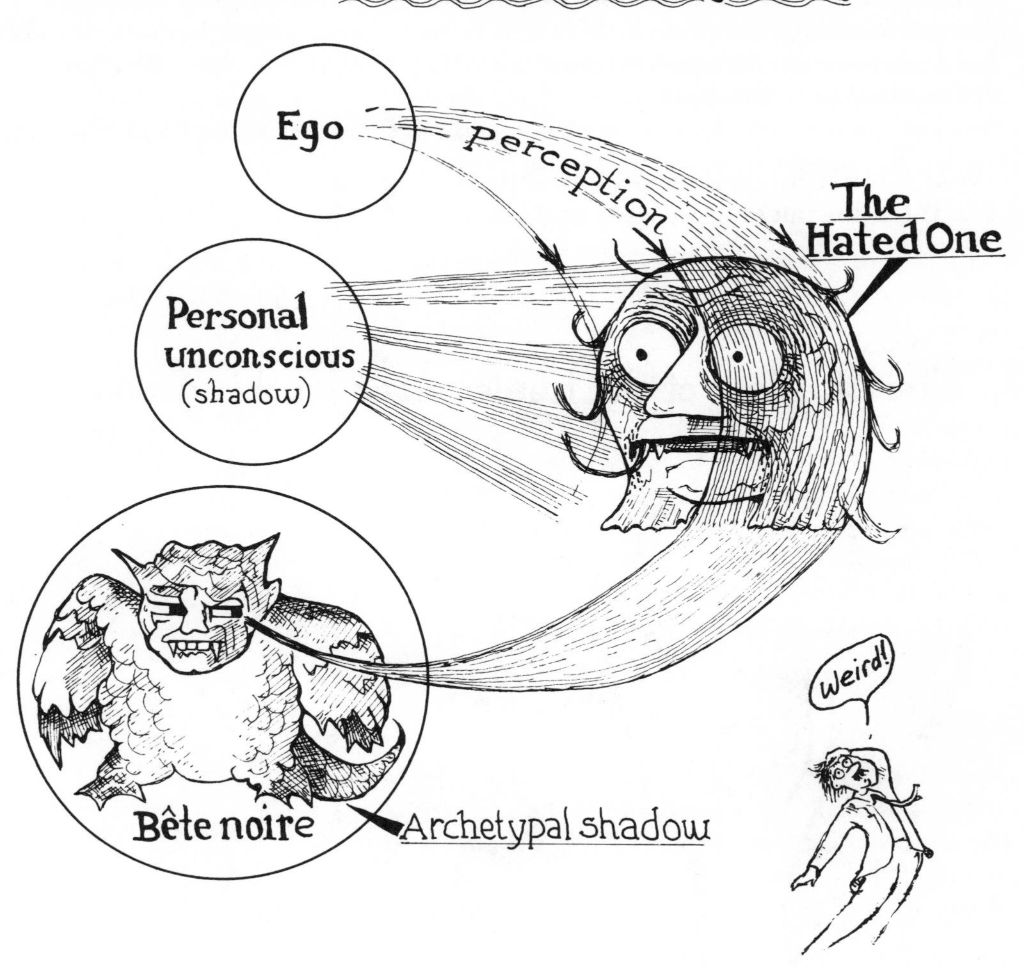

How appetizing is the next shadow
after you have one under your belt!

There is such a thing as a positive shadow.
It eats the negative shadow.
In ancient Rome it was the custom of the
conquering hero to ride triumphantly through the city.
By his side in the chariot sat a wise man
whispering into the hero's ear, over and over
"You are mortal. Remember you are mortal."

Jung wrote in a letter:
If Job succeeds in swallowing his shadow he will be deeply ashamed of the things which happened. He will see that he has only to accuse himself, for it is his complacency, his righteousness, his literal-mindedness, etc., which have brought all evil down upon him.

(Jung, *Collected Letters*, Vol. 2 p. 545)

What is the technique for dealing with the Shadow?
For this Jung offers us no nuts and bolts

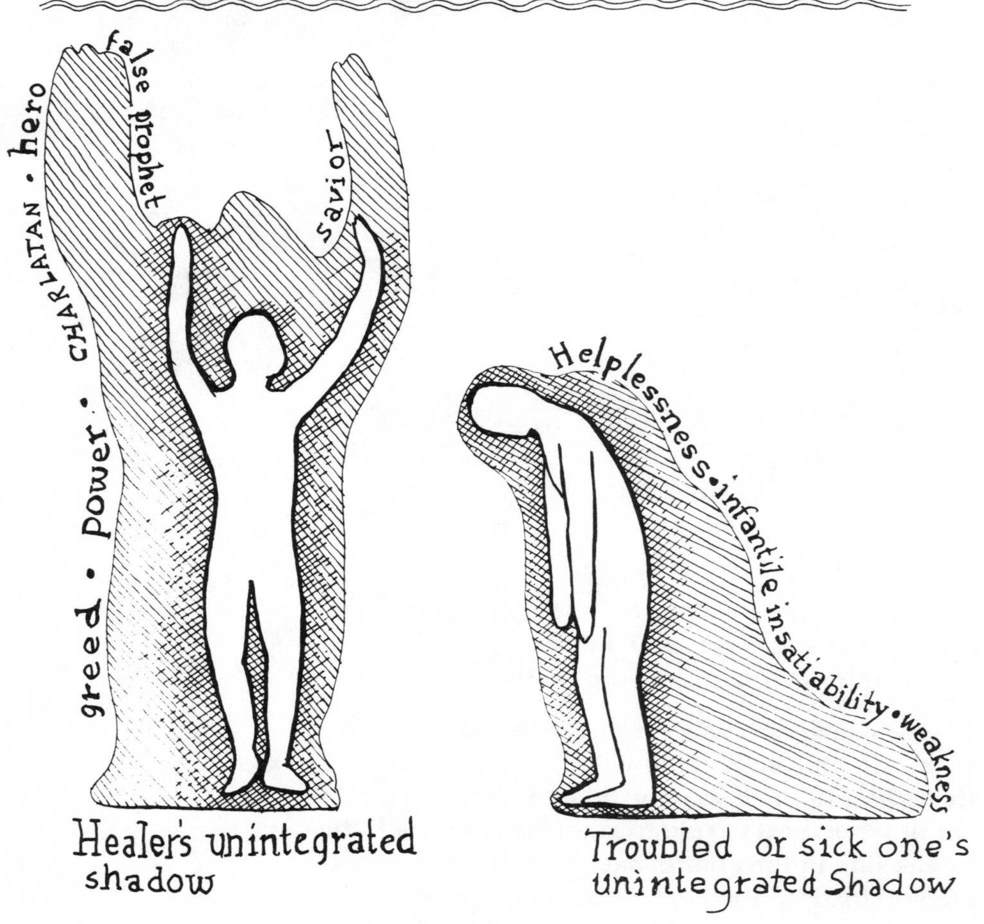

It is a very difficult and important question, what you call the technique of dealing with the shadow. There is, as a matter of fact, no technique at all, inasmuch as technique means that there is a known and perhaps even prescribable way to deal with a certain difficulty or task. It is rather a dealing comparable to diplomacy or statesmanship. There is, for instance, no particular technique that would help us to reconcile two political parties opposing each other. It can be a question of good will, or diplomatic cunning or civil war or anything. If one can speak of a technique at all, it consists solely in an attitude. First of all one has to accept and to take seriously into account the existence of the shadow. Secondly, it is necessary to be informed about its qualities and intentions. Thirdly, long and difficult negotiations will be unavoidable. Nobody can know what the final outcome of such negotiations will be. One only knows that through careful collaboration the problem itself becomes changed. . . . It is rather a result of the conflict one has to suffer. Such conflicts are never solved by a clever trick or by an intelligent invention but by enduring them.

(Jung, *Collected Letters*, Vol. 1, p. 234)

One of the problems of recognizing and facing our shadow,
owning it, eating it, and withdrawing it from projection
is that the shadow becomes a serious problem to oneself.
Withdrawing and acknowledging our shadow
is only the first step.
Then there is the long painful negotiation with it.
However, it is quite obvious from dreams
that when one faces a shadow which one has denied or run from
it diminishes in power, and size,
and ultimately becomes a positive force.

Our friends show us what we can do,
our enemies teach us what we must do. (Goethe)

The first view of any monster is apt to be
the most unnerving.
When we finally bring ourselves to see the shadow
we project as our own,
we are literally appalled and overwhelmed by the shadow,
the evil out there so plain to see.
At the moment of taking it back within ourselves
we are apt to be filled with self-recrimination,
guilt, and depression.
Little wonder we want to leave it out there
hanging on someone or something or some other whatever.

The Shadow · Evasion and Confrontation

Recognizing the Shadow

Running from the Shadow

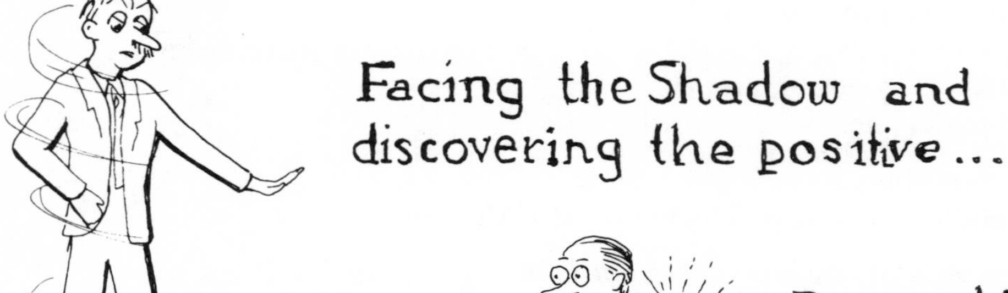

Facing the Shadow and discovering the positive . . .

. . . Pure gold of the Shadow

Repeat: We perceive the shadow as if it belongs to the other.
We withdraw our projection and our own shadow becomes enormous.
After prolonged negotiation we are able to befriend the shadow.
But even then it is not over because
the shadow will always be there, always be a part of our psyche.
We had best make a truce with it,
for the shadow
alerts us to particular kinds of danger or evil.
It is our personal and collective CIA.
Shudder the thought.

Since everybody is blindly convinced that he is nothing more than his own extremely unassuming and insignificant conscious self, which performs its duties decently and earns a moderate living, nobody is aware that this whole rationalistically organized conglomeration we call a state of a nation is driven on by seemingly impersonal, invisible but terrifying power which nobody and nothing can check. This ghastly power is mostly explained as fear of the neighboring nation, which is supposed to be possessed by a malevolent fiend. Since nobody is capable of recognizing just where and how much he himself is possessed and unconscious, he simply projects his own condition upon his neighbor, and thus it becomes a sacred duty to have the biggest guns and the most poisonous gas. The worst of it is that he is quite right. All one's neighbors are in the grip of some uncontrolled and uncontrollable fear, just like oneself. In lunatic asylums it is a well-known fact that patients are far more dangerous when suffering from fear than when moved by rage or hatred.

(Jung, CW 11:85)

"Es tu, Brute?"
The others out there also have their shadow.
So be it, they are hooks on which we hang our shadows.
This does not liberate us from recognizing
the legitimate shadows of the other.
Only now we know whose is whose.

We don't have to be paranoid to have enemies.
Paranoia is projection of hatred and evil
almost anywhere, even without hooks.

THE PSYCHIATRIST'S SHADOW: A Story

Those psychiatrists who know,
would just as soon forget.
Those who do not remember should be reminded.
Those who never knew read on.

In 1964 Senator Barry Goldwater was a candidate
for the presidency of the United States.
The magazine *fact* sent a questionnaire to the nation's
12,356 psychiatrists which asked:
Do you believe Barry Goldwater is psychologically
fit to serve as President of the United States?
1,189 psychiatrists wrote back that
he was not fit to be president;
657 said he was fit.
They submitted over one million words of professional opinion
without knowing or examining Mr. Goldwater.
I call it the "Great Patsy Shrinkapade."

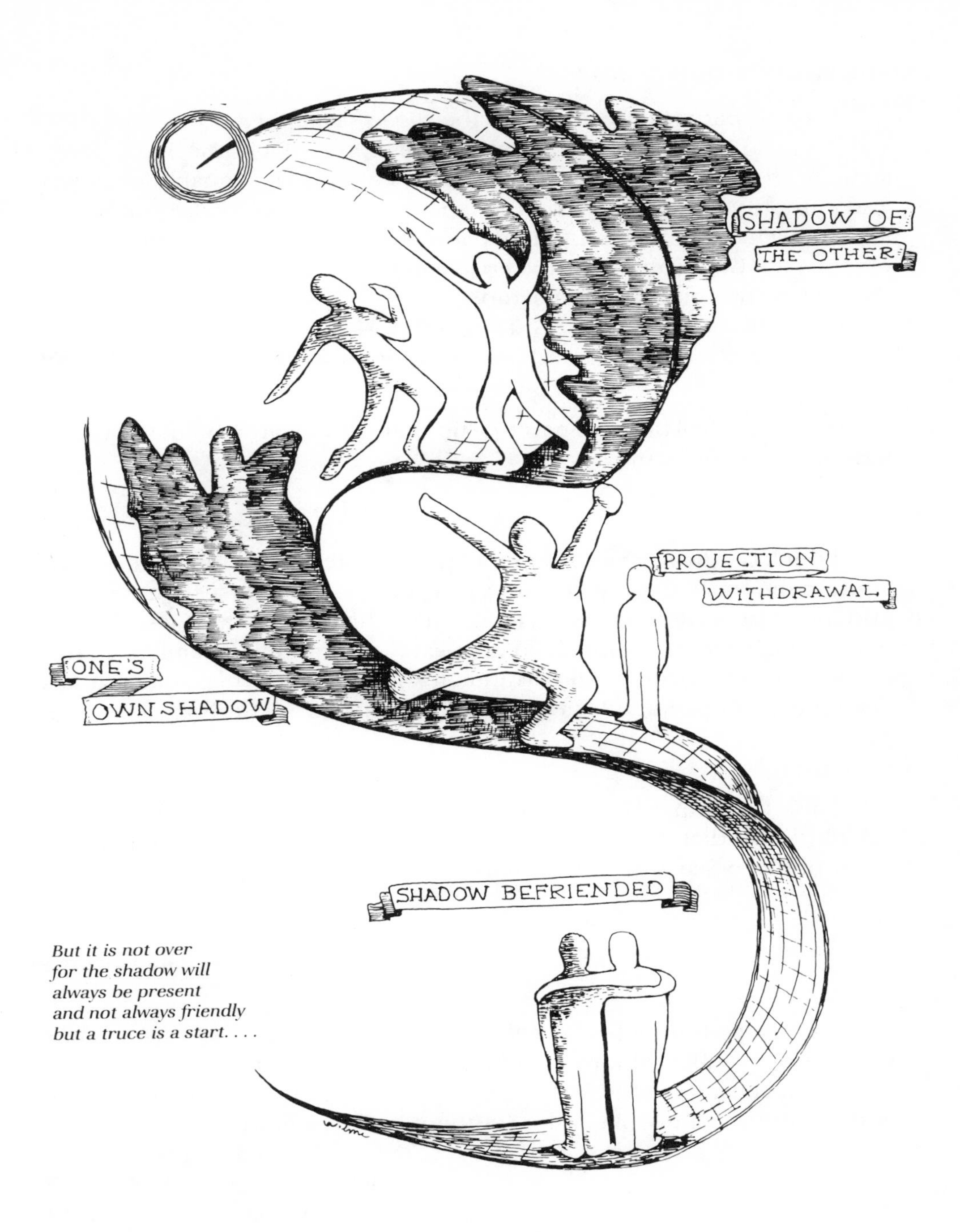
SHADOW OF
THE OTHER
PROJECTION
WITHDRAWAL
ONE'S
OWN SHADOW
SHADOW BEFRIENDED
But it is not over
for the shadow will
always be present
and not always friendly
but a truce is a start. . . .

Befriending the Shadow

This is what the experts wrote:

> Senator Barry Goldwater gives the *superficial* appearance of solidity, stability, and honesty. However, my impression is of a brittle, rigid, personality structure, based on a soft-spoken continuous demand for power and authority and capable of either shattering like crystal glass or bolstering itself by the assumption of paranoid stances and more power over others. . . . If Goldwater wins the Presidency, both you and I will be among the first in the concentration camps.
>
> G. Templeton, M.D.
> Director, Community Hospital Mental Clinic
> Glen Cove, NY
>
> ---
>
> Basically I feel he has a narcissistic character disorder with not too latent paranoid elements.
>
> Carl B. Younger, M.D.
> Los Angeles
>
> ---
>
> I think Goldwater has a paranoid personality which shows itself by rigidity, a tendency to project blame, fear of internal impulses breaking out and inherent contradictions in almost all of his statements. I feel he is dangerous because, although compensated at present, he could—and probably will—become more irrational and paranoid when under attack during the campaign. He is very much like Senator McCarthy.
>
> Alan M. Levy, M.D.
> New York
>
> ---
>
> Barry Goldwater is in my opinion emotionally unstable, immature, volatile, unpredictable, hostile, and mentally unbalanced. He is totally unfit for public office and a menace to society.
>
> Renatus Hartogs, M.D.
> Medical Director
> Community Guidance Service
> New York
>
> ---
>
> Word slips during his talks lead me to feel Senator Goldwater is grandiose and unstable, with tremendous self-investment. I feel he is destructive to himself and would be to others. His popularity is based on the fears and prejudices of people in the Southern and Western United States.
>
> Otto N. Raths, Jr., M.D.
> Chief Psychiatrist, V.A. Hospital
> Associate Professor of Psychiatry
> University of Minnesota, St. Paul
>
> ---
>
> (*fact* 1, no. 5 [Sept.–Oct. 1964])

There were some rational non-patsy shrinks.

One wrote,

> "If you will send me written authorization from Senator Goldwater and arrange for an appointment, I shall be happy to send you a report considering his mental status. The same goes for you." (*ibid.*)

Another wrote,

> "Your questionnaire is one of the most asinine, insulting documents I have ever been confronted with through the U.S. mails. Obviously, you and your informants believe that psychiatry is somewhat on the order of necromancy, soothsaying, glass-bell peering, and tea-leaf reading. I can assure you that no self-respecting, clinically minded, and sincere physician or psychiatrist will answer it. (*ibid.*)

But droves of therapists did answer.
They were roundly condemned by the embarrassed
American Psychiatric Association
and lampooned by the press.
The charlatan shadow of the psychiatric diagnostician
was conspicuous.

Whenever our opinions are solicited,
someone will appear
with the *first finger singular*.
Oh, great Logos, I have spoken.

WILMER

what is the collective unconscious?

Read the text!

The Dream Shadow

In a dream a person of the same sex,
usually unidentifiable as a real person who is
known in the dreamer's current life
and who has certain negative attributes
or is wholly bad or sinister,
is known as the shadow dream figure.

The shadow figure can turn out to be positive
and helpful.
The shadow has been called one's best enemy
because it makes us aware of our dark side,
the dark brother- or sister-twin within us.
It is a shadowy helpful figure.
Don't we learn by our mistakes?
If we value our failures as necessary steps
in becoming conscious, we are all the more human.

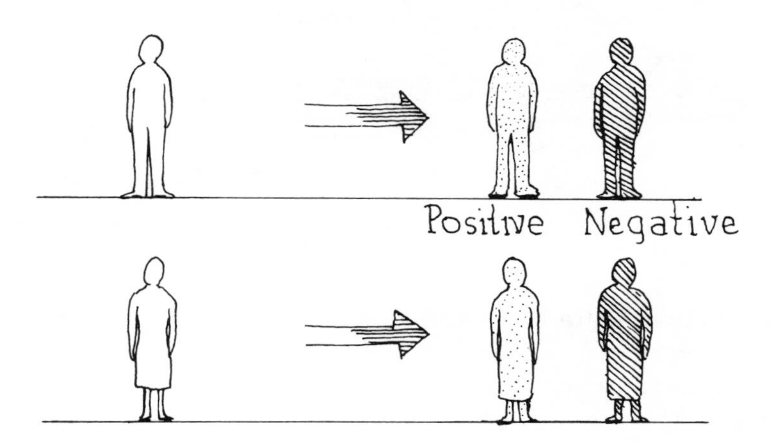

The dream shadow is ultimately a mediator between
the dream ego and the dark powers of the unconscious.
At one extreme it is absolute evil.
To complicate the picture, the symbolic dream shadow
may not be a person but
may be any animal, monster, or image of destructive force.

The Hero Archetype

The hero's main task is to overcome the monster of darkness,
to achieve victory over the powers of darkness,
to bring the triumph of good over evil,
and the dominance of consciousness over the unconscious.

Rites of passage,
and rites of initiation
are associated with the mythological progression of the hero
from a primitive trickster to
the redeemer hero.

St. George and the Dragon

Let us look at an illustration of the
stages of the hero myth cycle:

1. miraculous humble birth
2. early superhuman power and strength
3. rapid rise to prominence
4. triumphant struggle with the forces of evil
5. fallibility to sin, pride, and hubris
6. fall through betrayal, heroic sacrifice, and death

(Rank, *Myth of the Birth of the Hero*, ch. 3)

The hero has been called the collective ego.
He or she is also the archetype of the collective unconscious.

The Hero Myth

the six stages

Enantiodromia

Sooner or later everything runs into its opposite:
shadow to hero and hero to shadow,
trickster to redeemer, and good to bad.
The word *enantiodromia* means running contrariwise,
this business of everything turning into its opposite.

Old Heraclitus, who was indeed a very great sage, discovered the most marvellous of all psychological laws: the regulative function of opposites. He called it* enantiodromia, *a running contrariwise. . . . Thus the rational attitude of culture necessarily runs into its opposite, namely the irrational devastation of culture. We should never identify ourselves with reason, for man is not, and never will be, a creature of reason alone, a fact to be noted by all pedantic culture-mongers. The irrational cannot be and must not be extirpated. The gods cannot and must not die.*

(Jung, CW 7:111)

Every psychological extreme secretly contains its own opposite or stands in some sort of intimate and essential relation to it. Indeed, it is from this tension that it derives its peculiar dynamism. There is no hallowed custom that cannot on occasion turn into its opposite, and the more extreme a position is, the more easily may we expect an enantiodromia, *a conversion of something into its opposite. The best is most threatened with some devilish perversion just because it has done the most to suppress evil.*

(Jung, CW 5:581)

Jung once said that there can be up to
eighty percent pure gold in our shadow,
but curiously enough it is just the people
with the pure gold in their shadow
who show the most resistance to digging it out.
(in Hannah, B., "Ego and shadow," p.18)

The shadow and the hero are archetypes,
arche + *type* meaning prime imprinter.
Archetypes are composed of potentials for oppositeness,
and there we are back to old enantiodromia.
The cycle of initiation of the hero,
hero redeemer, and hero trickster

---

* Heraclitus (fl. c. 500 B.C.) conceived the universe as a conflict of opposites controlled by eternal Justice. In this conflict he found the apparent relativity of nature and her hidden unity. He was the first mental philosopher. (*Oxford Classical Dictionary*, p 415)

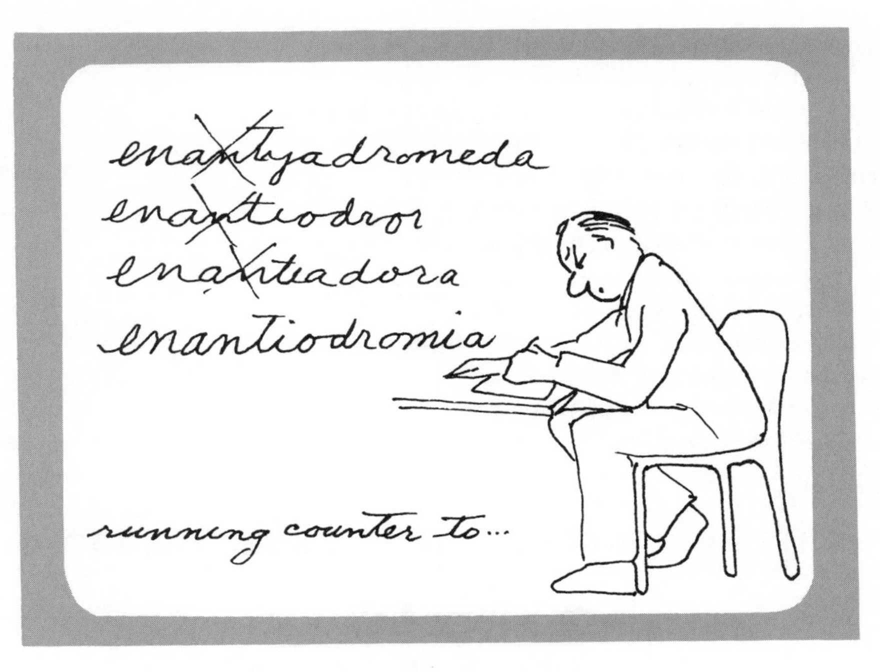

reveals that the hero is always at risk of regression,
the low ebb of the cycle is tricksterism,
and the high point, redeemer.
The cyclic flow is like a river:

> As all flowing rivers
> find peace in the ocean
> where they lose their name and form. (Upanishad)

A PSYCHOLOGY of OPPOSITES
Enantiodromia means "a running contrariwise" which means that every thing tends sooner or later to go over to its opposite –
tension of opposites

What is the trickster archetype?
He's the Charlie Chaplin in us,
the one who started out the nuts-and-bolts story,
the Little Tramp and the clown.
Hermes, whom we met with his caduceus,
is also a trickster. Ulysses is a trickster.
The trickster's characteristics are
chaotic caprice, malicious prankishness, and
meddlesome, cunning wit.
The trickster is both stupid and primitive,
unconscious and nonconforming,
a genuine 18-carat shadow but
divine and demonic, good and evil.

RITES OF INITIATION - CYCLIC MODEL

HERO REDEEMER
HERO
HERO
enantiodromia
enantiodromia
enantiodromia
enantiodromia
TEMENOS
HERO TRICKSTER

I don't get it!
MY HERO!

A Nuts-and-bolts Translation of Enantiodromia

It is a bewildering thing in human life that the thing that causes the greatest fear is the source of the greatest wisdom. One's greatest foolishness is one's biggest stepping stone. No one can become a wise man without being a terrible fool. Through Eros one learns the truth, through sins we learn virtue. Meister Eckehard says one shouldn't repent too much, that the value of sin is very great. In "Thais" Anatole France says that only a great sinner can become a great saint, the one cannot be without the other. How can man deal with this terrible paradox? He cannot say, "I will commit a sin and then I will be a saint," or: "I will be a fool in order to become a wise man." The question is, what to do when put into a complete impasse. Then the dream says, in the cauldron things are cooked together, and out of the things strange to each other, irreconcilable, something new comes forth. This is obviously the answer to the paradox, the impossible impasse.

(Jung, *Dream Analysis*, Vol. 3, p. 26)

Enantiodromia is a balance of the yin-yang opposites.
The opposites east and west are determined
by where you are, because facing north wherever you are
your right hand is east and your left hand is west,
even when you stand in the Far East or the West End.
There is no absolute east and west, just like
there is no absolute hot and cold.
Black and white, wise and stupid, yes and no.
Dear old enantiodromia, flow on,
yinning and yanging.

The Complex

The archetypal idea when actualized and experienced
becomes a complex of ideas.
The complex is held together by the
feeling tone common to all of the individual ideas.
Unconscious, feeling-toned trains of thought
determine our conscious associations.
Jung discovered that we have complexes
but more important, complexes can *have us.*
What is a feeling-toned complex?

It is the image *of a certain psychic situation which is strongly accentuated emotionally and is, moreover, incompatible with the habitual attitude of consciousness. This image has a powerful inner coherence, it has its own wholeness and, in addition, a relatively high degree of autonomy. . . and therefore behaves like an animated foreign body in the sphere of consciousness.*

(Jung, CW 8:201)

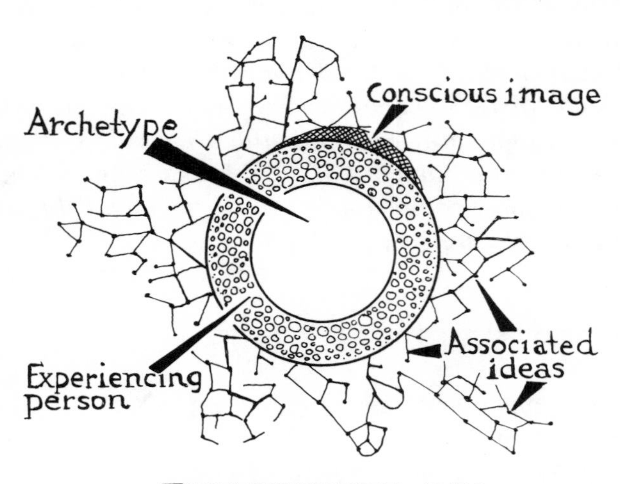

THE ARCHETYPAL IDEA

Jung discovered the complex in his important scientific work on the Word Association Test.
He observed that there was a prolonged time delay in responding to charged words associated with crucial conflicts.
Complexes interfere with conscious performance action, will, memory, and of course, associations.
Feeling tones attract ideas around archetypes, and memories, holding them as if by electromagnetic force.
This is a trim tab factor which determines how we guide ourselves.
It is the basis of the commonly used polygraph lie detector.

That is complex allright - a constellation of psychic elements grouped around feeling-toned contents, a nucleus and secondary associations

Sometimes Jungian psychology is called "complex psychology"

The Wounded Healer Archetype

This is an amalgam of opposites.
To see health and sickness as either/or is to
create an arbitrary total separation.
A wounded healer who sees the patient as wholly sick
does not see the healthy part.
When the doctor sees only the sickness in the other,
he assumes an all-healthy role himself.
The patient learns the sick role
as a way of surviving this one-sided connection.
The sick role can become a way of life.

At one extreme in the wounded healer archetype
is the medicine man, shaman, trickster, and charlatan.
At the other end is the healer of highest technical and human skills.
In the middle is the balanced, centered healer.

The wounds of the wounded healer who is unconscious of
his own wounds may be stirred up
when he devotes day in and day out to listening to
and helping others in psychological distress.
His tendency to see the patient as all-sick and
all-wounded blinds him to the inner physician.
It is the health-sickness archetype which is the
spectrum of all who are wounded.

In antiquity the entire art of healing
was the domain of the divine physician:

> *He* was the sickness *and* the remedy. These two conceptions were identical. Because he was the sickness, he himself was afflicted (wounded or persecuted like Asclepius or Trophonius); because he was the divine patient he also knew the way to healing.
> To such a god the oracle of Apollo applies: "He who wounds also heals."
> (Meier, *Ancient Incubation and Modern Psychotherapy,* p.5)

The eye of the balanced wounded healer sees both
the wounded and the healthy parts of the patient.
Not just organs and psychopathology, not just
a bevy of neurotransmitters and disease,
not, that is, a soulless body
but all being.

I would suggest that there is no special healer archetype or patient archetype. The healer and the patient are two aspects of the same. When a person becomes sick, the healer-patient archetype is constellated. This sick man seeks an external healer, but at the same time the intra-psychic healer is activated. We often refer to this intra-psychic healer in the ill as the "healing factor." It is the physician within the patient himself and its healing action is as great as that of the doctor who appears on the scene externally. Neither wounds nor diseases can heal without the curative action of the inner healer.

(Guggenbühl-Craig, *Power in the Helping Profession*, p. 90)

Wellness is not happiness.
Some happiness is just plain sick.
Sickness is not necessarily depression or anxiety.
Some depression and anxiety is just plain healthy.
Don't run for the antidepressant medication
nor the anxiolytic drugs.
Just be patient and take your medicine of mire and dumps,
and maybe it will enantiodromia itself.

But if you are now in the dumps and up to your ears in the mire, you must tell yourself that you were obviously flying too high and that a dose of undiluted hellish blackness was indicated. The pickle you are in is certainly something you couldn't have brought on yourself. This shows that someone "out there" is surrounding you with provident thoughts and doing you the necessary wrong.

You should regard your present situation as a mud bath from which after a while a small morning sun will burst forth again. "Patience be damned," says Faust, and you need it most of all. For your age and your circumstances you are still too fractious. The devil can best be beaten with patience, having none himself.

(Jung, *Collected Letters*, Vol. 1, p. 427)

The Wounded Healer
the Split Health-Sickness Archetype

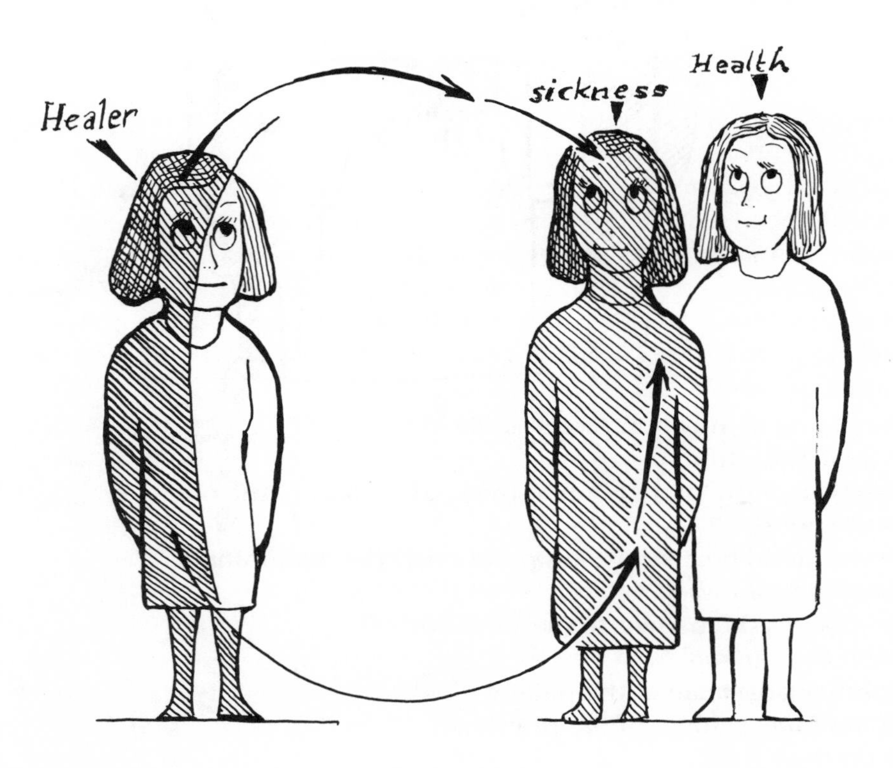

The inner voice of the healing self is the *daimonion*
in contrast to the demon.
Such a *daimonion* whispered into Socrates' ear,
"Thou shouldst make more music, Socrates."
Socrates took the advice literally and bought himself a flute.
The *daimonion* meant he should practice the art of feeling
in contrast to his preoccupation with reason.
Jung's interpretation of Socrates' *daimonion* was
"*To hell with the Ego-world! Listen to the voice of your daimonion. It has a say now, not you.*"
(Jung, *Collected Letters*, Vol. 2, pp 531–32)

THE WOUNDED HEALER

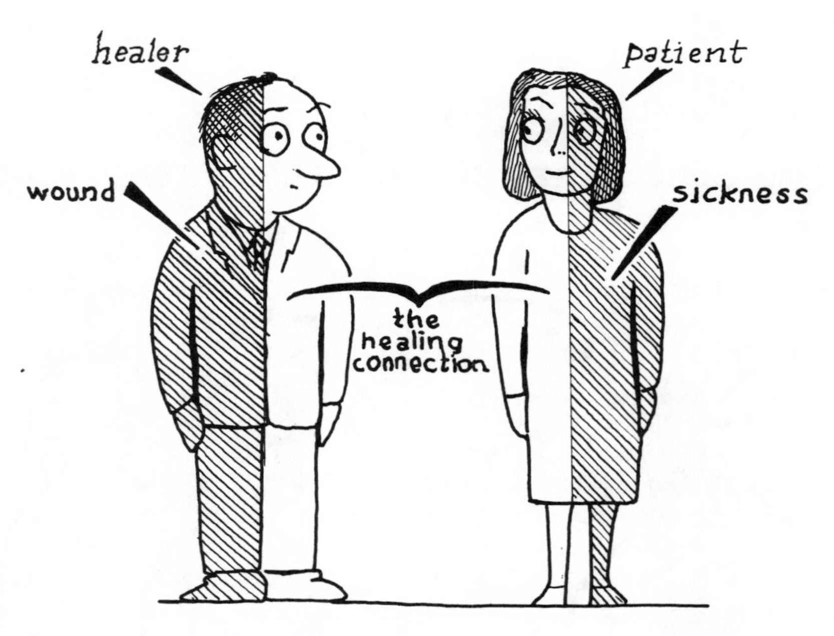

The healing connection pictured above
has a bird-like touch
from the healthy part of one to the healthy part of the other.
It is the bond.
The wounded healer has comprehended the admonition,
physician heal thyself.
This enables the patient to understand,
patient heal thyself.
The inner physician of the patient
and the inner patient of the physician
can do their work.

I keep saying *patient*, and I must repeat
what I said in the introduction:
Doctor, physician, and *patient*
are good and great words.
They have historic dignity.
Some therapists prefer the word *client*.
This had its origins in medical-practice laws
which designate formal rights to treat patients.
But to treat clients
did not require medical qualification.
Some of my medical and psychiatric colleagues
refer to their clients and not patients.
Clients are serviced like customers.
Come to think of it, there is a move afoot
for doctors to have customers.
To me the word *client* has the negative connotation
of a straight business relationship.
Lawyers have clients.
Advertising agencies have clients.
Doctors have patients.
A rose is a rose is a rose.
Call it *them, he, she*, or what you will.
If you feel differently please substitute the word *client*
every time I say *patient*.

Dream of the Wounded Healer Archetype

A woman who is *not* a doctor dreams:

> *I am a doctor seeing newly admitted patients on a medical ward. I begin talking to a woman patient. I ask her to get out of bed because I want to see her gait. She refuses. I turn around and see her husband, a surly man, who says, "I have had a lot of orthopedic surgery." I ask him, "Where are the scars?" He seems terribly annoyed at my question and doesn't seem to know. I persist, asking him several times, "Where are the scars?" Then the scene fades as I hear a voice saying,* ***"A lot of swagger is maintained via the sick role."***

In this dream the patient has assumed
the role of the physician,
but she is also represented by the patient and the voice.
As a physician she wants to examine an uncooperative woman
with an unpleasant, self-centered husband
who identifies himself as having had
a lot of orthopedic surgery.

When challenged to show
proof that he is a surgical patient,
he doesn't have the scars to do so.

One might say that the inner physician of this woman
is trying to see how capable of movement her patient is.
Her inner man, or sham patient who is playing a patient role,
evokes a clever interpretation.
Her inner daimonion nails her arrogant animus.
Touché, a need to be sick is revealed.

The case of the archetype of the wounded healer,
is told dramatically in a book I wrote
when I was a tuberculosis patient in a TB sanatorium
at the time of my internship at a hospital in Panama.
I was, indeed, the wounded healer
and came to terms with the self-healing phenomenon.

Huber proposed to Bovy at a fork in the Old Bronchial Tree.

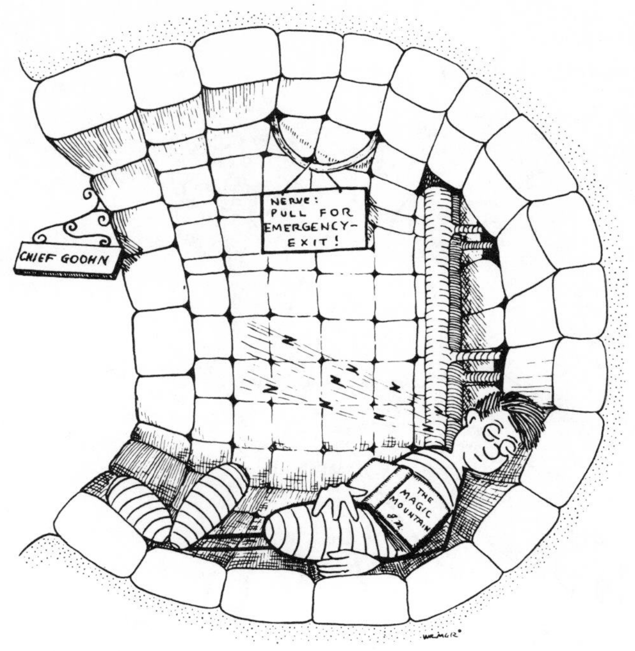

Huber the Tuber, asleep
in a calcified cell of the lung.
He has been reading Thomas
Mann's The Magic Mountain,
which I read in the sanatorium.
The sleeping hero-villain
is getting well.

In 1940 there were no drugs to help me,
only strict bed rest for a year.
My imagination came to my rescue in the images
or visions of a story which I wrote and illustrated,
in a book called *Huber the Tuber:*
The Lives and Loves of a Tubercle Bacillus.
In the beginning of the story Huber meets Bovy
(Bovine tubercle bacillus) in the old Bronchial Tree
where he proposes.

The story was created more or less unconsciously, as if
it wrote itself. Each day I drew one new picture
for the story. After 120 days the book was
illustrated and written.
I was possessed by my archetype muse.
I was Huber proposing marriage to my sick anima, Bovy.
It was a healing, funny book,
and it sold a great many copies
and was printed in many editions.

I had unconsciously discovered for myself
what Jung had already described as
active imagination.

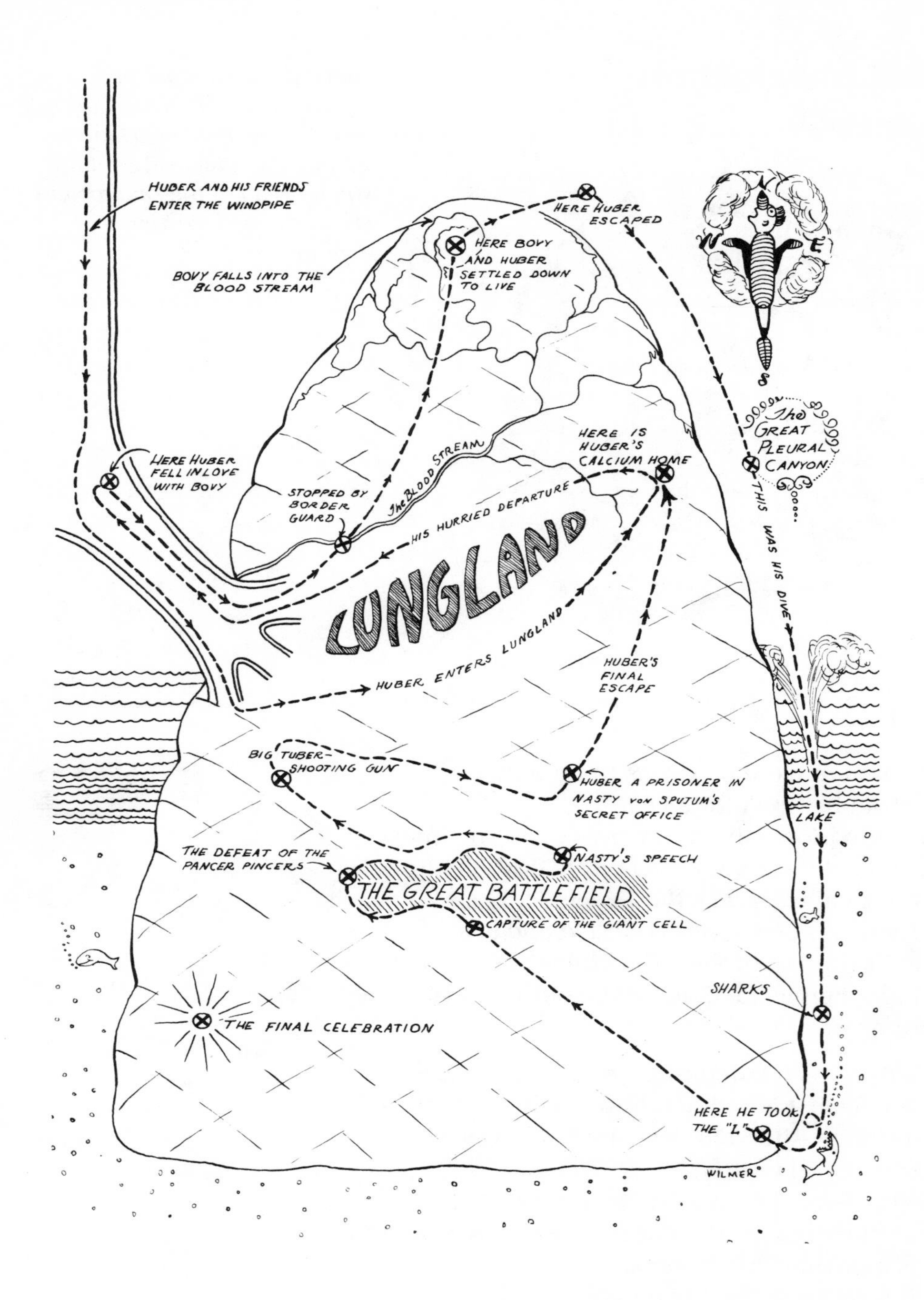

The final triumph of the White Cells in a great celebration of the liberation of Lungland. Long Live Lungland!

Active Imagination

These "visions" are far from being hallucinations or ecstatic states; they are spontaneous, visual images of fantasy or so-called active imagination. *The latter is a method (devised by myself) of introspection for observing the stream of interior images. One concentrates one's attention on some impressive but unintelligible dream-image, or on a spontaneous visual impression, and observes the changes taking place in it. Meanwhile, of course, all criticism must be suspended and the happening observed and noted with absolute objectivity. Obviously, too, the objection that the whole thing is "arbitrary" or "thought up" must be set aside, since it springs from the anxiety of an ego-consciousness which brooks no master besides itself in its own house. In other words, it is the inhibition exerted by the conscious mind on the unconscious. . . . Under these conditions, long and often very dramatic series of fantasies ensue. The advantage of this method is that it brings a mass of unconscious material to light. . . . The aim of the method is naturally therapeutic in the first place, while in the second it also furnishes rich empirical material.*

(Jung, *CW 9i: 319, 320)*

Active imagination can be painting, drawing,
sculpting, poetry, drama, dancing, or any other use of
color and form.
The seemingly unmanageable chaos of one's situation
is visualized and objectified,
observed by the conscious mind, and analyzed.
Active imagination is a fascinating blend of unconscious, preconscious,
and ego-consciousness in action.

What is the source of all this creative energy?
The symbol of birth and creation is the mother.
The image of the mother-of-us-all is the earth.
The earth mother is the archetypal mother.
Creation of life and life energy is also
rooted in biology and our inborn instincts.
Our directed fantasies and
creative works of art, poetry, fiction, and dance
make conscious the realization of
the mother archetype.

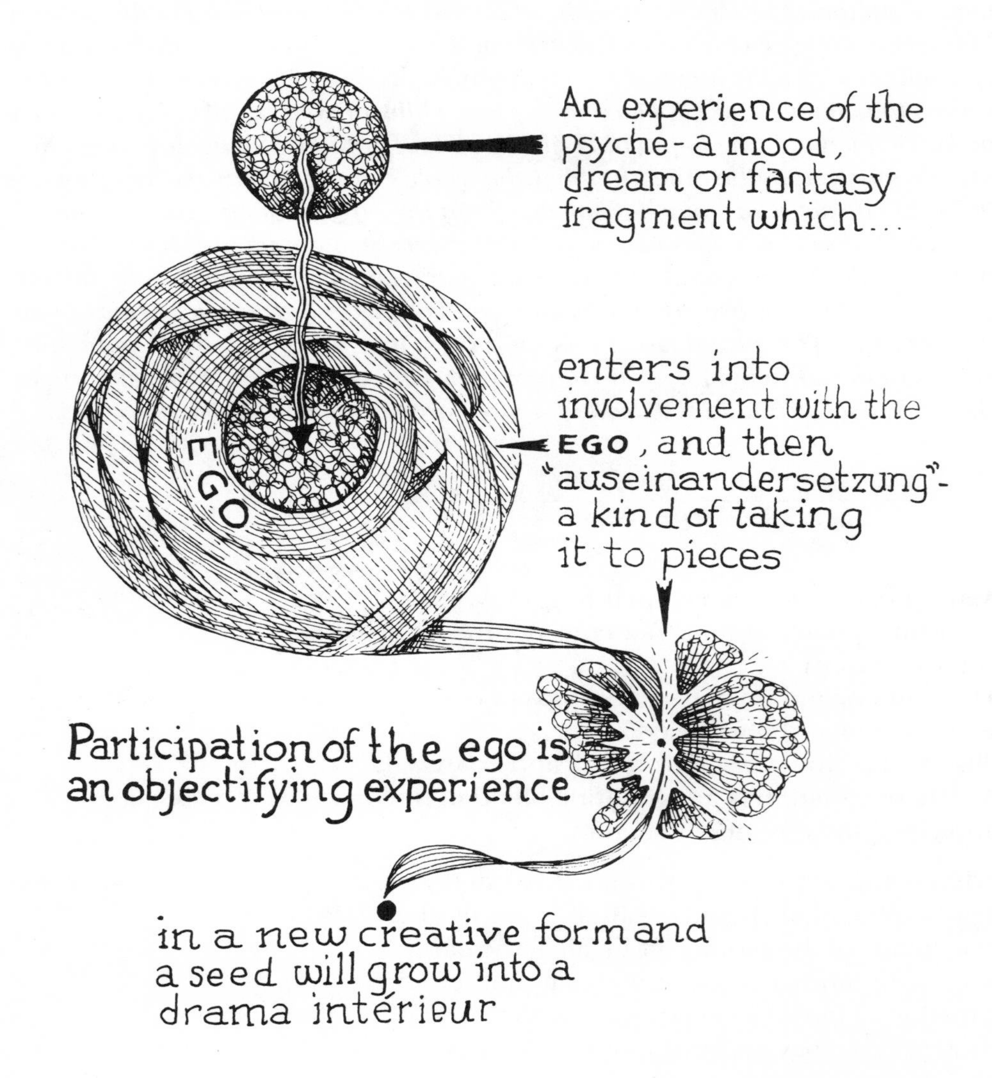

Active Imagination
one must let it happen to see where and to what it leads and why
An experience of the psyche - a mood, dream or fantasy fragment which...
EGO
enters into involvement with the EGO, and then "auseinandersetzung"*- a kind of taking it to pieces
Participation of the ego is an objectifying experience
in a new creative form and a seed will grow into a drama intérieur

---

Auseinandersetzung is a German word used often by Jung. It is almost untranslatable but its meaning is approximately "having it out." It is a kind of taking to pieces but different from *zerrissenheit* which means torn to pieces. It is letting the non-I world have its sway under the watchful, disciplined eye and not just wandering hither and thither. It is taking something apart powerfully.

CREATIVE FANTASY. species specific mother archetype

FORM

preformed, preexisting, inborn reality. Inherited primordial image-form for mother archetype

BIRTH

Conscious image manifest

EXPERIENCING PERSON

personal experiences in early life give the archetype its content

DIRECTED FANTASY MAKES CONSCIOUS THE REALIZATION AND MEANING OF ARCHETYPE

The world of creative fantasy needs roots
in the here and now;
the earth mother is an exquisite symbol of that.
Acceptance of the here and now
is living in the present, the eternal moment.
"Give us this day our daily bread"
is asking for sustenance for this one day,
not for tomorrow or the hereafter.
One patient told me that to balance that sacred prayer
he sometimes said under his breath,
"Give us this day our daily shit."
This is not a sacrilege but a natural process
in taking in and giving out.
Understood in this life context
it was a liberating metaphor for him.

Active Imagination at Work

One day I fell into a glum mood
and drew this picture.

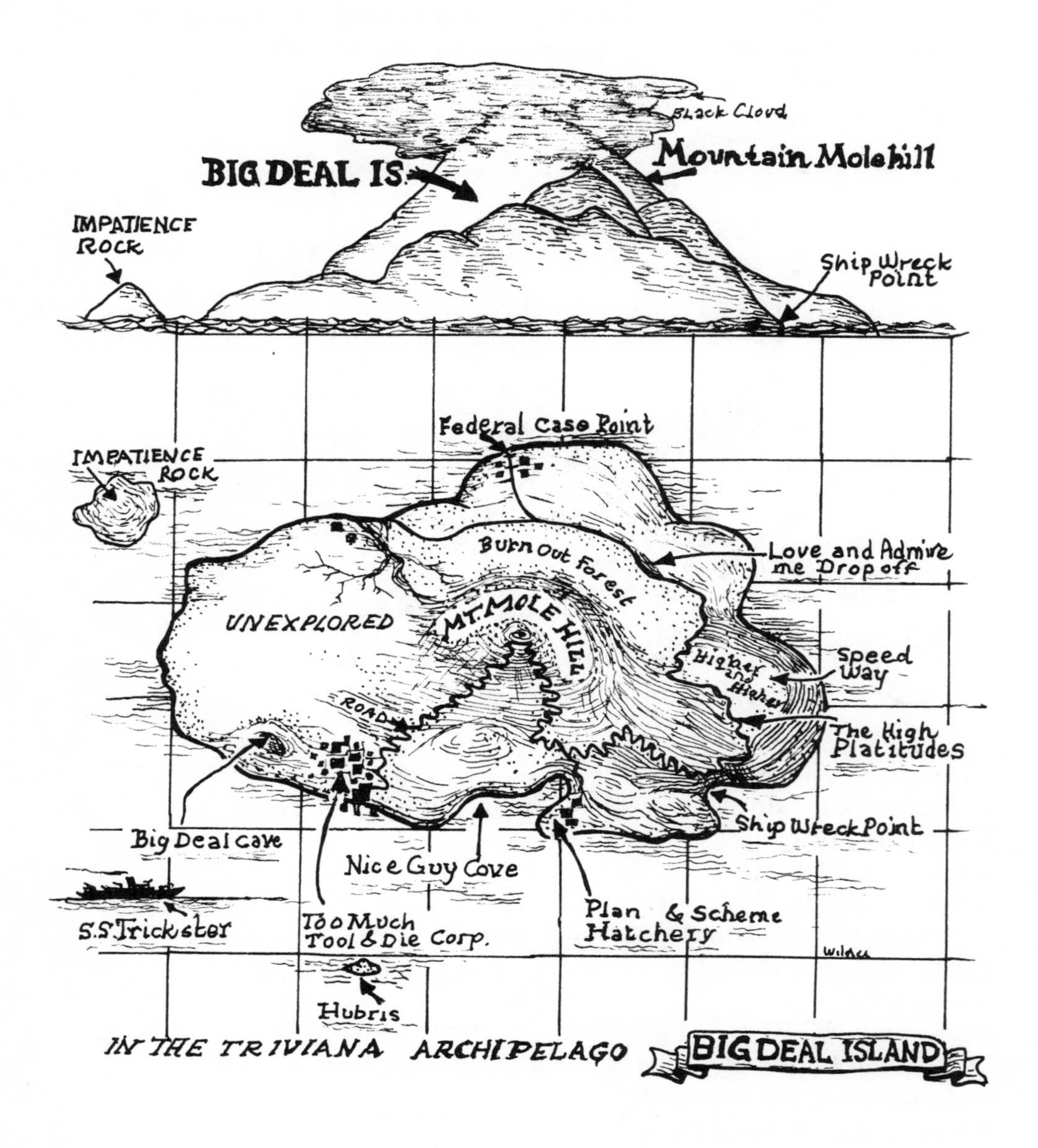

It is an Island called Big Deal with hills, cities,
inlets, cliffs, rivers, and in the center
Mole Hill Mountain. I said to myself,
"When anyone asks me, 'Where are you coming from?'
I will say, 'I'm coming from Mole Hill Mountain on Big Deal Island.'"
This *mental map* immediately transformed my mood to
a good feeling. I had mapped all the pitfalls
and risks I was navigating. I realized from the picture
that I had done well and kept myself from ego inflation.

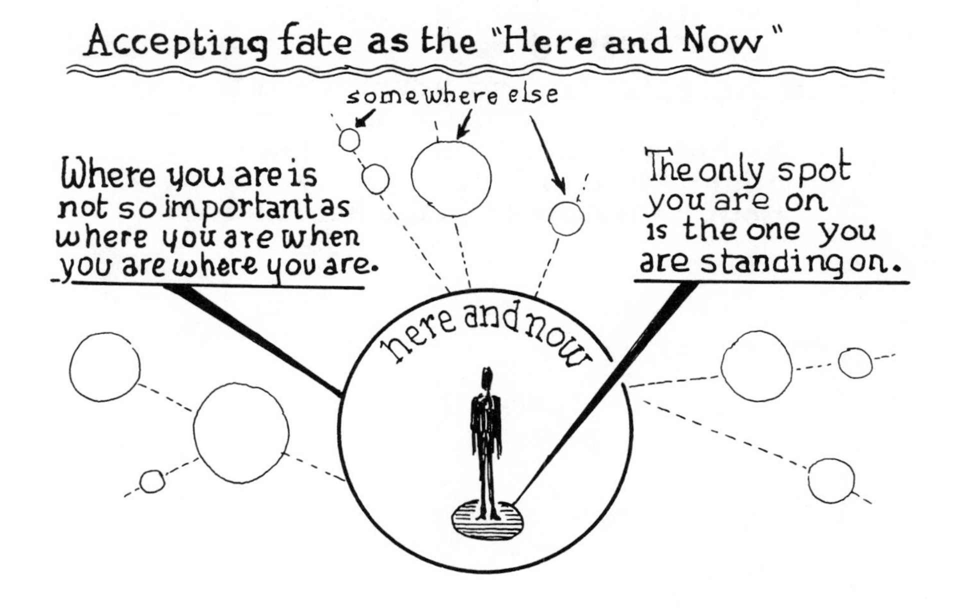

Accepting fate as the "Here and Now"
somewhere else
Where you are is not so important as where you are when you are where you are.
The only spot you are on is the one you are standing on.
here and now

This moment is the only reality
we will ever know.
Fully lived it is our whole life.
We are not just carrying on for a better tomorrow
but are accepting fate as being this being
as it is given to us, *hic et nunc*.
Accepting fate in this sense is not being fatalistic.
Quite the contrary, it allows us our only opportunity
to influence our destiny, which at each moment
in the future will be our fate
in the here and now.

I once had a psychiatric resident who refused to come back
to my seminar after I talked about fate in this way.
Tragically, a few months later
he committed suicide.
He had an appointment in Samara.*

- When you accept your present "fate"
you may be able to change
your destiny.
- Acceptance and adaptation to
your inner reality is as important
and may be more important than
adaptation to outer reality –
both being givens in the here and now.

---

*According to legend a merchant in Bagdad sent his servant into the market place. The servant came running home begging his master to give him a horse so he could ride to Samara, since he had seen Death in the market and Death had stared at him with a strange expression. He was given the horse and rode as fast as he could. The master rode into the market place where he met Death. He asked Death why he had looked at his servant with such strangeness in Bagdad. Death replied that he was startled to see him there because he had an appointment with him that evening in Samara.

Messages from Time Immemorial

The great sagas, the great myths, the divine symbols, and
the creativity of geniuses and great men and women
symbolize the archetype of the Self,
reminding us of the god-head within each of us.

From the sun and moon
the stars and planets,
the springs and rivers, the highest mountains
and deepest valleys,
the numinous moments,
the vast oceans and the endless sky,
and the healing spirit of transcendent experiences
come messages from time immemorial.

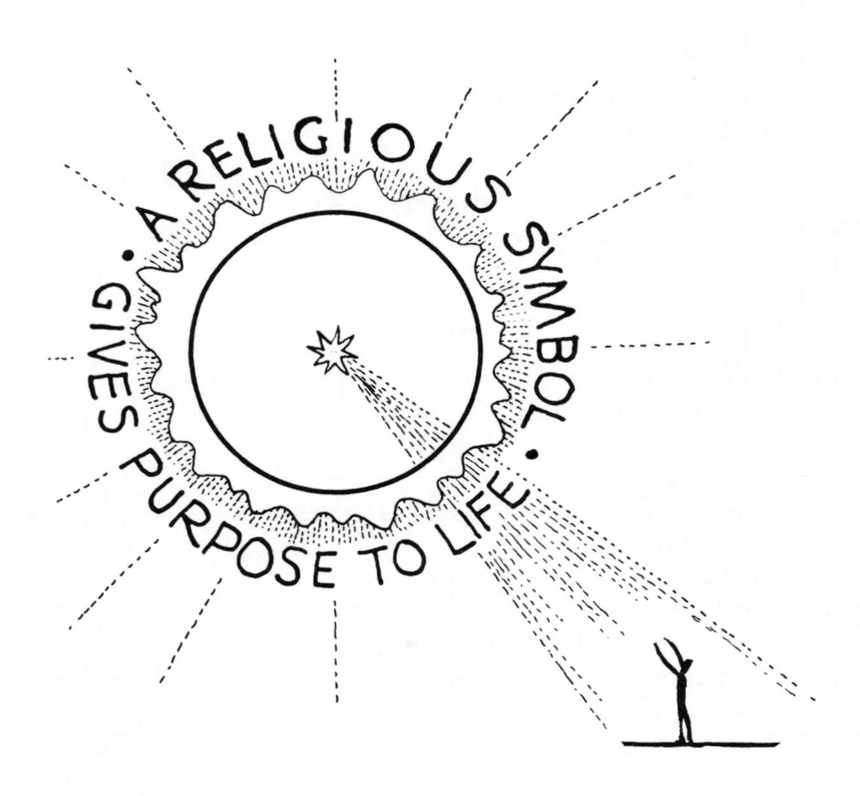

The impact of an archetype, whether it takes the form of immediate experience or is expressed through the spoken word, stirs us because it summons up a voice stronger than our own. Whoever speaks in primordial images speaks with a thousand voices; he enthrals and overpowers, while at the same time he lifts the idea he is seeking to express out of the occasional and the transitory into the realm of the ever-enduring.

He transmutes our personal destiny into the destiny of mankind, and evokes in us all those beneficent forces that ever and anon have enabled humanity to find a refuge from every peril and to outlive the longest night.

(Jung, CW 15:129)

Religious symbols have come from time before history.
A primitive person seeing the heavens,
eclipses, tornados, and lightning or hearing thunder
was in a world of magic and divine power.
That world is now lost in the delusions that
we have mastered space,
conquered mountains,
and are hot on the clues to the mystery of life itself.
But we have not even begun to conquer ourselves.

The Couch

In the pursuit of this great unknown, inner darkness,
Freud created psychoanalysis.
There were some problems
that were insurmountable,
but he tried a kind of space travel called the couch.
This became a new religion,
dogma, and doctrine with new altars and idols,
the couch and the chair:
the patient lying down, the analyst sitting elevated
and unseen in anonymous seclusion.

RULE OF THUMB: the Couch

A couch for the patient to lie down on
is not *verboten*.
Use a couch if you have one, when

- the patient has a rather intact ego,
- the transference is sticky,
- you don't want to look at the patient,
- you don't want the patient to look at you,
- you think regression is in order,
- you sense something you want to hear is lurking near
  but never coming out in the clear.

They say (whoever they are) that now and then
Jungians should be Freudians and
dust off the couch.
Not that all Freudians are wedded to the couch.
There is a great storehouse of theory and practice,
anecdote and apologue
about the why and wherefores of the couch.
If it isn't your stock and trade
then it might be a special technique you try.

However, be prepared!
It may be experienced as a put-down
or as infantilizing.
From the point of view of practical Jung,
the reclining proclivity toward free association
may be useful
or a wingding opening sesame to
new vistas.
But the odds are not great!

RULE OF THUMB: Listening for Threads

Listen for connecting threads and
weaving themes, laced by associations of thought.
Amazing.
A follows B follows C follows D back to A then E.
So that's what is going on!
A meandering maze of talk.
A follows B follows C follows D back to A then E!
Ah E.
So that's the theme.

PART

IV

The Outer Manifestation of Things

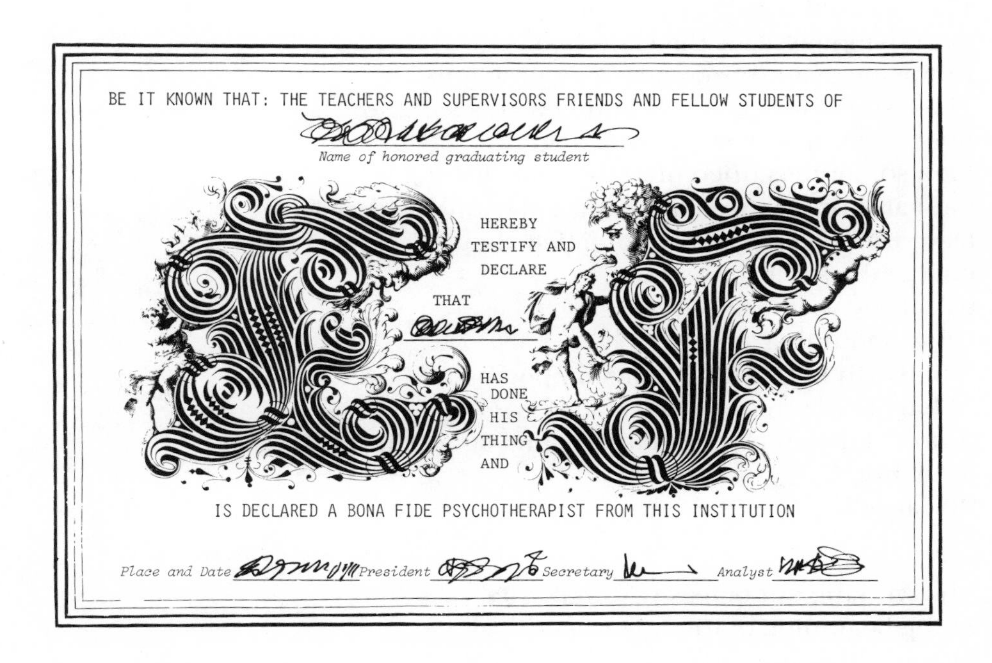

MIRABILE DICTU

I teach Jungian psychology
in a medical school.
My Jungian colleagues mostly don't work in universities.
You don't have to be a medical doctor to be a Jungian,
and few are.
On the other hand,
most American psychoanalysts are physicians.
Freudian psychoanalysis has deeply influenced
American psychiatric education.
Its influence is waning.

The Problem of Fees

This subject is a bit of a drag for most residents.
They avoid the problem and let the fee be set
by someone else, or they ignore it.
In the long run this creates new problems.
The issue of fees bedevils and bewitches therapists.
After all of these years of practice
I am sometimes uncomfortable establishing fees.
I am also uncomfortable that the day my residents
leave training and go into practice, they
charge the same fee as I do
with forty years experience.
"How about that?"
"I'm worth it!" one resident snapped back.
"What about a reduced fee?" I ask.
"I don't know if I would take anyone at a reduced fee."
"Why not?"
"Because."

The working out of fees with patients
at the beginning of therapy is a critical
factor in therapy.
You deal with the sensitive subject of money.

MONEY.
Money complexes are part of the human condition.
In order to understand money and psychotherapy,
it is necessary simply to think of
various people who charge money for psychotherapy:

- psychiatrists
- psychologists
- social workers
- nurse practitioners
- pastoral counselors
- Gestalt therapists
- family therapists
- sex therapists
- marriage counselors
- family therapists
- transactional therapists
- psychoanalysts
- analytical psychologists
- general practitioners
- family practitioners
- physician assistants
- cognitive therapists
- and 346 other assortedly trained people.

Fees?
I am astonished that most psychiatric residents who are
about to go into practice have never worked through this issue.
If one wants to make a lot of money,
offering good psychotherapy is a bad professional choice
for a physician.

RULE OF THUMB: Fees, i

Have a going rate, a standard fee,
that can be modified up or down.
If the standard fee seems inappropriate,
and you wish to treat the patient, negotiate.
The patient's circumstances, your circumstances,
good luck, and wisdom reign until some
insurance company or government department intrudes
with dictatorial policies.

There are some odd arrangements.
I know one therapist who tells his *clients*
that they should pay him whatever they wish.
I know a rich therapist
who does not charge his patients anything.
Oh, the money complex!
One indulges the patient,
the other indulges himself.

RULE OF THUMB: Fees, ii

Very special fees
sooner or later become thorns in your side.
The rich, the gifted, the important,
the poor, the promising, the well-connected, and
the specially-referred-to-you patient
are problem cases.
Set your fees regardless of their specialness.
Patients who pay very high fees
and patients who pay very low fees
engender emotions and ideas that influence therapy.

Being special is a handicap.*
Being exceptional creates its own hazards.
Being rich adds to the problem of judgment of therapists.
Being famous is a problem when it comes to fees.
As a rule
I do not charge anyone a very large fee.
I do not charge anyone a very low fee.
If a patient who has been in treatment for a period of time
experiences extraordinary financial reverses, then
I will adjust the fees down.
For patients whose fortunes change favorably,
I increase my fee.

RULE OF THUMB: Fees, iii

Set a fee.
Collect your fee each month.
If it's not paid when due, ask why not.
Do not accumulate a large balance on your cuff or anywhere else.
If you treat people right,
they will treat you right—
80% of the time. (F.D. Roosevelt)

---

*See T.F. Main, "The Ailment," *British Journal of Medical Psychology*, 1957, pp. 137–8.

RULE OF THUMB: Fees, iv

The subject of fees can stop at some arbitrary point
like this:

Symbol of One Hour Full Fee, Texas, U.S.A. Circa 1986

I charge successful psychiatrists
what they charge their patients.
Most patients who terminate therapy without paying
their full bill
cough up sooner or later.
A few people never pay.
What do you do then?
Do you turn your delinquent bills over to a collection agency?
I do not. You may feel differently.
About one percent of my private patients
fail to pay their fees.
On the other hand, the way medicine, psychiatry, and health care
seem to be going, in a few years
it could all be an irrelevant question.

RULE OF THUMB: Fees, v

A universal law which is worth remembering:
Every unit of money loses its value over time.
Fees, therefore, must increase.
Low fees, very low fees, even 25 cents a session,
may be the going rate in a poverty clinic.
No fee is paid personally by patients in
military hospitals, most of the time in VA hospitals,
and in some other institutions.
A patient need not pay for therapy
to make it effective, but it helps.
Entitlements create weighty problems for therapists and patients.

Money, money, money makes the world go around.
Money, money, money is power, power, power.
Where money dominates, Eros retreats.

A truism: We live in a materialistic culture.
In America we live in an extraverted society.
Possessions possess us.
Money is the measure of success and envy,
but it does not bring peace and tranquility.
It does not give health.
It does not make for happiness.
Security is an illusion.

> *Where love reigns, there is no will to power; and where the will to power is paramount, love is lacking.*
> *The one is the shadow of the other.* (Jung, CW 7:78)

No one can realistically calculate
the financial value of successful psychotherapy or analysis.

> While the secrecy that cloaks money matters varies with each individual and culture, most people in the Western world conceal money matters one way or another. Often, we just lie. Like all tales about sexuality, stories about money fall short of the truth. The stories are a personal mythology. . . . I know a colleague—his practice has a special parking space for clients—who starts sweating with anxiety each time he notices that a new patient drives a very expensive car! . . . That we connect money with life-force is obvious. . . . Although economists often assume the profit motif to be a fundamental drive animating human behavior, we psychologists know that few people, especially successful ones, really work for money. . . . Money is a tremendous projection carrier. Because money is so faceless, so neutral, we tend to project on it more easily. . . . Nearly everything can be projected on money: power, security, sexuality, and, in some bizarre way, even reality. Some people think that money is the reality, the real thing.
>
> (Guggenbühl-Craig, *Soul and Money*, pp. 85–86)

Alchemy and Gold

The importance of alchemy
from a psychological point of view
is that the alchemists were not concerned
with the creation of *aurum vulgi*, or common gold,
but with *aurum nostrum*, the pure gold symbol of
an illumined soul.

Alchemy does not lend itself to adaptation to practical Jung.
It is a scholar's realm of symbolism and the divine,
of ancient chemistry and the search for gold.

> In the alchemy of man's soul, almost all noble attributes—courage, honor, love, hope, faith, duty, loyalty—can be transmuted into ruthlessness. Compassion alone stands between good and evil proceeding within us. . . . the survival of the species may depend on the ability to foster a boundless capacity for compassion.
>
> (E. Hoffer, *Family Week*)

> How can science unravel the chemistry of the soul when what we have here is actually an alchemy? Good and evil, beauty and ugliness, truth and error, love and hatred, the sublime and the ridiculous continually pass into each other. And alchemy is ruled out not by intellect but by magic.
>
> (E. Hoffer, *Before the Sabbath*, p. 78)

my studies of alchemy may seem obscure and baffle many people, but taken symbolically the symbolic gold of great worth, or the transforming philosopher's stone "lapis philosophorum" hunted for centuries by the alchemists is to be found in man.

JUNG

Jung found in the symbolism of the alchemist
validation of his hypothesis
of the universal nature of the symbols,
the collective unconscious.
There was a deeper, spiritual search of the alchemists
than the transmutation of base materials into gold.
This idea opened up a new vista for Jung
in Eastern philosophy, religion, and psychology.

Reconciliation of opposites : Alchemy

Unleashed forces of unconscious opposites like love and hate, light and dark, domination and submission, greed and altruism, transference and countertransference . . .

evoke the forces of reconciliation so that the words of ancient alchemists, "medicina catholica" may be born.

He found a validation of his ideas in such remote sources as *The Secret of the Golden Flower*, a medieval alchemy of China that was the link between Gnosis, the collective unconscious, Taoism, the Self, and the spirit.*

Jung in "Dream Symbolism in Relation to Alchemy" writes:

Dream: *The dreamer goes into a chemist's shop with his father. Valuable things can be bought there quite cheaply, above all a special water. His father tells him about the country the water comes from. Afterwards he crosses the Rubicon by train.*

---

*See Foreword to *The Secret of the Golden Flower*, pp. 81–137.

The traditional apothecary's shop, with its carboys and gallipots, its waters, its lapis divinus *and* infernalis *and its magisteries, is the last visible remnant of the kitchen paraphernalia of those alchemists who saw in the* donum spiritus sancti*—the precious gift—nothing beyond the chimera of goldmaking. The "special water" is literally the* aqua nostra non vulgi. *It is easy to understand why it is his father who leads the dreamer to the source of life, since he is the natural source of the latter's life. We could say that the father represents the country or soil from which that life sprang. But figuratively speaking, he is the "informing spirit" who initiates the dreamer into the meaning of life and explains its secrets according to the teachings of old.*

He is a transmitter of the traditional wisdom. But nowadays the fatherly pedagogue fulfils this function only in the dreams of his son, where he appears as the archetypal father figure, the "wise old man." . . . But the dreamer has noticed something and with vigorous determination crosses the Rubicon. He has realized that the flux and fire of life are not to be underrated and are absolutely necessary for the achievement of wholeness. But there is no recrossing the Rubicon.

(Jung, CW 12: 159, 161)

Written Records

Question: What do you write about your patient?
Answer: As little as possible or permissible.

What you write about a patient is determined by
the nature of the formal records required in your situation.
In some institutions detailed records
must be kept.
Meticulously rigid record forms become vexatious burdens.
What's more they are dehumanizing and ingenuous
ways of keeping your ass covered.

Some kinds of notes must be kept,
at least a brief record with
the gist of what was talked about, or happened
each time you see your patient.
This is a minimal necessity for legal purposes.

Signatures

Ah, now, for a matter seldom mentioned:
Illegible signatures betray confused identities
hiding out in grand egoistic flourishes.
At future dates it will be impossible
to know to whom what happened and who was there.
Elaborate undecipherable signatures are
cryptographs which any graphologist can interpret.
Projection test: Do you get the visual gestalt?

All residency programs
should require people who persist,
after warnings,
in signing their names and and writing their notes in hieroglyphs,
to display in their office a special graduation diploma
which I have designed.

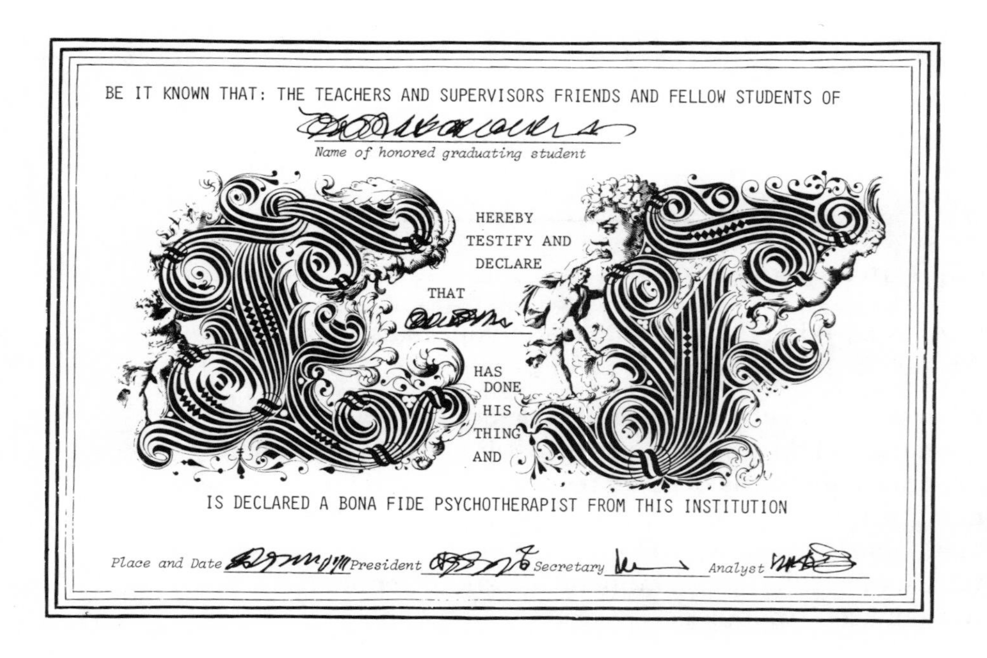
BE IT KNOWN THAT: THE TEACHERS AND SUPERVISORS FRIENDS AND FELLOW STUDENTS OF

Name of honored graduating student

HEREBY TESTIFY AND DECLARE

THAT

HAS DONE HIS THING AND

IS DECLARED A BONA FIDE PSYCHOTHERAPIST FROM THIS INSTITUTION

Place and Date *President* *Secretary* *Analyst*

The Wonderful World of Dreams

What do your patients write to you?

> Dear Harry,
> I am sorry I couldn't see you last time, but I am having so much financial trouble this month that I felt I couldn't afford you for a while, so we might meet April 5th if that's OK with you. I keep trying but nothing seems to affirm my efforts and give me any hope for the future. I dreamt last night that I arrived in Salado for an appointment and went to your home instead of your office (in the dream these were two separate places way across town from each other). You drove me to your office. I sat in the back seat right behind you. We chatted cheerfully of this and that. That's all.
>
> Sincerely,

Whatever a patient commits to paper is important
information.
Lists of complaints, which drive doctors up the wall,
are vital, meaningful documents.
We all make inference from such things.
How patients make out checks
and address their envelopes is important.

RULE OF THUMB: What You Write

Consider whatever you write about a patient
as a legal document, and ask yourself:
How would this sound if read in a courtroom?
There was a saying when I was in the navy:
    Never write anything in a patient's record that
    you would not want read over the PA system on a ship.

This reminds me of a story about a telephone call
with an incomprehensible meaning for the uninitiated.
A sailor who was admitted to my psychiatric ward
had been on the bridge of the USS Oriskany.
Just before he became psychotic,
he heard a voice through his headphone:
"CHILDSPLAY, THIS IS JEHOVAH."
It was the code word for the ship, and the
code word for the admiral.

"CHILDSPLAY, THIS IS JEHOVAH."

Elements of truth are the basis of delusions and hallucinations.
Some therapists navigate on the reality basis and
tell patients that these things are only in their minds.
On the other hand, delusions and hallucinations are real;
they are the language of another reality.
If you can see it this way,
appreciating the reality of the psyche
you can talk with your patients in a different mode
of understanding.
The spirit in which something is written or spoken
is betrayed in the rendition.
As the call, so the echo.

Write any appropriate note,
say almost anything, however direct,
provided you are free of hostility,
hidden agendas, innuendos, and oneupmanship.
Remember,
your reports, letters, and notes

may pass through many hands and before many eyes
even if they are marked **CONFIDENTIAL**.

Notes are useful to refresh your memory.
The requirements for notes are

- factual content
- merciful brevity
- common sense
- ethical and moral soundness
- usefulness
- nontriviality

Some analysts keep no notes at all. Zero.
Some doctors keep scrupulously compulsive notes
which say nothing.
Writing *pro forma* garbage fills the necessary space slots.
The wise one writes the right way.

During a psychotherapy session my mind wandered.
I jotted some notes on a piece of paper,
a list of things I wanted to do around the house.
My patient sensing that I was distracted,
brought me out of my reverie.
"A dozen eggs, a loaf of bread, a pound of butter,
and a bottle of horseradish," she said.

I caught on and we laughed.
She had hit home in a remarkably intuitive fashion.
I put my notes aside.
We got back to the business of her troubles.
Sic passem,
do not make notes that one day you would want to destroy
if legal problems arise.
Under no circumstances alter any record
because legal problems have raised their ugly head.
That is the worst kind of doctoring.
From time to time
destroy all the patient records you no longer want to keep.
Ask yourself: Do I need to keep this?
Who might read this record someday?
If you make off-the-record notes on patients,
destroy them as soon as they have served their purpose.
Do not, repeat, do not
keep two sets of records.

n the Bureaucracy

trusion of anyone or any power that dictates
ou will practice or what you will write
leads to negative transference to the institution.
In large organizations
we never escape from a modicum of adaptation
and conformity to the harness of organization and control.
Jungian psychology offers
a process of individuation, which
in our culture also means coping with bureaucracy
in one fashion or another.

It is deadly to the spirit to kowtow to sham.

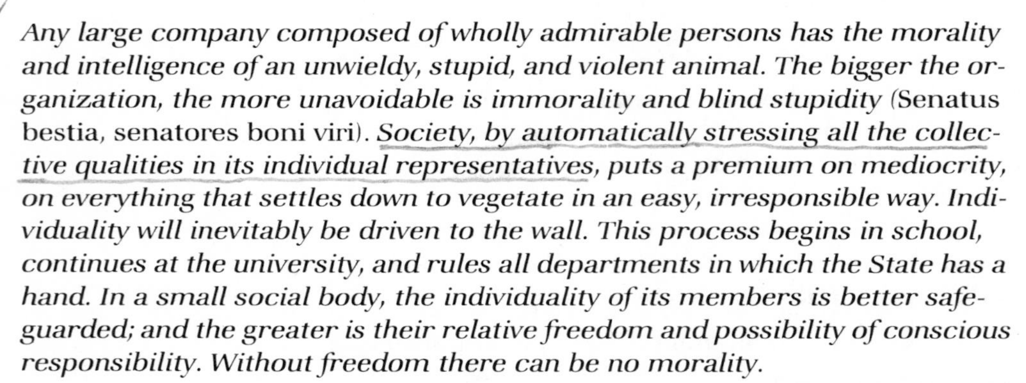

Any large company composed of wholly admirable persons has the morality and intelligence of an unwieldy, stupid, and violent animal. The bigger the organization, the more unavoidable is immorality and blind stupidity (Senatus bestia, senatores boni viri). *Society, by automatically stressing all the collective qualities in its individual representatives, puts a premium on mediocrity, on everything that settles down to vegetate in an easy, irresponsible way. Individuality will inevitably be driven to the wall. This process begins in school, continues at the university, and rules all departments in which the State has a hand. In a small social body, the individuality of its members is better safeguarded; and the greater is their relative freedom and possibility of conscious responsibility. Without freedom there can be no morality.*

(Jung, CW 7: 240)

Sham is based on the belief that
what we know to be false we accept as true,
and what we know to be true we pretend is false.
It is foolish to compromise with integrity
and dangerous to boot.

Nothing never happens.
In psychotherapy there is always change—
for the better or the worse, ups and downs.
If it is stuck, it is moving nowhere, but it is moving there.

It is easy and in accordance with human nature
to feel positive and caring for people who
are getting well and are grateful.

It is not difficult to like patients who are improving
and acting sensibly.
It is reassuring to have patients who
are achieving self-control and finding their way.
But we do better to care for those who
are not doing well, who are not mending,
whose pain seems unremitting, who cling
or project nasty things on us.
They are the ones whose problems need psychological
help.
If it weren't for them, you would be out of business,
if you have a conscientious practice.

RULE OF THUMB: Gossip

Do not gossip about your patients.
Do not talk about them to your friends.
Do not discuss patients in public places,
elevators, hallways, or common spaces.
Be careful what you tell your spouse.
Babbling or blabbing, divulging or betraying;
you must not prattle, tattle, or rattle.
In other words do not gossip.
A confidential relationship is the *sine qua non*
of psychotherapy.

The doctor-patient relationship is sacred.
Alas, it is becoming more and more pharmaceutical,
and sinking to customer-service contracts,
a trade, and a business to be advertised.
But the doctor-patient relationship is still sacred
to those who truly care.

RULE OF THUMB: Confidences

Whatever is told you freely is a professional confidence
with rare exceptions.
Never accept a confidence that is not freely given by a patient:
There is something I want to tell you,
but you must promise me that you will never
mention it to anyone.
Trouble is
you may hear some extraordinary things,
or they may be ordinary masquerading as portentous.
Warning: Do not bind yourself to a promise.
Promise me implies a lack of trust

And then I will tell you implies you are an accomplice,
not a confidant, therapist, or confessor.
Suppose what is about to be told you is
of grave or deadly consequence.
Then what
do you say or do if you have tied your own hands
and sealed your mouth?
Do you renege?
How good is your word?
In tight spots promises are blinders.

RULE OF THUMB: Promises

Nuts-and-bolts approach:
"I cannot listen to what you propose to tell me
and promise beforehand never to mention it.
You must trust me to use my discretion
as to whether I will keep a secret.
What transpires in this room is between you and me;
you can say anything you want, but
you must trust me because I do not make promises."
That's the idea. Say it in your own manner.
Maybe just "no" will suffice.
Betrayal is at stake.

PHINEAS PINCHBECK
SELLS
DOLLY-VARDEN ALARM
FOR HUSBANDS
APPRENTICES' TIMEKEEPERS
FOR MANUFACTURERS,
ELECTION REPEAT
FOR POLITICIANS

Time Pieces

Where do you keep yours? On the desk?
What do you do when a patient plops her handbag
in front of your clock?
Do you say something simple like, "Pardon me,
but I can't see the clock," or curse silently?
Some therapists sneak looks at their wrist watchs.
Others sense the time with an unerring accuracy,
especially if they keep to a tight schedule,
almost to the minute.
Not a bad idea. But,
"Wham! Time's up. See you same time next week,"—
cutting off saber-sharp is offensive.

Some therapists keep two clocks in their office.
Then it's not obvious when they are looking at the clock.
But you gotta keep time.
If you're in the real world,
you gotta keep time.
Keeping time is not the same as being a timekeeper,
anymore than a Venetian blind is the same as
a blind Venetian.

RULE OF THUMB: Schedules

Keep to a schedule.
See patients as close to the exact time of the appointment
as is humanly possible.
End the sessions at the designated time.
It is easy to be seduced
into running over time
by a patient who wittingly or unwittingly starts to tell
a tale at the very end of the hour.
Oh, Scheherazade:

> *It hath reached me, O auspicious King . . . before the hour of night she came to him, wrapped in a veil. . . .*

There is the hot item,
the dream about Thee,
at the moment of the hour's end.

Starting and stopping on time is one of the most valuable
rituals of psychotherapy.
It is a simple model of control and containment,
the boundaries of promised time and safe space
in which the patient can talk freely and candidly.

Some Questions Have No Answers

"How much time will my treatment take?"
"How long will we be working together in therapy?"
Unless therapy begins with a firm agreement on a time limit,
there is no way to be sure how long it will take.
Averages are easy to give,
but no one is an average.
It depends on where one starts,
and how fast one moves.
It depends on unforeseen detours and obstacles,
on chance and fate.
It depends on the economy.
It depends on the psyche's own sweet time.
Sometimes it is wise to set a time limit,
or once the journey is underway, to set an ending time,
but sometimes it is foolish to do so.

Psychotherapy is not only a healing process,
it is also a learning process,
and learning takes a lifetime.

> Life is fired at us point-blank. I have said it before: where and when we are born, or happen to find ourselves after we are born, there and then, like it or not, we must sink or swim. At this moment, every one of you finds him-

self submerged in an ambient that is an interval in which he must willy-nilly come to terms with . . . something of which he does not know whether it interests him or not, whether he understands it or not, which is portentously devouring an hour of his life—an irreplaceable hour, for the hours of his life are numbered. This is his circumstance, his here and his now. What will he do? For something he *must* do; either listen to me, or, on the contrary, dismiss me and attend to his own meditations, think of his business or his clients, remember his sweetheart. What will he do? Get up and go, or remain, accepting the fate of spending this hour of his life.
(Ortega y Gasset, *Man and People*, pp. 42–43)

The Here and Now, Again and Again

Here and now is our fate,
a pragmatic definition.
Not fate preordained, predetermined,
but our present lot.
Here and now is all there ever is.
It is out of this that each one of us creates his or her reality.
To that degree reality is a fantasy that
depends on our personality, mood, hunger, desire,
and life experience.
This here-and-now fate is not the fate
of the acts of God such as lightning and tornadoes.
Once they have struck they are past
and the past is dead, and
the here and now is what is left.

Primary Fate

Primary Fate is the present happening that
we could not have changed nor had a hand in making,
such as sibling order,
mother, father, and family tree.

Rather than being born in America,
you might have been born in Beirut or Johannesburg,
or Hiroshima, at 8:15 A.M. on August 6, 1945,
or Bhopal, India, at 11:40 A.M. on December 3, 1984.

We had no say in the color of our eyes
or our skin.
We are red, white, black, brown,
or Alzheimer through our Primary Fate.
This is not fatalism. *Per contra*
we come upon Secondary Fate, the one we
have a part in making happen:

Do we decide to drive to Dallas on Tuesday, and if so
at what hour?
If you scream, "You are to blame!",
the echo in the valley always comes back to you.

It is self-evident that as we feel
so we see the world:
mean, bright, cheery, empty, good, bad, or whatever.
Not to say that there isn't another reality out there:

> Shut your eyes, reader . . . and you can hear the water gurgling—those are prisoners' barges moving on and on. And the motors of the Black Marias roar. They are arresting someone all the time, cramming him in somewhere, moving him about. And what is that hum you hear? The overcrowded cells of the transit prisons. And that cry? The complaints of those who have been plundered, raped, beaten to within an inch of their lives.
> (Solzhenitsyn, *The Gulag Archipelago*, p. 586)

When we are self-confident and in good spirits,
the outside world either shines on us or
we can manage it, most of the time.
But there are restless people always looking for some place
to be other than where they are
as if the outside would do the trick. To repeat:
Where you are is not so important as
where you are when you are where you are.
Jung wrote a letter to one of his patients:

It is not altogether clear to me what you mean when you say that you are "looking for the right place." There is no sense in your expecting to be expected anywhere. Rather you can be quite certain that you are not expected and can say it nevertheless. If you wish to speak of these things you must also be able to talk to your stove, which cannot even give an understanding nod. Above all you cannot hope to "collaborate" is some way, for where in our time and our society would you find a person who knew how to express what your uniqueness alone can express? This is the jewel that must not get lost. But collaboration and especially "teamwork" are the quickest possible way of losing it. You can guard it only by enduring the solitude that is its due. This is the achievement for which the whole world, in its heart of hearts, is expectantly waiting.*

(Jung, *Collected Letters*, Vol. 2, pp. 480–481)

---

*In Grimm's fairytale "The Goose Girl" the princess whose place was taken by an evil maidservant pours out her grief to an iron stove.

Typology

"People are people everywhere."
"Oh, are they?"
"You know, basically people are the same."
"You mean like us?"
"Yes, like you and me. Everywhere in the world
people are just people like us."
"That's what you *think*."
"Of course, it is a logical, rational observation."
"I *feel* different."
"You do?"
"Yes, I feel they are not basically the same,
and I like those who are like me."
"I have a hunch that people are like birds,
some are migratory, some are in cages,
some are free as the spirit, and some are flightless."
"That's far out, and maybe it's true for you,
but for me there are mesomorphs, ectomorphs, and
endomorphs. You can get the statistical breakdown.
They are very different on any scale. And there
are differences in people in different socioeconomic groups."
"Yes, of course, but basically people are people everywhere."
"Oh are they?"
"I *think* this is where I came in."

TYPOLOGY: Attitude Types

How we relate to the world around us.

There are two attitude types that are diametrically opposite.
They view both the inner world and the outer world differently.
One is an extravert.
The other is an introvert.
In the case of extraverts, their energy flows outward
to the objects of the outer world.
Extraverts reach out eagerly to embrace
new ideas, new people, new things, big doings, and crowds,
and they enjoy a good argument.
To them the *other* kind (introverts),
are narcissistic, wooly-minded, and selfish,
not good, outgoing types like the extraverts.

Introverts, however creative, are not worth much
on the American scene.

Introverts tend to withdraw from outer objects.
It is as if they are instinctively saying
"no" at first to everything.
They distrust the extraverts
and see them as shallow, wasteful, untrustworthy, and
just not down there where life really is
with all its meaning.
The introverts usually try to escape clashes,
but they are often very good at encounters and confrontations.
The introvert is, by definition, drawn inward
into himself or herself.
Their psychic energy flows to the realm of the inner world.
America is predominantly an extraverted country.
Switzerland is an introverted country.
With his Swiss psychology, Jung was not
know-how and how-to oriented,
as this book mostly is.

The introvert extracts experiences from outer world for inner needs, and has a subjective attitude toward the outside. This is seen by the extravert as undisciplined, wooly-mindedness, and as not normal.

The extravert produces impressions on Outer world which is the reality. The extravert has greatest interest in the outside and is seen by the introvert as trivial and relatively meaningless, and as not normal.

Extraverts and introverts live in the same world
but their attitudes are worlds apart.
Usually they fail to understand each other.

In an extraverted country like America,
being convivial, object-related, materialistic,
ready to slap the other guy on the back
are cultural norms.
Extraverts have gobs of friends, tend to be optimistic,
ebullient, and are often caring people.
They are usually likable, interesting individuals.

On the other side of the room are the introverts,
just as normal as the extraverts, but more
introspectively interested in subjective things.
They feel like misfits in an extraverted culture.
They often learn how to play extravert.
In a sense the appreciation of the
normality of introversion by Jungian psychology
is a kind of Introverts-Lib movement.

In introverted Switzerland,
the extravert is more of a misfit and a bit peculiar
while the introvert shines quietly.

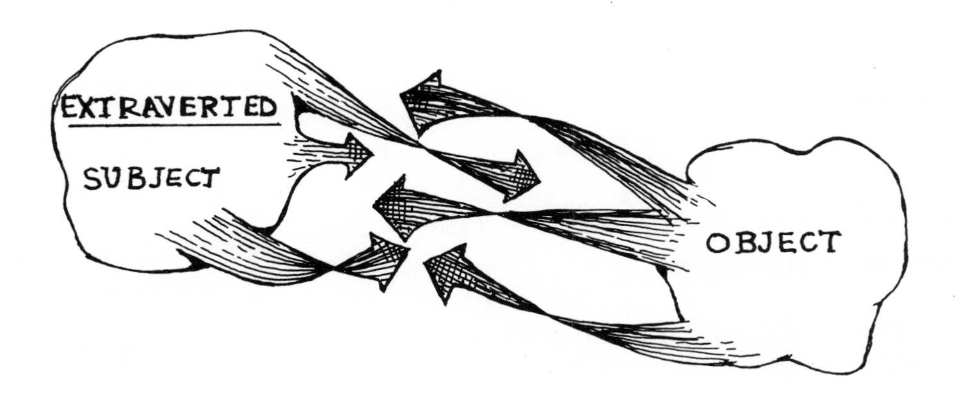

Extremes

To be too withdrawn is to be schizoid.
To be totally withdrawn is schizophrenic.
Ordinary introverts take a serious view of things
and tend to have good and deep friends.
Introverts are fascinated by their subjective reflections.
A cocktail party tends to slink them off.

The basic attitude type of extraversion
is diametrically opposite to introversion.
An extraverted friend had a big birthday party.
Each of fifty guests were given a button
on which was written "DeeDee's Best Friend."

The dominance of either Introversion or Extraversion
seems to be inborn. They come that way.
Typology, however, is not static and may vary
or change over time.

TYPOLOGY: Functional types

In addition to the two attitude types Jung identified four functional types:

- Thinking
- Feeling
- Intuition
- Sensation

Personality is characterized by
or you might say character is personalized by
one dominant attitude type and one dominant function type.
These factors determine much of our life script.

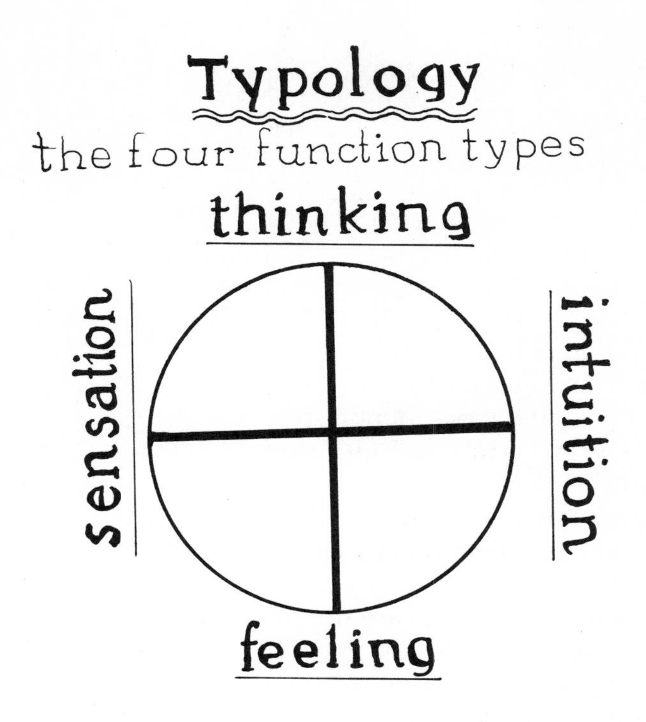

No other human type can equal the extraverted sensation type in realism. His sense for objective facts is extraordinarily developed. His life is an accumulation of actual experiences of concrete objects, and the more pronounced his type, the less use does he make of his experience. In certain cases the events in his life hardly deserve the name "experience" at all. What he experiences serves at most as a guide to fresh sensations; anything new that comes within his range of interest is acquired by way of sensation and has to serve its ends.

Since one is inclined to regard a highly developed reality-sense as a sign of rationality, such people will be esteemed as very rational. But in actual fact this is not the case, since they are just as much at the mercy of their sensations in the face of irrational, chance happenings as they are in the face of rational ones.

(Jung, *CW 6: 606*)

An individual is either a thinking type
or a feeling type.
You can't be both at the same time.
If you are not one of those two types
you are either an intuition or sensation type,
but you can't be both of those either,
not at the same time.

Check your dominant attitude type:
- ☐ *Extravert*
- ☐ *Introvert*

Now check your conscious dominant function type:
- ☐ *Thinking*
- ☐ *Feeling*
- ☐ *Intuition*
- ☐ *Sensation*

There is one more item in your basic typology.
In addition to one dominant function you have
at your disposal one auxiliary function
that is either one of the other two opposites.
The former is your strong suit;
the latter is your second strength.
The so-called auxiliary function is less well developed
than the dominant type.
The alternate opposite functions are unconscious,
and less well developed.
Psychological growth implies more consciousness of
your unconscious functions.
The more conscious we are,
the less we are at the mercy of our unconscious.

Prejudice

"People are people everywhere."
"Oh are they?"
"You know people are basically the same."
"You mean like us?"

Understanding different outlooks on life
permits us to comprehend our patients and our neighbors,
our friends, and those we love or are bound to.
It doesn't do much good for a thinking therapist
to keep hammering at getting feelings first
from another thinking type patient,
or a feeling type to want to get out feelings first
from a sensation-minded patient.
The opposite typologies in others are mighty good remedies
for one-sidedness in ourselves.

Functional Types Again

Each of the pair of opposites is antithetical to the other.
Only one of them can function at any time.
They are polar opposites.
Jungian psychology is a psychology of opposites
that aims toward centering and creating a balance and
reconciliation of opposites toward individuation.
Bearing the tension of opposites
is an aim of psychotherapy.
To know that the opposite, the other,
is legitimate and real is an insight.

> The ancient Greeks, nothing if not logical, began the great quest. They argued some twenty-four hundred years ago that the known continents of the north must necessarily be balanced by other land to the south. The northern part of the world lay under the constellation Arctos, the Bear, and hence was called *Arktikos*. The unknown land in the south, then, must be *Antarktikos*, the total opposite.
>
> (Chapman, *Antarctic Conquest*, p.3)

Intuition led the Greeks to this speculation.
Both intuition and sensation are ways of *perceiving*.
On the other hand, thinking and feeling are ways of *evaluating*.
A scientist must rely principally upon the thinking function
in order to work rationally.
His perception must be evaluated by the sensation
or reality function.
Thus, in his work things are balanced in his mind.

If the scientist gives way to feeling judgments,
his thinking gets muddled and sentimental.
One just can't scientifically feel one's way to an answer;
One must grope by cerebrating.
Experimental scientific evaluation
relies wholly on sensation—factual and sense perception.
No fantasy. No wild hunches when it gets down to experiments.
"Just the facts, ma'am," as TV detective Joe Friday droned
over and over on "Dragnet."
Ideas for discovery come from brilliant intuition,
but hunches are no good when it comes to facts of evidence.

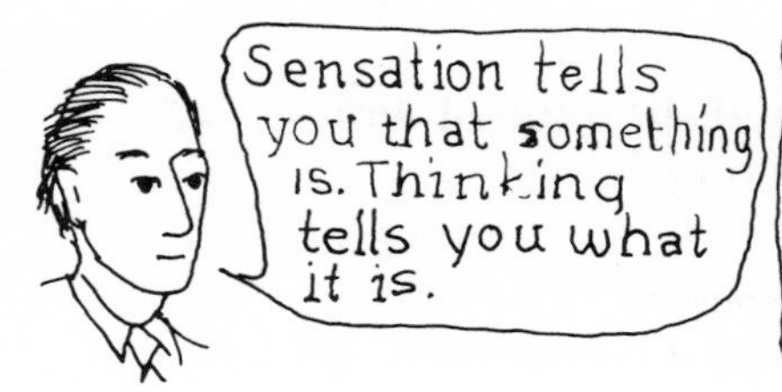

The thinker is the expert in reasoning,
in cognitive exploration.
The feeler comes to conclusions because it feels right.
Ask him and he'll say that's just the way it is.
One way of perceiving can be as valid as the other.

The intuitive strides all over the factual world
in seven-league boots.
But why seven?

Fool: The reason why the seven stars are no more than seven is a pretty reason.
Lear: Because they are not eight?
Fool: Yes, indeed: thou wouldst make a good fool.

(*King Lear*)

Flights of intuition are accompanied by
a capacity to see around corners and into the future
beyond a time and place.

Jung says every intellectual formula can never be anything more
than a partial truth and can never claim general validity. (CW 6:591)
In practice the formula often gains such an ascendency
that all other possible standpoints are thrust into the background.

The more feelings are repressed, the more deleterious is their secret influence on thinking that is otherwise beyond reproach. The intellectual formula, which because of its intrinsic value might justifiably claim general recognition, undergoes a characteristic alteration as a result of this unconscious personal sensitiveness: it becomes rigidly dogmatic. The self-assertion of the personality is transferred to the formula. Truth is no longer allowed to speak for itself; it is identified with the subject and treated like a sensitive darling whom an evil-minded critic has wronged. The critic is demolished, if possible with personal invective, and no argument is too gross to be used against him. The truth must be trotted out, until finally it begins to dawn on the public that it is not so much a question of truth as of its personal begetter.

(Jung, *CW 6:590*)

For balance:

- Intuition nurtures, feeds, and develops sensation function.
- Sensation grows and points out things to intuition.
- Thinking learns to value feeling opinions and relationships.
- Feeling learns the rules of thinking and head-using.
- Extravert learns to be at home with introversion.
- Introvert learns to be at home with extraversion.

This adds up to the process of individuation, which is
the actualization of the potential within the personality
to become what is within it to become.
This requires assertion and questioning and
acceptance and challenge
without intimidation by oneself or another.

"They may be your ideas professor,
but we the people reserve the right
to make our own comments."

THINKING AND FEELING: A Pair of Opposites

If you are a thinking type, you are using your brains;
most of the time you are rational, and reason triumphs.
Three cheers for reason! Thinking is Logos.
There is no consciousness without
Logos and the discernment of opposites.

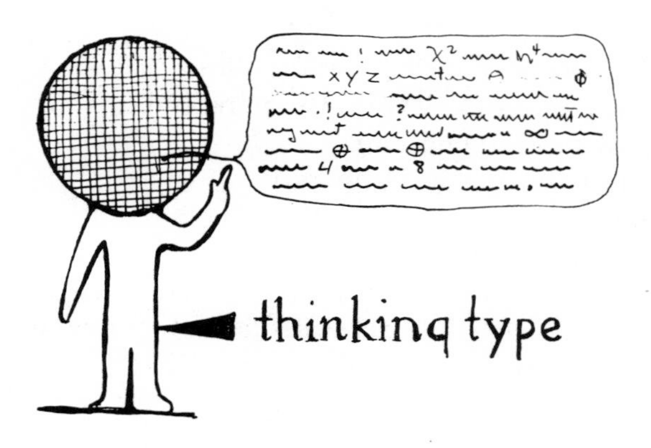

Logos is a philosophical abstraction of the
dynamic power of thoughts and words.
The *Logos was in the beginning, and God was the Logos.* (Jung, *CW 9ii:294)*

Feeling types feel that something is true
with the same conviction as thinker's reason.
It carries the power of conviction,
a kind of belief system.
Feeling is also characterized by relationships, or Eros.
Logos is the masculine principle
and Eros the feminine principle.

RULE OF THUMB: Expect a Type to be a Type

In psychotherapy don't push for feelings
from thinkers, or for thinking from feelers;
don't push for sensation facts from intuitives,
nor for hunches from reality-sensing types—
at least not until you have met them in their strong suit!
When the time is right later on, the unconscious type
can be confronted.

Think of it this way:
if you are an intuitive therapist,
a sensation patient may find you incomprehensible,
unless you begin with reason.

This is the origin of lots of negative transference
and conflict between lovers and spouses.
What is labeled as resistance by a psychotherapist
may be a type problem which the analyst does not understand.
A psychotherapist's formulations may not make sense
because the patient is a different type.

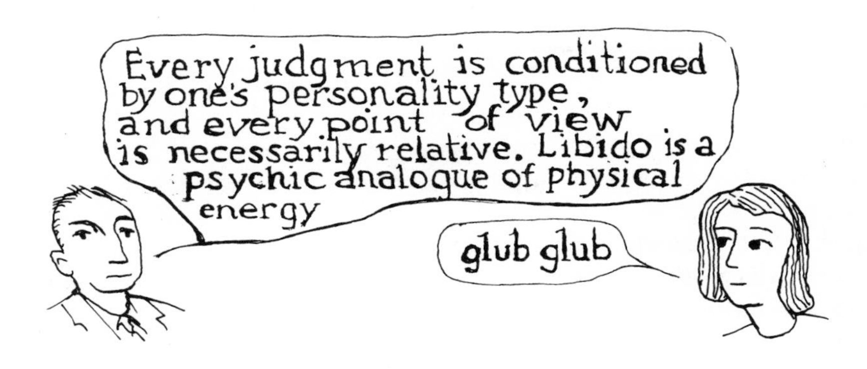

INTUITION AND SENSATION: A Pair of Opposites

We perceive the world by our senses (sensation)
or by our impressions (intuition).
Intuition flashes ideas and leaps to conclusions
regardless of the seeming facts.
Of course, the intuitive person might actually see beyond facts.
Honor to the hard facts, says the sensation person,
root out guesswork, anecdote, and sentiment.

The Introverted Intuitive Type:

The peculiar nature of introverted intuition, if it gains the ascendency, produces a peculiar type of man: the mystical dreamer and seer on the one hand, the artist and the crank on the other. The artist might be regarded as the normal representative of this type, which tends to confine itself to the perceptive character of intuition. As a rule, the intuitive stops at perception; perception is his main problem, and—in the case of a creative artist—the shaping of his perception. But the crank is content with a visionary idea by which he himself is shaped and determined. Naturally the intensification of intuition often results in an extraordinary aloofness of the individual from tangible reality; he may even become a complete enigma to his immediate circle. . . .

What the introverted intuitive represses most of all is the sensation of the object, and this colors his whole unconscious.

(Jung, *CW 6:661 and 663*)

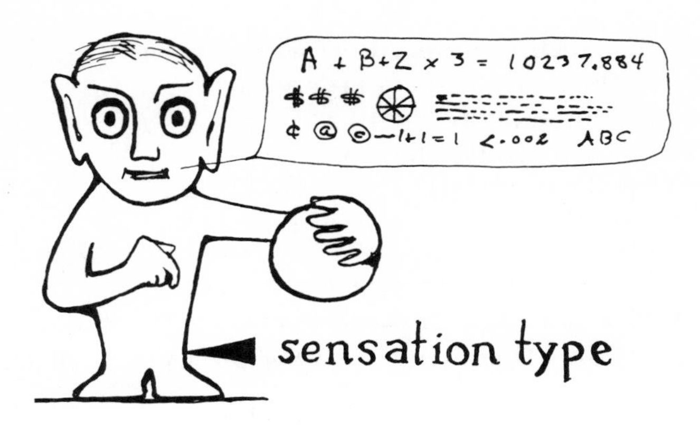

Sensation mediates the perception of physical stimuli.
It perceives stimuli from the outer world
and from our physical body.
It is strongly developed in children and primitive people.
Sensation is chiefly conditioned by the object.

It is natural for people of the same typology to be drawn together,
like birds of a feather, but opposites also attract.
The strongest bonds are woven between opposites.
There is powerful unconscious attraction because
one completes the other.

Lovers are drawn together by forces which
promise a total fulfillment, a completeness,
a uniting of the two in one.
Love transcends reason.
Pascal wrote that the heart has reason
that reason does not know.
The sensation of love epitomizes
the overwhelming, mysterious power of an unconscious function.

Wrap Up of Typology

The two attitude types of
- extraversion and introversion

are complemented by four function types
- thinking and feeling
- intuition and sensation

These are neither all or none; we have
some of the qualities of each type
but have a dominant personality type.

While psychological testing is the surest way
to identify the typology, one can come very close
by observation and interaction.
There are eight various combinations which are
either extraverted or introverted:

EXTRAVERTS

Function:	Dominant	—	Secondary or auxiliary
	Intuitive	—	Feeling
	Feeling	—	Intuitive
	Intuitive	—	Thinking
	Thinking	—	Intuitive
	Sensation	—	Feeling
	Feeling	—	Sensation
	Sensation	—	Thinking
	Thinking	—	Sensation

INTROVERTS

Function:	Dominant	—	Secondary or auxiliary
	Intuitive	—	Feeling
	Feeling	—	Intuitive
	Intuitive	—	Thinking
	Thinking	—	Intuitive
	Sensation	—	Feeling
	Feeling	—	Sensation
	Sensation	—	Thinking
	Thinking	—	Sensation

An individual may be classified in any of these 16 types.
However, typology is not absolute.
Putting people into pigeon holes is a misuse of typology.
In people of extreme types,
it is fairly certain that there is
a diametrically opposite character in their unconscious.
Our days and nights
lubb dubb their regular systole and diastole,
and in the end our lives fall into a place.

Synchronicity

An acausal meaningful relationship
of an inner and an outer world event.

Synchronicity is not the same as synchronous or coincidence.
The synchronistic principle asserts a meaningful
relationship with no possible causal connection
between a subjective experience within the human psyche
and an objective event which occurs at the same time
but at a distant place in the outer world of reality.

Jung wrote that he often came up
against this phenomenon in his practice.
The connection of events by other than cause and effect
is a central feature in modern physics.
Jung and Nobel Laureate physicist W. Pauli
wrote a book on this subject.

> *In most cases they were things which people do not talk about for fear of exposing themselves to thoughtless ridicule. I was amazed to see how many people have had experiences of this kind and how carefully the secret was guarded. So my interest in this problem has a human as well as a scientific foundation.*
>
> (Jung and Pauli, *Interpretation of Nature and the Psyche*, p. 6)

> When Norman Mailer began his novel *Barbary Shore* there was no Russian spy in it. As he worked on it, a Russian spy became a minor character. As the work progressed, the spy became the dominant character. After the novel was finished, the Immigration Service arrested a man who lived one flight below Mailer in the same building. He was Colonel Rudolph Abel, named as the top Russian spy in the United States at that time.
>
> (Wilson, *Science Digest*, p. 84)

In contrast to synchronicity, Jung cites
the following story as an example of *coincidence*:
A wife gives a man a new pipe for his birthday.
He takes a walk and sits under a tree in a park.
Sitting next to him is a man smoking the same kind of pipe.
He tells the man that his wife gave him his pipe
for his birthday.
The man says, "Mine did too,"
It turns out that they both have the same birthday.
They introduce themselves.
They have identical Christian names.
This is not a synchronisitic event
because there is no simultaneous, inner-meaningful, subjective event.

SYNCHRONICITY

acausal relationship

An inwardly perceived psychic event has a corresponding physical external event

SIMULTANEITY

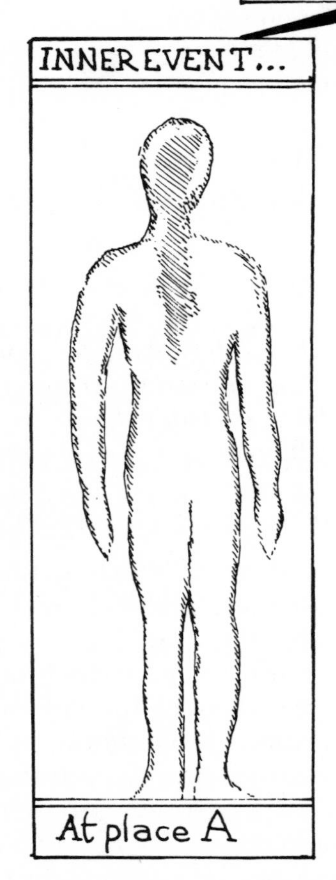

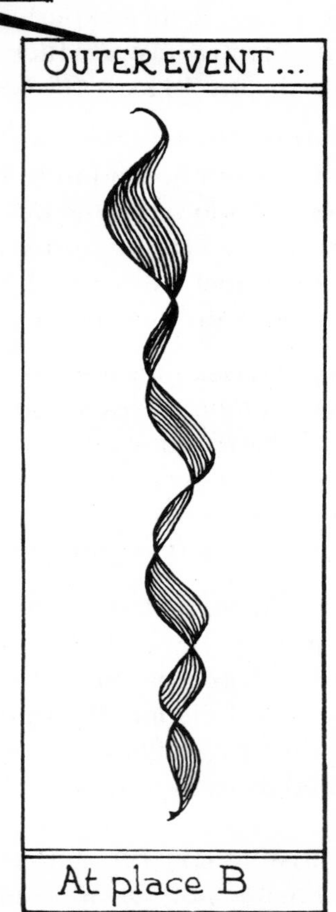

it's not that they can't be explained, it's that a cause is intellectually unthinkable - it's like discontinuities in physics.

the two events occurring at the same time have the same or similar meanings: on the other hand synchronism merely means similar events

SIMULTANEOUS OCCURRENCE OF TWO MEANINGFUL EVENTS WITH NO CAUSAL RELATIONSHIP

In contrast to the synchonous, simple
simultaneous occurrence of two events,
synchronicity is the simultaneous occurrence of two
meaningfully but not causally connected events
in which an inner psychic subjective state or event
parallels an outer event in the objective world.
Not only is the cause unknown,
but the cause is not even thinkable.

A dog suddenly barks and whimpers in the night and
wanders bereft and aimlessly through the house.
The next day it is found out that the dog's master
had been slain in another city at the very time that
the dog was siezed by the paroxysm of crying.

One does not need to produce ten thousand duckbilled platypi in order to prove they exist. It seems to me synchronicity represents a direct act of creation *which manifests itself as chance. The statistical proof of natural conformity to law is therefore only a very limited way of describing nature, since it grasps only uniform events. But nature is essentially discontinuous, i.e., subject to chance. To describe it we need a principle of discontinuity. In psychology this is the drive to individuation, in biology it is differentiation, but in nature it is the "meaningful coincidence," that is to say synchronicity.*

(Jung, *CW 18:1198*)

Arthur Koestler (London *Times*, 1974) related this story: After landing the leading role in the movie *The Girl from Petrovka*, English actor Anthony Hopkins tried without success to find a copy of the book in London. Then one day as he was passing through Leicester Square he noticed a book lying discarded on a bench. It was *The Girl from Petrovka*. During the movie's filming Hopkins met the book's author, George Feifer, who mentioned in passing that he no longer had a copy of his own novel. Feifer said he had loaned his last copy to a friend who had lost it in London. Hopkins showed Feifer the book he had found. Feifer looked inside and discovered notes in his handwriting. It was the same book.

(Bryson, *American Way*, May 1982)

A patient of mine traveled to her mother's deathbed in the hospital,
hoping for reconciliation.
Her mother had opposed her psychotherapy and
ridiculed her dream analysis.
During the patient's analysis
her mother had fallen ill with terminal cancer.
The night before she died, the patient saw her in the hospital.
The patient had prayed for a dream to help her understand
this tragic separation.
To the patient's surprise, her mother was eager to tell her a dream
she had had the previous night:

I am writing a new constitution for a new country
in big black letters on very heavy parchment.
It was very very important.

Her mother died the next day.
The mother confided the dream as a great truth
that had been sent to comfort her.
It was a profound gift to her daughter.

PART

V

Psychotherapy

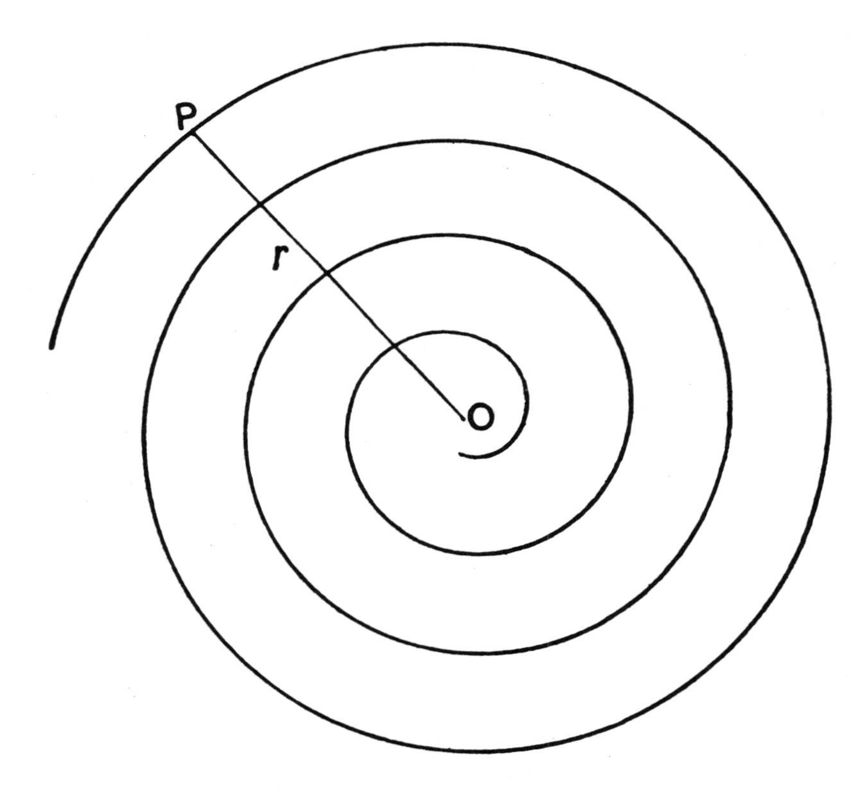

The spiral of Archimedes

We speak of the point of origin (O) as the pole of the spiral; a straight line having an extremity in the pole and revolving around it we call the radius vector, and the point (P) traveling along the radius vector under definite conditions of velocity. It is roughly illustrated by the way a sailor coils a rope of uniform thickness on a deck, and each whorl is of the same breadth as that which precedes and that which follows it.
(Thompson, p. 753)

Many of my psychiatric colleagues are bewildered
by the notion of *practical* Jung as if it were a nonsequitur.
Those who have read deeply into Jung's original writings
know better.
There is a great deal that is obfuscating,
but basically Jung was a pragmatic, straight-talking analyst.
He wrote to a distraught doctor patient:

I have the feeling that you are really going a bit too far. We should make a halt before something destructive. You know what my attitude is to the unconscious. There is no point in delivering oneself over to it to the last drop. If that were the right procedure, nature would never have invented consciousness, and then animals would be the ideal embodiments of the unconscious. In my view it is absolutely essential always to have our consciousness well enough in hand to pay sufficient attention to our reality, to the Here and Now. Otherwise we are in danger of being overrun by an unconscious which knows nothing of this human world of ours. The unconscious can realize itself only with the help of consciousness and under its constant control. At the same time consciousness must keep one eye on the unconscious and the other focussed just as clearly on the potentialities of human existence and human relationships.

I certainly don't want to interfere, but before I go to India I would beg you to reflect on this warning.

(Jung, *Collected Letters*, Vol. 1, pp. 239–40)

Perilous Odyssey of a Psychotherapist

I have drawn a picture map of a journey
though the land of psychotherapy with all its
predictable pitfalls, pratfalls, encounters with sirens,
trials, and tribulations.

The therapist enters though the gate in the Wall of Defense
and passes the Watchtower of Resistance.
Directly ahead is the Hot Point Geyser
gushing hot air vapors
near the Selfish Sea.

The therapist wends his way between
the frozen Tundra of Denial and
the Obsessive-Compulsive Foothills,
beyond Echo Canyon and Perseveration Pinnacles,
where high achievers risk impalement on Spike's Speaks,
and the Pointless Recitative
of words memorized to pass examinations
in the Valley Beyond Rote.

Alone in the hills to the east
stands the castle of the Kingdom of Detach
wherein rise the Ivory Towers of the Castle Keep
above the burrows of the Pigeon Holers.
The therapist may get stuck here
on the incestuous Olympian Heights
where the Institute Falls drown ordinary mortals
beneath the Cathexis Plexis.

If the therapist continues his journey,
the way leads past Shadowland
with its dark Forest of the Give-ups
and the Desert of Despair.
One last trial beyond despondency
is the Organic Range of Super Science Biology
which under certain circumstances
lures the traveler down Cop-Out Valley.

A final achievement is to pass undaunted
the High Platitudes where countless
Hubrisians have disappeared in avalanches.
Now at last the therapist is free and responsible
to travel along the plateau of the Great Plains Talk
where curmudgeons and metaphysicians*
are left behind.
In the end the Odyssey leads to the light
of the rising in its unending cycle.

---

*A metaphysician is one who, when you remark that twice two makes four, demands to know what you mean by twice, what you mean by two, and what by four. For asking such questions metaphysicians are supported in oriental luxury in the universities and respected as educated and intelligent men." (H.L. Mencken)

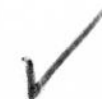

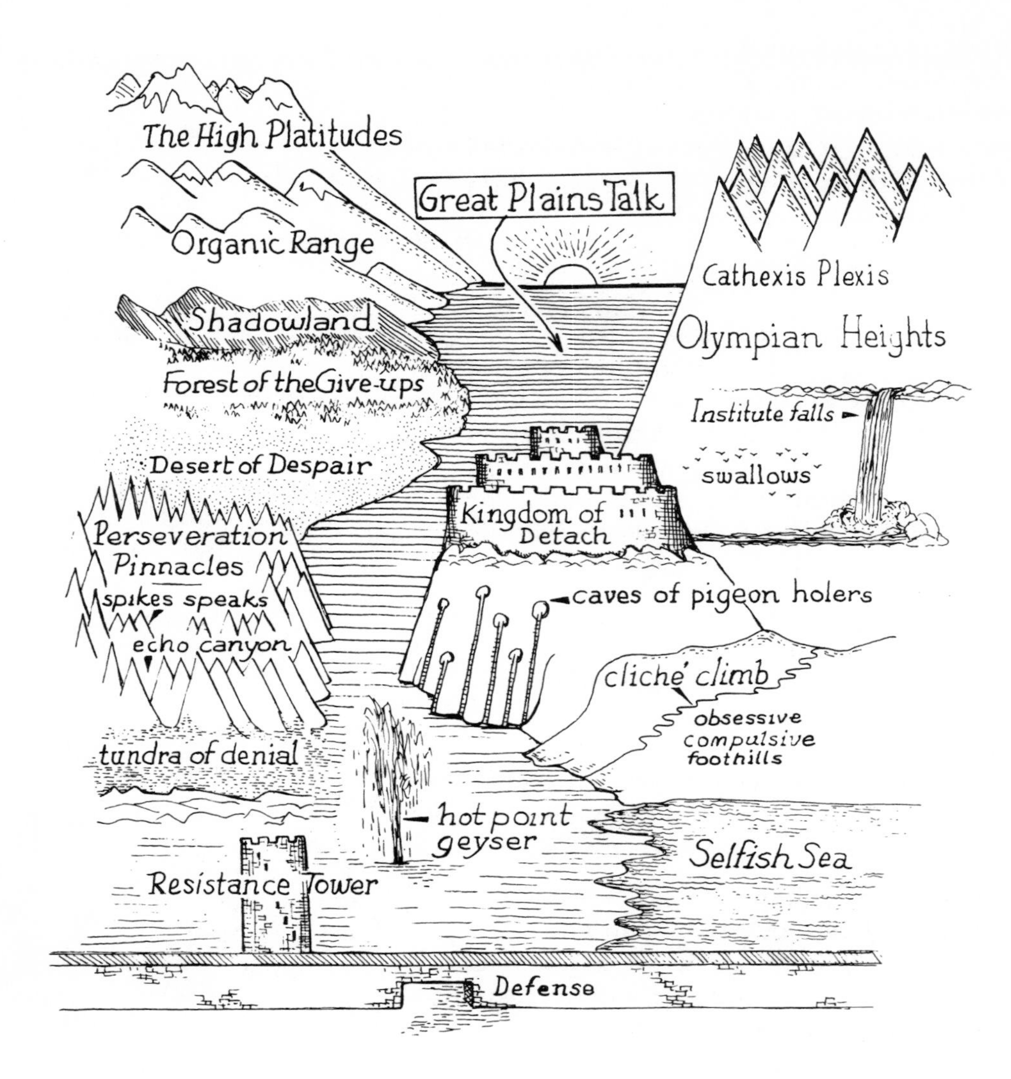

Odyssey of a psychotherapist

Reflections on the Psychotherapist's Perilous Journey

We learn by our mistakes.
Jung said that the right way to wholeness is made up
of many fateful detours and wrong turnings. (*Centenary Brochure*)

There are occupational hazards, harmful to your health
such as,

- discomposure
- disquisition
- disesteem

"Of two things," wrote Goethe, "we cannot sufficiently beware:

- of obstinancy if we confine ourselves to our proper field,
- of inadequacy if we desert it."

I would add

- burnout, *
- cult of the tentative,
- envy and avarice,
- not reading what is being written in your field.

On the *positive* side, after reaching the Great Plains Talk, there is

- self-respect,
- satisfaction,
- self-confidence,
- simplicity,
- caring,
- self-directedness.

Stop making lists.

---

*Burnout literally means the point at which missile fuel is completely burned out and damage is caused by overheating. "The commonplace 'burnt out' might refer to the 'burnt men' who, like the bush before Moses, were set ablaze by the fire of God's presence, yet were not wholly consumed." (Mott, *The Seven Mountains of Thomas Merton*, p. 255)

More Psychotherapy

It is said that D. W. Winnicott, a British psychoanalyst,
was so independent that he refused to join
the Society of Independent Analysts in London.
Three cheers for good old Winnicott!

When Margaret Little was seeking a second analyst
after some bad experiences,
she found Winnicott.
With relief and joy she cried, "I wish I had found you sooner."
He replied, "I couldn't have done your analysis sooner
because I didn't know enough then."

> Did he really say "done" her analysis?
> Oh God, when is an analysis done?
> And who done it?
> If he done it, then it done her in.
> But if she done it,
> she done right good.

A patient of mine cursed that he didn't know anything,
that he was stupid and a failure,
and if only he were different.
He was surprised when I told him that
he was like most achievement-conscious people
who are haunted by the obsession that they
do not know anything.
Even the most accomplished and renowned achievers
slip into feeling "I don't know anything,
I am a failure, I'm stupid."

"I am in the declining years," a fifty-year old patient said to me.
"How is that?" I asked.
With a tone of cutting sarcasm he retorted,
"*You're* getting old, too, you know."
"I don't see it that way."
He sat silently pondering.
I thought, "Yes, I am far into the second half of life."
The second half of life is just as long as the first half.

And I felt older ten years ago
when I was old.

BURNOUT

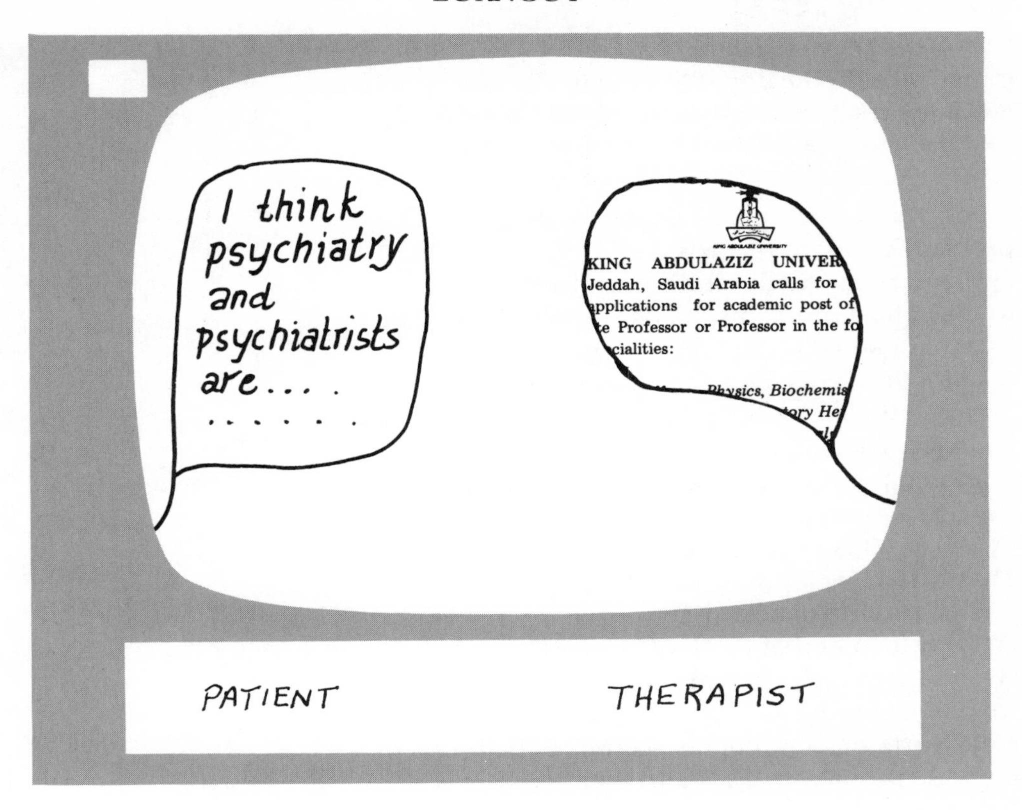

She was embarrassed to say, "I have something to confess:
I like frogs. I like to crouch down and look them in the eye.
I sometimes talk to frogs. I say,
'Will you talk to me? Where have you been?'"

I replied, "What's wrong with liking frogs?
You talk to your dog, why not to a lovely frog?
And besides frogs are very positive figures,
representing the creative beginning of things.
They have been tadpoles swimming in the water like fish,
then they turn into land creatures.
They are symbols of metamorphosis, change,
and they are peaceful little creatures.
You know the fairy story of the princess and the frog?
Why do you think it is such a universal story?"

"It's OK," she said, "to like frogs."

Psychotherapy Problems

It may not be a *problem,*
it may be a *predicament* like life itself.
Problem-oriented thinking demands or assumes
that there is a problem.

Today it is a widespread policy to have
problem-oriented records
for insurance and for audit purposes,
to crystallize problems, plans, and implementations.
I saw a hospital chart filled out on admission.
It said, "Problems: depression, insomnia, and anxiety.
Treatment Plan: reduce depression, diminish insomnia,
control anxiety.
Implementation: Desiprimine for depression,
Halcion for sleep, Valium for anxiety.
Goals: diminish symptoms, discharge in two weeks."
That in itself is a predicament.
It is called box-checking ☑
Write-rote in lieu of thinking.
Where there are problems, it is implied that
there are solutions;
sometimes the solution is to endure the problem,
and one problem passes and another appears.
But there are some insoluble predicaments
which we must transcend.

Psychotherapy is a healing interlude in a life story.
If you expect complete and stable cures
of complex human problems and emotional illnesses,
that is the problem.
Some old-fashioned strategies are still preferable.
The Swiss army uses carrier pigeons.
They can't be detected by radar.
They spirit the message home.

An old-fashioned commitment to honesty helps psychotherapy.
Authentic suffering evokes psychotherapeutic urge to growth.

Loaded Questions

Patient: What would you say about what I just told you,
if you were a friend rather than my therapist?

Lights flash in my mental switchboard.

- Do you answer at all?
- Do you answer right away?
- Do you ask what the patient thinks?
- Do you affirm that, in a way, a therapist is a friend?
- Do you ask for elaboration as a play for time?
- Do you act distant and anonymous?
- Do you pretend to be a friend?
- Do you put on your super-professional garb and ask, "Why do you ask that?"
- Do you play comforting mother?
- Do you play authoritative father?
- Do you sit and wait in silence?
- Do you say, "I'll answer your question, but first. . . ."
- Do you ask why you are needed as a friend rather than a therapist?
- Do you do what?

RULE OF THUMB: Loaded Questions

Loaded questions aren't fired straight.
Your job is to get them in line.
So don't give an immediate answer.
But don't play coy games of clever interpretation.
Get it straight first.

Figure out what is being asked of which of your personae and by whom.
Try to avoid cliché professionalism with such questions as,
"I wonder why you ask me that question."
Assume you have a good idea why the patient is asking the question,
because if you don't and act as if you do,
loaded questions may go off in your face.

The patient is testing the water.
He or she is testing you and telling you something,
such as, "I am scared" or "Please be my friend."
In such a spot
you can always say,
"I will answer your question later, but first
let's see if we can figure out
what your question is all about."

Sometimes the therapist is wise to answer a question directly
and as completely as the situation warrants.
Answering questions with the proper attitude
is teaching. Teaching is understanding.
A good part of psychotherapy is sensitive teaching;
it is also giving hope,
    conveying equanimity,
        and facilitating the strength to endure.

Sometimes it is necessary to affirm
and in affirming to give reassurance.
Advice is notoriously slippery,
to be avoided like thin ice,
except
in situations where the patient
is on a self-destructive course impelled by powers
beyond his comprehension.
Then, sometimes, advice and counsel are
life-giving holding operations
until understanding and strength set in.

For example, you might want to tell a depressed patient
not to make any major life decisions,
not to change where he or she lives or works,
or to change any key relationship.
You might say the equivalent of
don't run, don't jump, don't move, don't buy a fantasy,
or sometimes say, "Why not? What do you have really to fear?"
Advice like tabasco sauce is to be used sparingly, if at all.

RULE OF THUMB: Depression

Depressed patients are to be cautioned,
and if necessary advised that any major move
is not to be undertaken because the patient believes
it will relieve the depression.
(This is a rule of thumb par excellence.)

ASIDE: Advice to Therapists

It takes a lot of solitary thinking
to understand your patients.
When bollixed, try writing exactly what
your patient said and what you said.
It's a form of self-supervision
if you look critically and not admiringly
at your dialogue.

ACHTUNG! Warning to Psychotherapists

Right off the bat
I can name four foolish things that are counterproductive:

- nasty tongue of sarcasm, contentiousness, condescension;
- saying things that are basically stupid;
- nosey intrusions in sticky situations;
- being seductive under any guise;

and four angry things:

- falling asleep;
- talking too much
- talking too little;
- thinking how wonderful you are;

and four greedy things:

- arrogance
- knowing everything
- sham
- exploitation.

> These three—greed, anger and foolishness—are, therefore, the sources of all human woe. To get rid of these sources of woe, one must observe the precepts, must practice concentration of mind and must have wisdom. Observance of the precepts will remove the impurities of greed; right concentration of mind will remove the impurities of anger; and wisdom will remove the impurities of foolishness. (*The Teachings of Buddha,* p. 166)

ranscendent Function

nscendent function represents the uniting symbol.
ates the union of opposites by
restoring balance between ego and the unconscious.
All the symbols and archetypes are vehicles of this function.

THE TRANSCENDENT FUNCTION

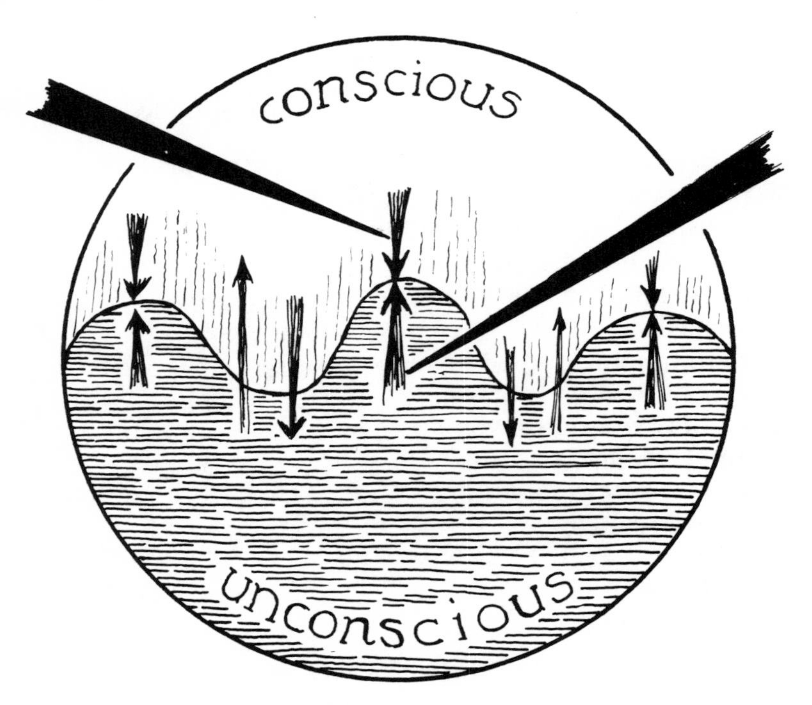

the trained analyst mediates this function and thus helps to bring conscious and unconscious together so as to arrive at **a new attitude**

The mandala is a symbol of the transcendent function.
Jung did not wish to designate any metaphysical quality
by the use of the word transcendent, but
merely that this function makes a transition
from one attitude to another attitude.

It's not only big or great things that count,
it's the little things

meaning and purpose of the unconscious gives insight into the transcendent function, but how?
Tension between opposites are brought into complementary relationship to free the individual to work with neglected and undeveloped parts of the personality.

that mean something big,
the ordinary little things we don't think about.
For example,
when someone is giving me his history,
I am not *taking* a history.
One can take a history in order to get the
hard data of medical and personal facts.
However, one *gives* a history of one's personal life.
You *give* your attention.
You are paid to give it.
The patient pays to give it to you.
It makes sense to take some things.
It is important to give others.

RULE OF THUMB: Asking Names

I always ask the names of the patient's children,
brothers, sisters, parents, and spouse.
Patients appreciate this simple, small touch.
And later on when these people are discussed,
I have already been introduced to them by name.

When patients tell me about important relationships,
intimacies, and sensitive memories,
I always ask for the other person's name.
If the intimacy is an affair or involves someone
whose name the patient might not want to disclose,
I specifically ask for the first name.
You might be surprised how much more human this makes our talks,
and avoids the awkward "he-she-him-and-her."
By saying, "Tell me her (his) first name,"
I am giving the patient tacit permission not to reveal more than he (she)
wishes now.

When a patient conveys a childhood vividly
with pictorial images
I ask for some photographs
or an album of pictures to show to me.

RULE OF THUMB: Violent Patients

Take not only enough time but use enough words
in managing potentially violent patients.
This is a subtle, artful business.
Regardless of whether or not drugs are used
the human relationship is the key to control.

When I was in charge of the psychiatric admission ward
of the U.S. Naval Hospital at Oakland, California,
about a hundred new patients were admitted each week.
In one year 200 out of 1000 patients came in restraints,
many in straightjackets.

A large, muscular, acutely psychotic marine sergeant
was brought in by an armed guard.
He had been charged with assault
and was hallucinating and delusional.
I had the corpsman remove his leather restraints
and I asked him to come into my office.

His severe agitation and panic diminished.
I talked with him for about an hour,
staying after my duty time.
As we talked he became tranquil.
I thought to myself,
at last, we've really made a connection.
We can talk more tomorrow, but not now
because I was late for an engagement.

I said to him,
"Let's continue talking tomorrow."
I didn't explain anything. I just said,
"Let's continue talking tomorrow," like that. Abruptly.
It might have been a good and proper time to stop.
But it would have been better
had I explained why I was stopping talking then
and reflected on what he had been telling me
so he knew for sure I had been listening.
Instead it was just, "Plop! Time's up! Finis!"

Making of People Need People, *Revue Studios, 1961. The marine, played by Lee Marvin, arrives on the psychiatric ward in restraints. Narrator Fred Astaire stands by. Dr. Harry Wilmer was played by Arthur Kennedy. Story adapted from Dr. Wilmer's book,* Social Psychiatry in Action.

The emergency seemed to be over.
In my fatigue and relief I said, in effect,
the old cliché, "Time's up. See you tomorrow."

He felt suddenly betrayed and abandoned.
He might have said to himself,
"Just as I thought! He's a fake. A sham. I'm a fool
to have trusted this doctor or whatever he is.
Fool! Shithead! Crazy! Sonovabitch!"
He stood bolt upright, glared at me and said,
"You're not the man I thought you were."
He bolted from my office into the locked ward
in a rage. All hell broke loose.

There was quite a scene.
I had to stay longer than
had I listened to him and talked to him about my leaving.
I am not advocating martyrdom and masochism,
but being genuine and consistent.
I could have said the truth, "Look, Sergeant,
I don't have any more time. I'm tired. I have to leave,
but I want to reflect briefly about what you and I have said."
I had suddenly switched persona from caring physician
to uncaring naval officer.
Being genuine and authentic
seems a small thing, but it turns out to be a big thing.
It takes more time, not a lot really,
but it is fully-attentive time so that you turn out to be
the man the patient thought you were

and not the person he fears you might be.

Joseph Henderson designed the above Logo
for the C. G. Jung Institute of San Francisco.
There are four snails moving around the center
symbolizing the slow pace of deep understanding.

BIG THINGS

During the psychoanalysis of one of my first patients,
she came into the room, lay down on the couch,
and fell into a profound, prolonged silence.

I began, "Why don't you talk about where
you left off last time, you know . . ."
She suddenly began to sob and said,
"My father was killed in an accident last night."
The room seemed to get dark.
I felt a sense of shame
that I had not waited to hear what she had to say.
With remorse I tried to comfort her,
"I know how you feel."
Obviously I had said exactly the wrong thing to her.
"You don't know how I feel! You don't know how
anybody feels! You don't know!"
She was right, of course.
How insensitive I had been.
I never forget that lesson.
Since that day I have never said to a patient in pain or anguish,
"I know how you feel."

We do not *know* how another person feels.
At best we can connect empathically.
If we are empathic we don't say,
"I know how you feel.
Yes, my father died too, but. . . ."
The object is not to intrude yourself.
"I know how you feel" is sympathetic,
but it doesn't invite her to tell about her feelings,
the tragic accident, and her grief and about her father.

A therapy hour begins
with the patient having the first say.
After "Hello" or "How are you?" or any
other salutation,
the Rule of Thumb is to wait to see what the patient
has to say: opening lines and filling lines.

Announcements are best left for later in the hour.

I once said, "I will be awake June 3rd through the 7th."
Without blinking an eye, my patient replied solicitously,
"I am so sorry. All that time?"

Patients have the best last word.
Slips of the tongue are apt to be a riot.
It doesn't take much of a wit to know how meaningful they are
or how embarrassing.
One of my analysands was explaining his professional relations
and he said,
"I am afflicted with the San Francisco Psychoanalytic Society."
"Affiliated?"
"Oh."
One of my patients at the Mayo Clinic said to me,
"This is the bless'd clinic in the world."
I replied, "Yes, true."

Inner Dialogue

There is an inner rehearsal that goes on in the mind
of the attentive, listening psychotherapist.
Before he speaks aloud, he tries out various things to say.
It is a more or less automatic inner speech,
a dialogue with oneself, the patient, or anyone.
This inner speech is associated with exquisite listening
and follows intuitive clues to dialogue
and the voice of the inner *daimonian*.
The Wise Old Man, or the Wise Old Woman within
will nudge and whisper proper metaphors.
This inner dialogue can be cultivated, but
it seems to come
naturally to empathic people.
I am not sanguine about how much empathy
can be taught if there isn't an inborn high potential.

Eric Hoffer once said, "It is safe to assume
that people are more subtle and less sensitive
than they seem." (*The Passionate State of Mind*)
That always struck me as profound insight.

How good it is to reach a point
when you don't have to ask yourself,
"Should I say this?" or "Should I say that?"
or wonder if it is in accordance with someone's gospel.
There comes a time when you have learned
to speak spontaneously in your own idiom
sans jargon,
in phrases that are your very own,
and with spontaneous words,

Things are always better
than they are.

not repeating anything exactly like you ever said before.
It is a BIG THING when you realize one day
that you have been talking
just right,
not wondering if you should or ought, but just
talking to the point.
That is the point.
Big things come in few words.
Words in inner dialogue are played with, discarded,
taken up, elaborated, and silently articulated.
You are author, script writer, director,
prompter, producer, and audience in a secret, tryout performance.
In the cybernetic networks of the mind,
messages zip back and forth in automatic feedback
keeping things in equilibrium.

Sometimes I think the model of the good psychotherapist
resembles a Seeing Eye dog who is
trained to cross intersections,
to be alert to signals, sounds, dangers,
sniffing, nudging and guiding,
acting naturally and instinctually with monumental discipline.
If there is such a thing as instantaneous inner dialogue,
the Seeing Eye dog has it.
Barking, yipping, moving, stopping, signalling,
the dog does what it is trained to do for another.
Altruism without expectation: unconditioned love.

At the end of a moving analytical hour,
one of my patients stood up to leave my office and said,
"You have helped bring me into the light."

The inner dialogue whirled and instantly
delivered a reply,
"Maybe I just helped you to see the light you were in."

She looked at me for a moment of penetrating thought
and nodded, "Gracias."

It was getting dark,
as she stepped out of the office.
I offered to turn on the patio lights.
"Oh, never mind," she reassured me, "It's lighter than you think."

She had made an unconscious reference to the patio sundial
on which was inscribed,
"It is later than you think."

Such rich metaphors come spontaneously from the unconscious.
Once, during a personally difficult time,
I was attending a service at the Stanford University Chapel.
Out of nowhere words came into my head:
"Things are better than they are!"
I often remember those words
when life is hard and they lift my spirits
every time.

Such powerful one-line messages occur frequently in dreams.
It is little wonder that in ancient times
people thought
somnia a Deo missa: Dreams are sent by God.
Another patient who was preparing to leave my office
at the end of her session began picking up
a clutter of typed dreams, notes, books, and a purse
she had set down on the floor by her chair.
"Messy Lady!" she scolded herself.
"A lot of interesting material," I replied.
"Thank you."
Simple? Yes. A cognitive switch from subjective personal judgment
to valuing what represents herself and her labor.

A patient returned from a long ocean voyage
which she had taken to help cure a serious depression
on the advice of her medical physician.
I had thought the journey was foolish, impetuous,
and a dangerous flight from psychotherapy.
"Take a long sea voyage!"
To my surprise she returned buoyant.
She came for her first appointment,
sat down, slowly and meticulously
folded her diaphanous scarf, and laid it on my desk.
Then she looked me in the eye, smiling, sighed,
"Good grief!"
Her depression had lifted.
I was wrong. It had been a positive grief experience.

Principles of Practical Psychotherapy

More than one patient had admitted to me that he has learned to accept his neurotic symptoms with gratitude, because, like a barometer, they invariably told him when and where he was straying from his individual path, and also whether he had let important things remain unconscious.

(Jung, CW 16:11)

I do not know which is the more difficult: to accumulate a wide knowledge or to renounce one's professional authority and anonymity. At all events the latter necessity involves a moral strain that makes the profession of psychotherapist not exactly an enviable one. Among laymen one frequently meets with the prejudice that psychotherapy is the easiest thing in the world and consists in the art of putting something over on people or wheedling money out of them. But actually it is a tricky and not undangerous calling. Just as all doctors are exposed to infections and other occupational hazarads, so the psychotherapist runs the risk of psychic infections which are no less menacing. On the one hand he is often in danger of getting entangled in the neuroses of his patients; on the other hand if he tries too hard to guard against their influence, he robs himself of his therapeutic efficacy. Between this Scylla and this Charybdis lies the peril, but also the healing power.

(Jung, CW 16: 23)

Giving the Patient an Image from the Symbol of an Archetype

Unable to help a patient see
how she was always obviously falling into the same kind of
self-defeating and self-destructive traps,
I sank into mute frustration and looked at her,
thinking that she had almost transferred her sense of helplessness
onto me.
Week after week, hour after hour, for months, it had been
variations on the same story.
She went blindly on her miserable way.
Now this day was going to be one more glum day.
She couldn't use my words or
really listen to her own words.
Nothing seemed to register.
Something had to change.
Figuratively I threw up my hands as if in supplication
for some wisdom beyond my ken. It came in an image:
She was down once more in the proverbial hole
that she kept falling into.
In exasperation I took my pen and a piece of paper
and drew a picture of her situation for her.

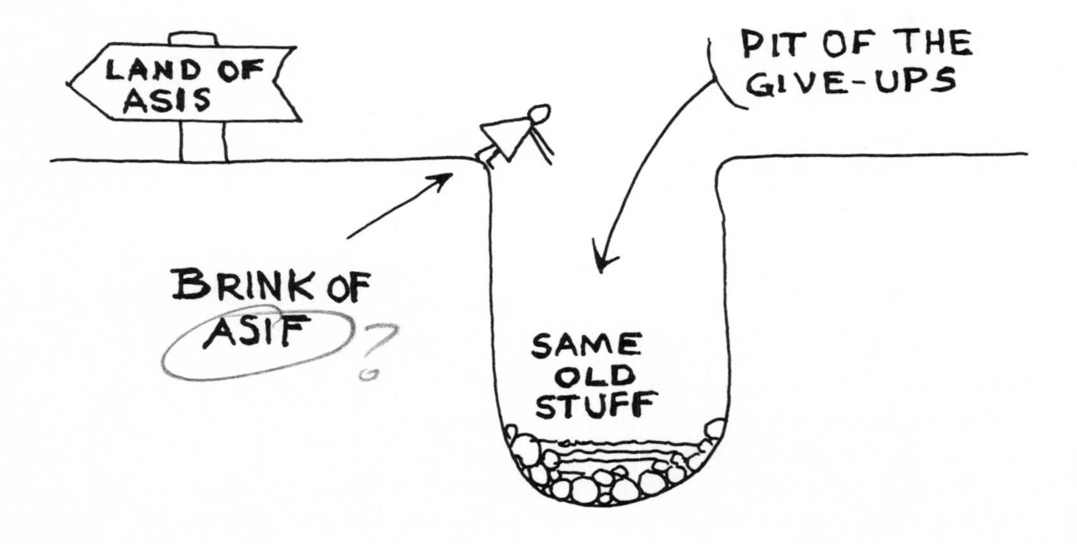

"*There it is!*" I said,
"Do you see it now?"
She gazed at the sketch in fascination
"Yes. I see it."
"Well then look how you keep edging up
to the brink and falling over
into the *Hole of the Give-Ups*,
into the mess of debris and trivia.
See the sign pointing to the good *Land of Asis!*
The pile of old stuff in the pit is in
the *Land of Asif*.
You need to keep your feet on the earth
and stay back from the edge!
Above all, don't lean over too far
because you will keep falling in."

She listened without a word of reply,
then she took the picture, folded it,
and put it in her purse.
That was the end of the session.
I forgot about the picture until she reminded me
a few weeks later that she carried it
with her all the time.
When she got into a self-defeating mood or situation
she took the picture out, looked at it,
and stopped herself from falling into the hole.
It was good medicine.
Just what the doctor ordered.
She used it that way for several years.
Most of the time it worked,
not the picture per se
but a creation for her objectifying our work
in a visual metaphor, a story.
That I could do something in an impasse,
not being passive but a model of active mastery,
gave her the strength to do something for herself.

Necessity is said to be the Mother of Invention,
and giving birth to something, even a drawing,
makes it our symbolic offspring.
It is noteworthy that in the very first dream she told me
she was buried in a tomb as if she had fallen into a sepulcher.
There was no apparent way out.

In her subsequent therapy she did not seem to be able
to come out of her depression.
It was as if she drew me in after her
until I drew a map which was a way out for both of us.

Jung called fantasy the mother of all possibilities
in which the inner and outer worlds,
like all psychological antitheses,
are joined in living union:
The psyche creates reality every day.
The only expression I can use for this activity
is fantasy. (Jung, CW 6: 78)

The First and the Second Half of Life

The first half of life is a period
when the ego becomes differentiated
and separated from the Self
with which it was united at birth.
At midlife the ego has achieved a high point
of conscious development in its separation
from the Self.

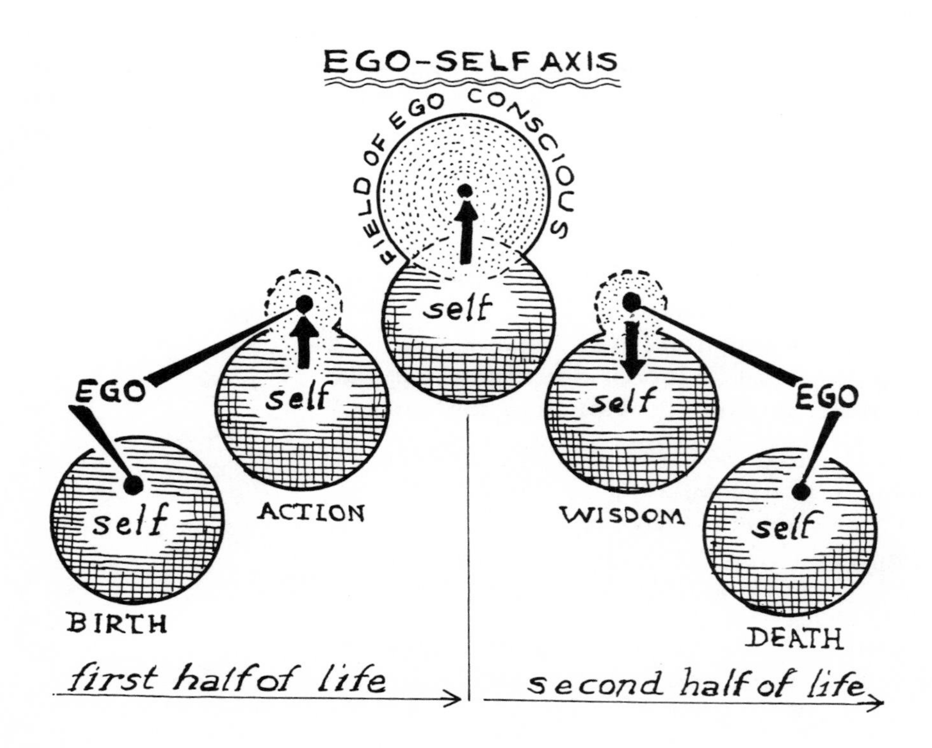

It is as separate as it ever will be
along the ego-Self axis.

In the second half of life the ego is drawn back
into the Self.
The growing union of a highly conscious ego
and the Self creates an aura of wisdom.
At death, as at birth, ego and Self are again one.
The cycle is complete.

To be conscious at the moment of dying
may be the utmost completeness of living
and the closest consciousness to eternity,
as one becomes one in the Self,
imago Dei, the image of God into which ego is submerged.

> The Self as the center and totality of the psyche which is able to reconcile all opposites can be considered as the organ of acceptance *par excellence*. Since it includes the totality, it must be able to accept all elements of psychic life no matter how antithetical they may be. It is this sense of acceptance of the Self that gives the ego its strength and stability. This sense of acceptance is conveyed to the ego via the ego-Self axis. A symptom of damage to this axis is lack of self-acceptance. The individual feels he is not worthy to exist or be himself. Psychotherapy offers such a person an opportunity to experience acceptance. In successful cases this can amount to the repair of the ego-Self axis which restores contact with the inner sources of strength and acceptance, leaving the patient free to live and grow. (Edinger, *Ego and Archetype*, p. 40)

The first half of life is like a sphere
which overlaps slightly with the sphere
of the second half of life.
The midlife time from 35 to 40
is a betwixt time of
unique biological and psychological stress.
The conscious life sphere encompasses
all but the beginning and the ending of life,
although in a fashion consciousness exists
from alpha to omega,
from the first to the last breath.
The midlife portion of overlapping spheres, an almond-shaped space,
is called a *mandorla*.
It may surround a sacred personage in religious art
or define the midlife holy battleground.

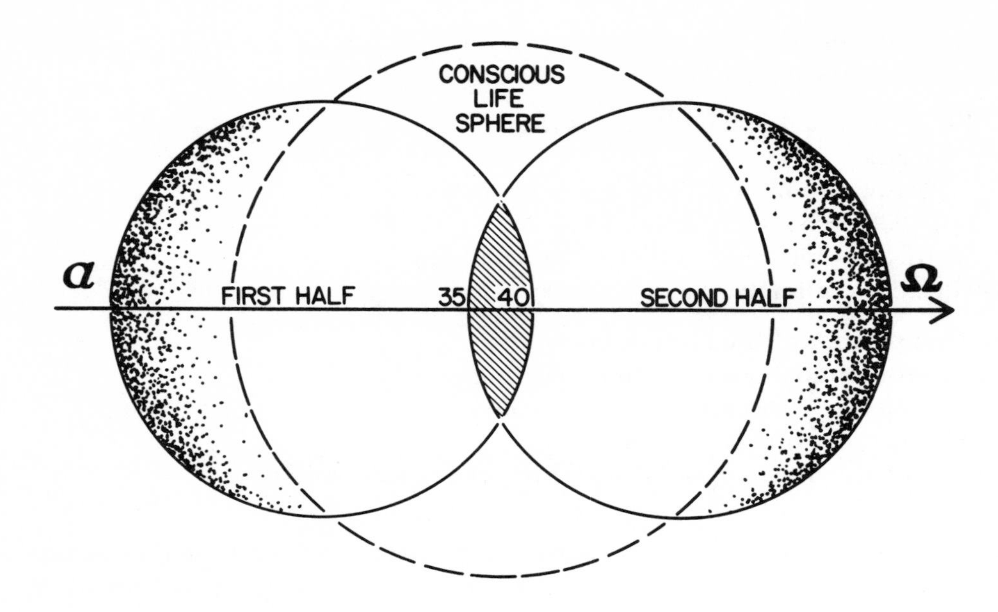

Schopenhauer (*Essays*, p. 102) compared life to a piece of embroidery:
during the first half one sees the right side
and during the second half, the wrong side,

which is not so lovely
but is more instructive since
one can see the way in which
the threads have been worked together.

The latter part of life
is not all going downhill.
Those who cross the midpoint
and bemoan the coming of the end should remind themselves
that one half of anything is always as long as the other half.

The first half of life is characterized by unfolding activity,
striving for accomplishments and achievements,
the acquisition of material things, and
usually, the creation of a family.
It is a time of developing maturity,
reaching for personal power, and an ever-widening
expansion of life.

The second half of life is ushered in by
the normal midlife crisis,
the transformation of life patterns to new challenges
in the face of which many people become melancholy.

Not a few lose their way
and life becomes meaningless,
an existential void,
a personal theater of the absurd.
In the throes of this angst
individuals begin to rethink their lives,
going back over the past wondering
where they went wrong,
why they missed this or that golden opportunity.
They mourn lost relationships and loves,
and they fear death and are unprepared for dying.

At midlife some parents experience the empty nest syndrome
when all of the children have left home.
Suddenly two parents are sitting, looking at each other,
wondering what it has all been about,
and what now?

The midlife crisis,
even when it brings on depression, anxiety, fear, or despair,
is a time of great challenge,
out of which come symbols of transformation,
tinctured with a sweet poison of nostalgia.
Psychologically, some individuals never pass the boundary
of midlife.
Their growth is arrested, new challenges are pushed away,
and ennui sets in.

The natural and normal introspection of midlife hangs on
distorted in obsessive rumination and retrospection.
Like Lot's wife looking back, they turn to pillars of salt.
Darkness comes over their existence.
They are swallowed up by the past.

A surprisingly large number of people try to live
the second half of life as if it were the first half.
This perverts the normal grace of aging.
Hating wrinkles, bemoaning physical deterioration,

sexual changes, aches and pains, and illnesses,
they hide or deny aging,
clown their way through life, playing perennial youths,
seeking the thrills and action of being young.
They are robbing themselves of the treasures of growing old
which compensate for its frailties and infirmities.

Midlife depression may be quite serious;
it may lead to suicide.
It is a normal life crisis
which, if extreme, needs psychiatric attention.
But this disorder can be made worse by classic psychoanalysis,

in my experience, and such treatment is contraindicated.
It may add a disastrous burden.

Freud devoted his life to understanding
the first half of life.
Jung devoted his life to understanding
the second half of life.
Midlife depressions are fueled by reawakened
adolescent despair and unresolved sexual conflicts.
The way through this maze
is not running from the reality that actually is one's midlife lot,
and not seeking

- intoxication of drugs and alcohol
- excitement of promiscuous sex
- greener pastures
- power, glory, and notoriety
- new job, new wife, new husband, new lover
- denial of the humdrum of everyday.

On the positive side, the way through is

- go towards the inner values
- seek development of what you have neglected
- follow the flow of life but do not float passively.

It is a truism that we all fear death,
but it is not so well known that
when we fear death we fear living.
In worries about aging some people
become obsessed by the four poisons:

- if-onlys
- what-ifs
- should-haves
- could-haves.

Life tragedies are arranged by a power of events
beyond individual control.
Aimless homeless wanderers,
street people turned out of mental hospitals,
demoralized, impoverished who have lost their jobs,

hungry and starving people,
all are suffering in ways most people try not to think about.

I see a new meanness afoot in this country,
a shrinking of the generosity of spirit
which has characterized America.
There is a growing selfish, hedonistic callousness.
The saving power of compassion is atrophying.
Atomic bombs are hypertrophying.
Atomic war threatens our destruction.
Animals are slaughtered by poachers.
Nature is blighted.
Our toxic, noxious wastes proliferate.
Our consuming society is consuming itself.
Acid rain, gluttony, greed,
power, lying, cheating, spying abound.

Life's predicaments require
an acquiescence to life as it is and
the courage to examine that life and our part in it
and to make of each day a life.
But we must try to change what is evil and unjust.
Those in the second half of life
have a greater responsibility to remedy evils
because they have had a longer stake
in perpetuating them.

RULE OF THUMB: Shut off the Past

"Shut off the past. 'Let the dead past bury its dead.'"
It is easy to say, so hard to realize.
Shut out the yesterdays, which have lighted for fools
the way to dusty death, and have no concern for yourself
personally, that is, consciously.
The petty annoyances, the real and fancied slights,
the trivial mistakes, the disappointments, the sins,
the sorrows, even the joys—bury them deep in the
oblivion of each night.
To look back, except on rare occasions for taking stock
is to risk the fate of Lot's wife.
To die daily, after the manner of St. Paul, ensures
the resurrection of a new person, who makes each
day the epitome of life." (Osler, "A Way of Life", p. 241)

Retirement

Today as we grow old, we must carry the burdens
of leaving old, established, well-worn patterns,
and joining the ranks of aging people
in a culture which discounts them while at the same time
offering discounts to them,
in a culture which honors them little
and revels in youth and youthful tastes and pocketbooks.

> *Say not thou, What is the cause that the former days were better than these? for thou dost not inquire wisely concerning this.* (Eccles. 7:10)

Retirement absolves nobody of responsibility
for life, culture, and human values.
Peace of mind which comes from
shutting off the past and letting the past bury their dead
does not diminish our living involvement in the present
and the need to inquire wisely concerning this.

Jung Writes on the Stages of Life

Natural life is the nourishing soil of the soul. Anyone who fails to go along with life remains suspended, stiff and rigid in midair. That is why so many people get wooden in old age; they look back and cling to the past with a secret fear of death in their hearts. They withdraw from the life-process, at least psychologically, and consequently remain fixed like nostalgic pillars of salt, with vivid recollections of youth but no living relation to the present. From the middle of life onward, only he remains vitally alive who is ready to die with life. For in the secret hour of life's midday the parabola is reversed, death is born. The second half of life does not signify ascent, unfolding, increase, exuberance, but death, since the end is its goal. The negation of life's fulfilment is synonymous with the refusal to accept its ending. Both mean not wanting to live, and not wanting to live is identical with not wanting to die. Waxing and waning make one curve.

(Jung, CW 8: 800)

In my rather long psychological experience I have observed a great many people whose unconscious psychic activity I was able to follow into the immediate presence of death. As a rule the approaching end was indicated by those symbols which, in normal life also, proclaim changes of psychological condition—rebirth symbols such as change of locality, journeys, and the like. I have frequently been able to trace back for over a year, in a dream-series, the indications of approaching death, even in cases where such thoughts were not prompted by the outward situation. Dying, therefore, has its onset long before actual death. Moreover, this often shows itself in peculiar change of personality which may precede death for quite a long time. On the whole, I was astonished to see how little ado the unconscious psyche makes of death. It would seem as though death were something relatively unimportant, or perhaps our psyche does not bother about what happens to the individual. But it seems that the unconscious is all the more interested in how *one dies; that is, whether the attitude of consciousness is adjusted to dying or not.*

(Jung, CW 8: 809)

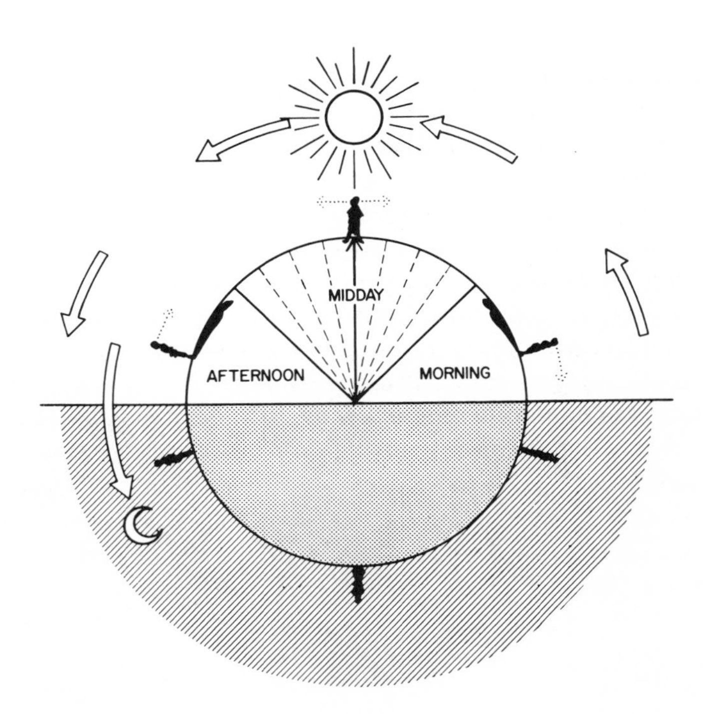

The one hundred and eighty degrees of the arc of life are divisible into four parts. The first quarter, lying to the east, is childhood, that state in which we are a problem for others but not yet conscious of any problems of our own. Conscious problems fill out the second and third quarters; while in the last, in extreme old age, we descend again into that condition where, regardless of our state of consciousness, we once more become something of a problem to others. Childhood and extreme old age are, of course, utterly different, and yet they have one thing in common: submersion in the unconscious psychic happenings.

(Jung, CW 8: 795)

Fortunately we are not rising and setting suns, for then it would fare badly with our cultural values. But there is something sunlike within us, and to speak of the morning and spring, of the evening and autumn of life is not mere sentimental jargon. We thus give expression to psychological truths and, even more, to physiological facts, for the reversal of the sun at noon changes even bodily characteristics.

(Jung, CW 8: 780)

Middle life is the moment of greatest unfolding, when a man still gives himself to his work with his whole strength and his whole will. But in this very moment evening is born, and the second half of life begins. Passion now changes her face and is called duty; 'I want' becomes the inexorable 'I must,' and the turnings of the pathway that once brought surprise and discovery become dulled by custom. The wine has fermented and begins to settle and clear. Conservative tendencies develop if all goes well; instead of looking forward one looks backward, most of the time involuntarily, and one begins to take stock, to see how one's life has developed up to this point. The real motivations are sought and real discoveries are made. The critical survey of himself and his fate enables a man to recognize his pecularities. But these insights do not come to him easily; they are gained only through the severest shocks.

(Jung, CW 17: 331a)

Life is a constant struggle against extinction, a violent yet fleeting deliverance from ever-lurking night. This death is no external enemy, it is his own inner longing for the stillness and profound peace of all-knowing non-existence, for all-seeing sleep in the ocean of coming-to-be and passing away. Even in the highest strivings for harmony and balance, for the profundities of philosophy and the raptures of the artist, he seeks death, immobility, satiety, rest. If like Peirithous, he tarries too long in this abode of rest and peace, he is overcome by apathy, and the poison of the serpent paralyzes him for all time. If he is to live, he must fight and sacrifice his longing for the past in order to rise to his own heights. And having reached the noonday heights, he must sacrifice his love for his own achievement, for he may not loiter. The sun, too, sacrifices its greatest strength in order to hasten onward to the fruits of autumn, which are the seeds of rebirth.*

(Jung, CW 5: 553)

Our life is like the course of the sun. In the morning it gains continually in strength until it reaches the zenith-heat of high noon. Then comes the enantiodromia: the steady forward movement no longer denotes an increase, but a decrease, in strength. Thus our task in handling a young person is different from the task of handling an older person. In the former case, it is enough to clear away all the obstacles that hinder expansion and ascent; in the latter, we must nurture everything that assists the descent.

(Jung, CW 7: 114)

---

*In the Greek myth, Peirithous and Theseus swore an oath of eternal friendship. When they attempted to abduct Persephone from Hades, they were tricked into sitting on a magic bench from which they are unable to rise. After four years of torture Hercules descended into Hades and pulled Theseus from the bench; but when Hercules reached for Peirithous, the ground trembled, and he was left behind.

A human being would certainly not grow to be seventy or eighty years old if this longevity had no meaning for the species. The afternoon of human life must also have a significance of its own and cannot be merely a pitiful appendage to life's morning. The significance of the morning undoubtedly lies in the development of the individual, our entrenchment in the outer world, the propagation of our kind, and the care of our children. This is the obvious purpose of nature. But when this purpose has been attained—and more than attained—shall the earning of money, the extension of conquests, and the expansion of life go steadily on beyond the bounds of all reason and sense? Whoever carries over into the afternoon the law of the morning, or the natural aim, must pay for it with damage to his soul, just as surely as a growing youth who tries to carry over his childish egoism into adult life must pay for this mistake with social failure. Money-making, social achievement, family and posterity are nothing but plain nature, not culture. Culture lies outside the purpose of nature. Could by any chance culture be the meaning and purpose of the second half of life?

(Jung, CW, 8: 787)

I have often been asked what I believe about death, that unproblematical ending of individual existence. Death is known to us simply as the end. It is the period, often placed before the close of the sentence and followed only by memories or after-effects in others. For the reason concerned, however, the sand has run out of the glass; the rolling stone has come to rest. When death confronts us, life always seems like a downward flow or like a clock that has been wound up and whose eventual 'running down' is taken for granted. We are never more convinced of this 'running down' than when a human life comes to its end before our eyes, and the question of the meaning and worth of life never becomes more urgent or more agonizing than when we see the final breath leave a body which a moment before was living. How different does the meaning of life seem to us when we see a young person striving for distant goals and shaping the future, and compare this with an incurable invalid, or with an old man who is sinking reluctantly and impotently into the grave!

(Jung, CW 8: 796)

Like a projectile flying to its goal, life ends in death. Even its ascent and its zenith are only steps and means to this goal. This paradoxical formula is no more than a logical deduction from the fact that life strives towards a goal and is determined by an aim. I do not believe I am guilty here of playing with syllogisms. We grant goal and purpose to the ascent of life, why not to the descent? The birth of a human being is pregnant with meaning, why not death? For twenty years and more the growing man is being prepared for the complete unfolding of his individual nature, why should not the older man prepare himself twenty years and more for his death? Of course, with the zenith one has obviously reached something, one is it and has it. But what is attained with death?

(Jung, CW 8: 803)

---

23 December 1950

Dear Dr. [Hanna] Oeri,

The great tiredness I saw and felt in my friend on my visit to Basel has now run speedily to its end. The dead are surely not to be pitied—they have so infinitely much more before them than we do—but rather the living who are left behind, who must contemplate the fleetingness of existence and suffer parting, sorrow, and loneliness in time.

I know what Albert's death must mean to you, for with him my last living friend has also departed. We are but a remnant of the past, more and more so with each coming year. Our eyes turn away from the future of the human world in which our children, but not ourselves, will live. Enviable the lot of those who have crossed the threshold, yet my compassion goes out to those who, in the darkness of the world, hemmed in by a narrow horizon and the blindness of ignorance, must follow the river of their days, fulfilling life's task, only to see their whole existence, which once was the present brimming with power and vitality, crumbling bit by bit and crashing into the abyss. This spectacle of old age would be unendurable did we not know that our psyche reaches into a region held captive neither by change in time nor by limitation of place. In that form of being our birth is a death and our death is a birth. The scales of the whole hang balanced. With heartfelt sympathy,

Yours sincerely,
C. G. Jung

(Written to the wife of Jung's close, lifelong friend, in *Collected Letters*, vol. 1, p. 568)

PART

VI

The Meaning and Function of Dreams

The Meaning and Function of Dreams

Given the impossible impasse, then listen to what the dream says.
Dreams, as clues to understanding,
help us cope with daytime problems;
they provide helpful voices and images from
the two realms of the unconscious.
They are the only examples of memories and fears
that we process in our mind
without conscious distortion.
In fact, a night of dreaming helps undistort consciousness.

There is no censor in our unconscious distorting or telling us
we cannot dream about this or that or
cannot talk about one thing or another.
None of our conscious prejudices or ideas
are twisting, contorting, or falsifying
these memories or ideas when we are unconscious.

For those of you who want your dreams to help you,
write your dreams down in a bound notebook,
date them, and write out
what you think they are saying.
If you can remember only bits and pieces,
write these fragments and ask yourself,
"What is the dream trying to show me, tell me, or
help me see what I do not want to see or know?"
Really,
really,
really think about your dream.
Contemplate your dream and let it contemplate you.

If it seems incomprehensible,
it may keep coming to you.
If you miss the message one night,
it will come in a different light another night.
If you hang in there, it will speak to you.

If you can't decipher it
and your dreams seem important,
seek the help of some analyst who understands dreams.
Dream interpretation is
more an art than a science.
If it is a science, it is an embryonic science.
In the hands of a gifted, trained dream analyst
it is a mature art.

If one accepts the premise that dreams reveal meanings
hidden from our waking life,
then we must examine dreams exceedingly carefully.
Psychotherapy is impoverished if
dreams are not listened to.

"This sounds silly, but you're going to marry a pussycat."

RULE OF THUMB: What Do You Say?

Student: What do you say when a patient tells you a dream?
Teacher: Not very much, and that only after you have listened and thought a great deal.

Many people don't believe in Rules of Thumb.
I know plenty of Jungian analysts who
bridle at the idea of techniques and disciplined methods.
I have talked with them; they demand freedom.
I have worked with some of them who resent interference.
But discipline and method are of utmost importance
when dealing with ambiguous symbols,
paradoxical psychic events, and
mysterious matters such as dreams.
The freedom demanded is hatched in hubris.

Slick interpretations,
a Jungian bag of tricks,
a Freudian bag of tricks,
any kind of bag of tricks
is the hallmark of the trickster archetype.

I have not devised the
Trickster Dream Game just for kicks.
It depicts dream analysis
schematized in diagram
to avoid preaching
and resort to play.

RULE OF THUMB: Taking Yourself Too Seriously

In confronting the dream world,
don't take yourself too seriously
but take the dream seriously.
Honor the dream,
and at the same time learn to play.

Trickster Dream Game

Move 1: All functions are alert.

Move 2: The dream is placed in the context of the patient's history and culture.
(*If you meet the dream at this point with clichés, stereotyped perceptions, and evaluations, go back to Start.*)

Move 3: Take hold of the dream narrative with some method suitable to yourself, with some disciplined approach, and have some Rules of Thumb available for the predictable but unexpected things that happen.
(*If you meet the dream at this point with cookbook methods without a grain of salt and variation, go back to Move 1.*)

Move 4: Have some knowledge of symbols and the capacity to take meaning in pluralistic possibilities; know something about mythology.
(*If you get lost in the forest of trivia go back to Move 2. If on the other hand you get snookered by the trickster into a power game, go home! You are disqualified and cannot even go back to Start.*)

Move 5: Stay alert to transference and countertransference in dream stories and in your work with the dreamer about the dream content. Keep yourself out of it as much as possible, but don't shy away when you are actually in it.
(*If you try to pawn off a sham explanation of interpretation or if your intellectualizing is a manifestation of pseudo-understanding, go back to Move 3.*)

Move 6: The nitty-gritty of wisdom, prudence, understanding, and humility is called brevity.
(If you make some super interpretation that you just love and revel in, if your windbag energizes your verbal output, or if your hubris is showing, go back to Move 1.)

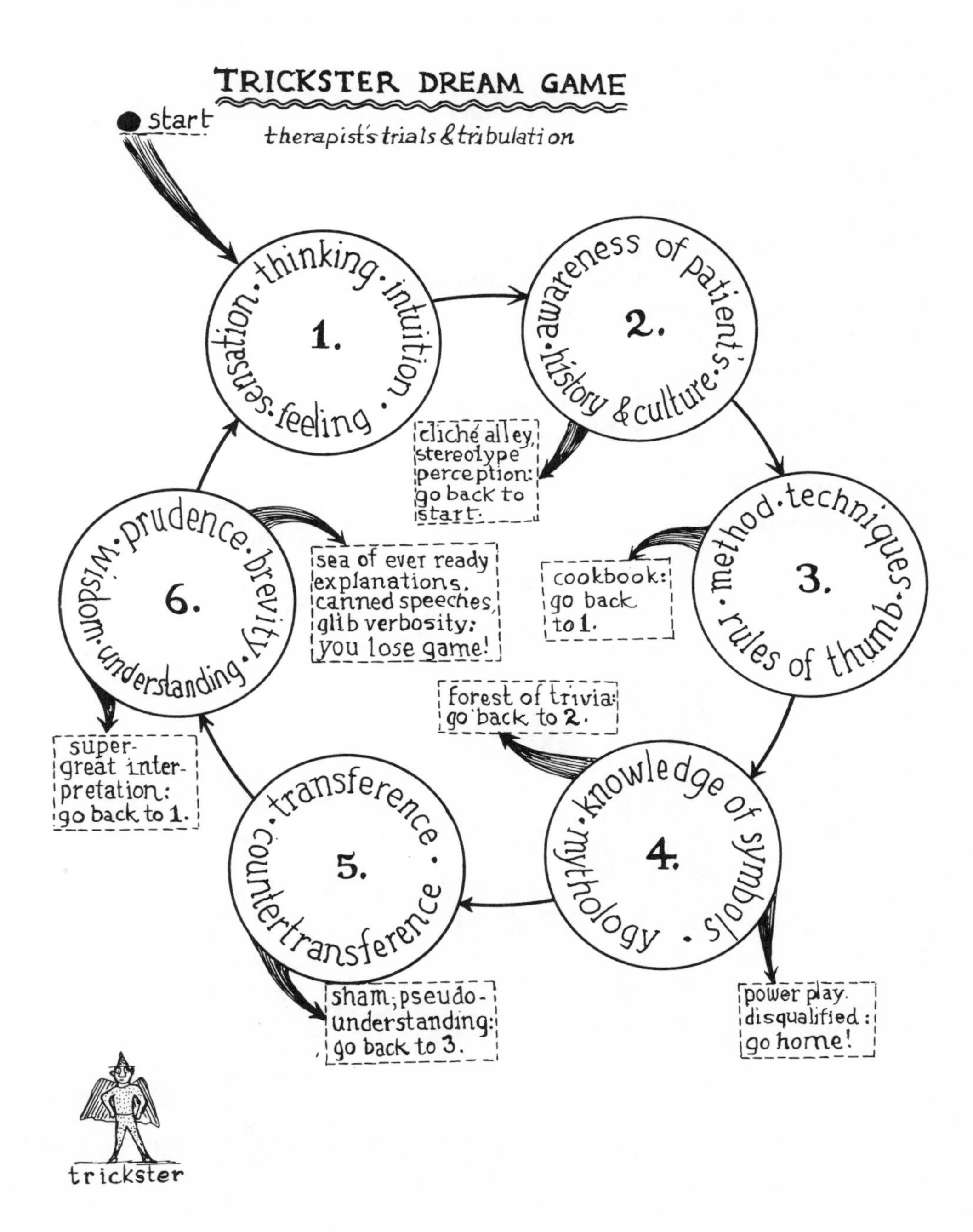

If you float on a sea of ever ready explanations, canned speeches,
glib verbosity, you lose the game.
If you make your point mercifully brief, succinct, and easily understandable, you are to be congratulated for winning the Trickster Dream Game.
A scientific method for the study of dreams and dreaming
is now applied.
In dream and sleep laboratories
and neuroscience experimental centers,
the emerging biological science of dreaming is growing.
The discovery of REM and rapid-eye-movement sleep
revolutionizes dream theory.

For now, and perhaps for always,
the comprehension of the meaning of dreams
is essentially a psychological matter.
That it is associated with physiologic
and molecular changes is not in question.
But the meaning of dreams remains subjective.
Science demands double-blind experiments
and statistical averages.
Only in the most general way can this apply
to interpretation.

"My psychiatrist is recalling all his old patients. They have a new theory about dream meanings."

Eight Dream Patterns

A practical look at dream patterns has led me
to classify the morphology or format of dreams
into eight categories.
Content and motifs are not involved in this method of
classification.

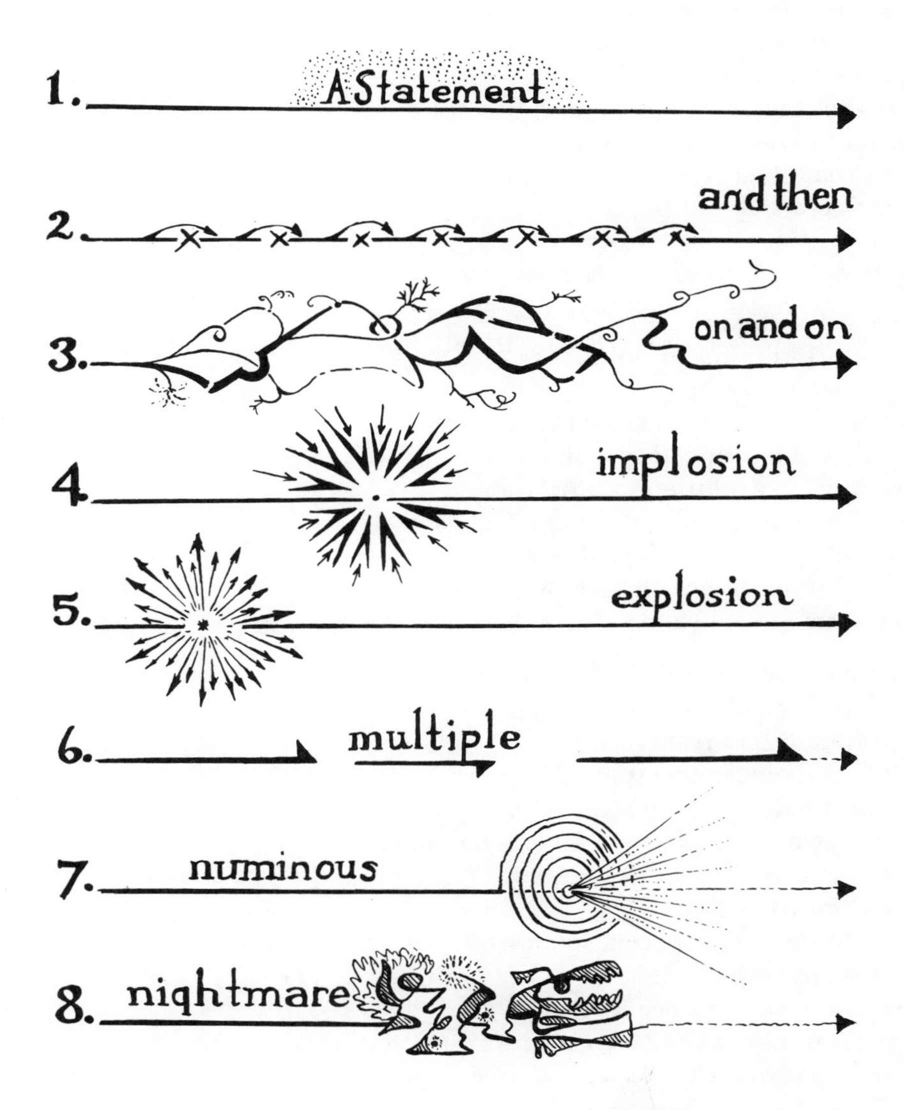

Type 1: The Statement Dream

This is a declarative revelation; usually
one pithy sentence is all it takes to make its point.
In more obscure forms the statement has the
somewhat bewildering quality of a Delphic oracle.
It grabs the dreamer.
The more obvious form is like a newspaper headline,
a clever metaphorical banner statement
of the story.
When you wake up it is as though you are reading
the front page of your morning dream newspaper;
but unlike the newspaper, the statement is almost always
at the end of the dream story.
This adds to its punch
since the dreamer doesn't have the option of
turning to another story in the paper.
Your dream has your full attention
while you are dreaming it.

Type 2: The And-then Dream

This kind of dream
goes on from point to point,
from place to place,
from sequence to sequence like a story
which can be reduced to a series of
"and then . . . and then . . . and then."
It is an arrangement of the happenings
with skilled juxtaposition of sequences.
The and-then dream almost always has an ending
that seems appropriate to both dreamer and analyst.

The dream moves from point A to B to C.
The skill of the therapist
is catching the narrative and
putting the pieces together like a whodunit.
The connections of the scenes and episodes
give an awareness of the story line or theme.
At its boring extreme it is a drag,
a story not well told.
These dreams, when brief, seem well edited by the psyche's
brilliant inner storyteller.
When these dreams are very long
the patient may take twenty minutes just telling it.
It is not so much that they are endless

as that they seem finally pointless.
Then do not try to make something out of it.
Wait. It will come out in a better edition
another day.

Type 3: The On-and-on Dream

On-and-on dreams differ from and-then dreams
in that they never get to the point.
They meander.
The on-and-on dream goes off here and there
in curlicues without plot to hold sequences together.
Parts seem obviously unconnected,
which is not to say that a clever analyst cannot find a thread.
It requires mental gymnastics and one must often stand on one's head.
While this is greatly admired by psychoanalytic colleagues,
it is not much use to the patient.

The and-then dream creates an ambience of "then what?" and at the end,
"oh!"
On-and-on reduces the listener to "so what else is new?"
It is hard to find a story line
when all is told.
It is a puzzle with parts from different puzzles
mixed in the same box
with no picture on the lid.
Viewed dynamically over time the on-and-on-dream
would seem to be like a first draft
of a good dream to follow.

Some patients are enraptured by their on-and-on dreams
with all their conglomerate mishmash.
In relating them they overwhelm their therapist
as if their dreams were *War and Peace*
or *One Thousand and One Nights.*
Best for the therapist to listen and say
as little as possible, or follow a—

RULE OF THUMB: Take One Portion Only

Focus on one portion, one image, or one sequence from the dream
and give it your best in a few words.
Then retreat.
Don't get sucked in to the quicksand of words and images.
Say what you have to say
and wait for future clarifications
in the nights to come.

Type 4: The Implosion Dream

A single action highlights a dramatic event in this dream
in which energy, power, and objects focus inwardly and
usually are directed into the patient.
Some element dramatically bursts inward.
A typical implosion dream is short and unsweet,
like a vortex of a whirlpool.

Type 5: The Explosion Dream

A gun fires; a bomb explodes.
Something, someplace, someone is suddenly shattered.
Dream elements fly apart.
Less sound and fury than a blowup
which instantly transforms the story.
Real or symbolic, the happening
is anything but subtle.

Type 6: Multiple Dreams

Several separate dreams or dream sequences may occur
in one night.
The dreamer may or may not wake up between the dreams.
Often the individual dreams
seem to bear little specific relationship to one another.
But if they are imagined as components of a single dream,
a hidden theme may suddenly emerge
or the dreamer may sense that he has been seeing
different facets of a stone or gem.
Occasionally you can examine it as narrative or drama.
Take the first dream as a prologue or preamble to the rest.
Take the next sequence(s) as elaboration and portrayal.
This may appear realistic and objective
or highly subjective and allegorical.
The final dream, if any, may be an epilogue.

RULE OF THUMB: Dreams As Plays

Sometimes think of multiple dreams as acts of a play
or segments of a parable.
In Act I the curtain rises and the narrator
sets the stage.
Act II is the principle action and reflection, and
the curtain may come down on a cliffhanger.
In Act III the predicament is now metaphor or exposition.
Act IV is the denouement.

Think of the sequences as parts of a coherent whole.
If the story line clicks with the patient,
there may be insight and new understanding.
If not, your effort may be only clever prattle
or at best a good try that didn't work.

Type 7: The Numinous Dream

Numinous means with mysterious power.
Some such dreams might be religious experiences.
It would be foolish to think that dreams
could not be such a thing.
Numen represents divine power or spirit,
hence *numinous* is supernatural or divine.
In antiquity numen signified a local diety
who often inhabited a particular object.
The numen was also the center of a sacred city;
in Roman times a symbolic object, called the numen,
was placed at the center of the city
and held the mysterious power which drew people
to the place.

A numinous or religious dream may relate to
the fish symbol of Christ. (Jung, CW 9ii: 86-149)

RULE OF THUMB: Fish and Fishermen

Jung was prudent enough to write:
"Canis panem somniat, piscator pisces"—
the fishes that the fisherman dreams are fishes
and nothing more. (Jung, CW 16:318)

Although science does not subscribe to the supernatural,
there is no evidence that the mind does not do so.
The dead live in our dreams,
and the sky is not the limit.

Type 8: Nightmares

Everyone knows what a nightmare is.
They are said to ride their victims
and have their own order of terror, horror, and pain.

> *Nightmare*: A female spirit or monster, supposed to beset people and animals at night, settling upon them when they are asleep, and producing a feeling of suffocation by its weight . . . . The spirits of the night called Incubi and Succubi, or else Night-mares.
> "It is to prevent the Night-mare, *viz.* the Hag, from riding the horses."
> (Compact Edition Oxford English Dictionary, vol. 1, p. 1926)

Dreams do not have definitive absolute interpretations.
They are open to many possibilities,
and different interpretations sometimes show us
that one interpretation is as psychologically valid as another.
But there is generally one that is better than others,
and I judge this one by what is most useful to the dreamer,
not necessarily agreeable but with a clear and cogent ring.

RULE OF THUMB: Multiple Working Hypotheses

Any interpretation should be challenged
in the mind of the interpreter by several totally different
and possibly diametrically opposite points of view.
This is an example of the method of
multiple working hypotheses.
If the only tool you have is a hammer,
you will hammer your interpretation home.
If the patient challenges your interpretation,
listen carefully because
you may need that guidance.
Opposition is often not resistance.

A logical system must contain a premise
which it cannot define
without contradicting itself.
A nightmare is a nightmare until it is understood.
Its symbolic logic may resemble a Zen koan.

Holding a short bamboo stick before some monks,
Chao-chou said, "If you call this a stick, you affirm;
if you call it not a stick, you negate. Beyond affirmation
and negation, what would you call it?"

When a monk said to Chao-chou, "What do you say
to one who has nothing to carry about?"
he was analyzing his own state of mind.
To this Chao-chou replied, "Carry it along."

A monk said to Yun-men, "What would you do when
no boundaries are seen, however wide the eyes are open?"
Said Men, "Look!"

(Suzuki, *Zen Buddhism*, pp. 141, 152, 153)

Monk: "How is it when one is not burdened with anything?"
Master Jōshū: "Throw it down!"
Monk: "How could one do that?"
Master Jōshū: "If you cannot, shoulder it away!"

(Suzuki, *What is Zen*, p. 26)

Examples of the Eight Patterns of Dream Morphology

EXAMPLES: The Statement Dream

A complicated dream ends with the dreamer hearing these words:
"*King Lear* interrupted by a Chinese fire drill."
The impact of this line was all the stronger and stranger
because it seemed at first to be a non sequitur.
It didn't seem to have anything to do with the rest of the dream
until the dreamer explained what a ludicrous, comic idea
the Chinese fire drill was to her
and how moving and profound Shakespeare's *King Lear* was to her.
Then she saw what the paradoxical statement meant
in her present life predicament.

I once had a two word statement dream.
I had given a lecture
which met with warm and enthusiastic response.
I was high on the happy experience.
That night I dreamed I went into a fashionable hat store.
"I want to buy a Tyrolian hat."
"What size do you wear, sir?"
"Size 54," I answered.

A gifted, intelligent, highly successful young man, who was
driven by ambitious fantasies of glory,
married a humble, modest woman with no ambition
except to live a good and full life.
He was continually irritated by his wife's pedestrian ways,
and although he loved and admired her,
he bridled at every critical comment she made.

Dream: *I am high in the mountains. It is gorgeous and reminds me of the opening idyllic alpine scene in the movie* Sound of Music. *I could even hear music in the distance. Then I am holding a magazine entitled* Love Story. *Suddenly I see my wife standing nearby. She has been there observing me all the time. When I wave to her she calls out, "You are W. C. Fields!"*

The dreamer was highly amused by the dream in which
his wife points out to him his inner redeeming fool,
W. C. Fields, the clown par excellence,
who personifies the intoxicated trickster.
His wife's punchline helped him recognize a shadow side of himself.
She brought him down to earth.

This dream was reported by Jung (CW 12:114–15):

Dream: *The dreamer is surrounded by nymphs. A voice says, "We were always there, only you did not notice us."*

Jung wrote that the phenomenon of the "voice" in dreams
always has for the dreamer the final
and indisputable character of "he said it himself,"
the phrase which originally alluded to
the authority of Pythagoras.
The voice, said Jung, expresses some truth
or condition that is beyond all doubt.*

EXAMPLES: The And-then Dream

This is a dream that a patient
had the night before a therapy session.
He had been in treatment for over a year
and despaired that his depression
and feeling of the meaninglessness of life
would never end.
In this discouraged state of mind, he had been considering
terminating treatment or reducing the frequency
of visits from once a week to once a month.
Then he had this dream:

Dream: *I am on a trip. I am going to travel back to where I started out. It seems to me that I am stationary; but I also have the sense that I am moving. A companion, whom I do not recognize, is trying to help me prepare for someone else's wedding. The bride and bridegroom are not there and I have no idea where they are. I am feeling happy to be at the wedding, and I am helping prepare a wedding feast on a table in an open space. There are a lot of people present. And then I have to travel across some barren territory. There was a time limit. I notice a woman silently observing the whole thing. She says nothing but I seem to be in telepathic communication with her.*

---

* See p. 121 dream line, "A lot of swagger is maintained via the sick role."

This is our discussion about the dream:

Doctor: It's about your journey. What do you think about it?
Patient: The travel is like my life journey and my treatment. "Going back to where I started" means that the journey is too much for me, like I am giving up. Nothing is moving, like I'm stuck.
Doctor: While it seems like you are stationary, you also sense that you are moving. Going back to where one began sometimes means a new beginning rather than giving up.
Patient: I like that. It was barren territory that I had to travel across. *Now I remember!* In the dream I was traveling West on a hard-packed desert. The time limit means that there is a time limit to my life. Maybe I have 20, 30 or 40 years left. I could piddle it away on my therapy. You can't survive on the desert forever. You have to keep on moving to survive.
Doctor: Notice that you have to travel the barren hard-packed desert *after* the preparation for the wedding feast. A wedding is a ritual of union or unity. There is still some emptiness, the barren feelings that brought you here. In the dream you are in touch with an observing woman who doesn't say anything but she knows intuitively exactly what is happening. She is part of you. Now there is a time limit to this journey. And there are other people in the dream. A companion is helping you prepare a wedding feast, but the bride and bridegroom are not yet there.
Patient: When I first came to see you, I wished I was dead. My life seemed to be at an end. The dream doesn't sound that way, does it?

A middle aged man consulted me because of a fear of losing his mind; he had various phobias and panic spells.

Dream: *I am near a high dam and am terrified because I think it is going to break. I hear strange crashing noises. I get into my car and race down the road which after a while turns into the river bed below the dam. It is a rough ride. I have the feeling that I have to go very fast before the dam breaks and the water roars down the valley.*

Suddenly I turn a corner and see you, Dr. Wilmer, sitting in a camp chair in the river bed just as if there is no danger. I speed on wondering why you are so calm.

The dream was reassuring to the patient.
The fear of an imminent psychic break had led him to see me.
In the dream the dam is not breaking.
It just sounds as if it is.

Jung used the image metaphor of a dry, old river bed
to describe the archetype
as a preformed potential pattern from ages past,
which when filled with water moulds its form.

The patient's dream doctor—
the one he projects onto me—
is unperturbed and sitting quietly,
camped out in the path of his journey.
He is not inundated by the unconscious which he fears.

And then this happens, *and then* that happens
because of the noise and sight of the dam,
and then he sees someone who and so on.

EXAMPLE: The On-and-on Dream

Dream: I am sailing on an old-fashioned, square-rigged sailing ship. It is rolling and pitching in high waves on a rough sea, blown by a gale from the west. All around the ship there are mountainous, endless waves. I am standing on the deck near the main mast, holding tightly onto heavy ropes. A sailor comes up to me and says, "Sir, the captain requests that you go below deck so you will not be washed overboard, and he asks you to report to his cabin."

I am walking through long, narrow, dimly lit, deserted ship passageways. I seem to be wandering for a long time, unable to find the captain's cabin. Suddenly a bell sounds and a voice calls out, "Now hear this! This is your captain speaking. You are now at my cabin. Come in." A door swings open on my right side, and I see the captain sitting at his desk under a bright light.

At that moment I realize that a young woman is standing at my left side. She takes my arm and says, "Come in and meet the captain. No one, except the captain, knows how to get the ship to its destination."

"Who are you?" I ask.

"I am the navigator, but I can't read maps," she replies. She pulls out a huge revolver, and to my dismay, shoots the captain. He disappears in the smoke and blaze of the gunfire.

I shout, "Oh my God! What is going to happen now?"

"How should I know?" the young woman says.

Then the scene changes and I am on an airplane that is rapidly losing altitude. A stewardess says over a loud speaker, "Please tighten your seat belts, put your seats in the upright position, and stow your hand luggage under the seat in front of you in preparation for landing." I look out the window. It is pitch black. There is not a light anywhere on the horizon. As I feel the wheels hit the runway, a passenger in the seat on my right, whom I had not seen before, turns to me. She is a very old, decrepit lady who is smiling at me.

"Hello," she says, "I'm Miss Probst, your third grade teacher. Welcome back home."

At that moment I hear the sound of a marching band playing "Seventy-Six Trombones" from The Music Man.

The pilot's voice over the loudspeaker booms out, "Welcome to River City!" I get up and start to walk out of the airplane but find myself back in long, dark, narrow passages similar to those on the sailing ship.

A deep masculine voice says slowly, "The captain is dead. Now where is the First Mate?"

Miss Probst appears, takes my hand, and says, "Don't be scared. Mother West Wind is always unpredictable. Look at the overhead monitor for your connecting flight." I look up and see a row of television monitors with long lists of planes, their flight numbers, gates, destinations, departure and arrival times. I can't figure out what I am looking for. I wake up bewildered.

EXAMPLES: The Implosion Dream

A young man, suffering from depression,
fixed ideas, and obsessive thoughts
that seemed to fly into his head for no reason at all,
told me this dream:

Dream: *I am walking along a beach. Suddenly a huge snake, six to eight feet long, flies through the air towards me. It comes at me almost like an arrow, right over my right shoulder and sinks its fangs into the back of my shoulders. There is no pain. But I am afraid I am going to die of poison. I don't know what to do. In desperation I bat the snake with my hand and it falls down and disappears.*

The snake represents the patient's self-paralyzing poisonous attitude.
It is an unconscious, thinking snake that comes
in a straight line across the sea through the air and
is related neither to the sea nor to the earth.
This is wrong for a snake.
It comes at him full face but
strikes him in the back, the shadow side of unconsciousness.

The right side
represents action, control, and consciousness.
The snake was flying at him like the attacks of demonic ideas
from the region of the ocean, that is, the unconscious.
It is a negative symbol but not poisonous.
It is the fear which seems to poison his mind
and strike him out of the blue.
Hitting at the snake is doing battle
with the serpent or monster in a hero-dragon myth.
The absence of pain indicates that it is not
really a dangerous shadow phenomenon.
The dream seems to say,
"Your fear of loss of control is unfounded.
It is really a fear you can bat down if you try."

EXAMPLES: The Explosion Dream

Two dreams from the same woman patient:

Dream: *It is really a crazy dream. I am standing on the front lawn of my home and suddenly there is danger. I put my arms around my son and hug him close to me as two large airplanes fly toward us. I think "Oh my God! They're going to kill us!" Just then one of the them zooms off to the left but the other keeps getting close to us. I notice that the landing wheels are not down. I think there is no way to escape. Suddenly the plane pulls up just as it is near us. It turns into a silver bird that flies over my house and crashes behind it, sending cars and big objects flying through the air towards us.*

The dreamer has a last minute reprieve from two deadly objects flying at her and her little son in the yard. The dream says she has escaped a deadly situation but still is in danger of being hurt from the near miss. She is not yet out of danger from the fallout of her precarious situation.

Dream: *I am walking into a room in my house which begins to get bigger and bigger. It becomes enormous and in the center of the room is a pile of rocks which grow into a high mountain. I think, "I have to go over that mountain." Then I notice a rocky ledge around the side of the mountain, and I begin walking around the mountain under the ledge, but as I go there is suddenly lightning and thunder, and an avalanche starts roaring down the mountain, and I think I am going to get killed.*

The dream gave the patient a dramatic picture of how
things got out of hand and how they are magnified
to huge proportions.
Her decision to take the short cut rather than

climb over the mountain made
the world seem to come crashing down on her.
It is an archetypal journey to the mountain.

EXAMPLES: Multiple Dreams

The following two dreams occurred the same night.
The patient was considering
hiring a new partner in his law firm.
He felt extremely positive towards a new prospect.
His previous partner had been malicious.

Dream: I am outside the door of a bank where I have gone to consult the president about whether or not I should hire Jeff as my new partner. The bank president is an old, trusted friend of mine. He greets me and tells me how much he admires me and how much he has used my advice. Just as I begin to ask him about Jeff, I wake up.

He felt the dream was incomplete
and he was relieved when he fell back to sleep
and the dream story continued in a symbolic statement.

Dream: I see Jeff as a large goose. He is lying on my stomach and I am stroking his long neck. The goose is looking up admiringly at me.

The dreamer took the first dream as commenting on
his real life intention to ask a banker friend for advice.
In the dream he never got around to that,
perhaps he was hung up in mutual admiration.
Maybe the dream told him to be alert and cautious
before asking more advice from outside.

The second dream is inside advice
from his unconscious.
Traditionally the goose is someone who doesn't have any sense,
is just not intelligent, and moves about in a collective way,
imprinted like the gosling who instinctively tags along
behind a person he mistakes for his mother.
The dream seems to be saying that the prospective partner
is a goose, countering the dreamer's inflated opinion of him.
One extreme in consciousness
is compensated by another in the unconscious.
This suggests that he needs to look at this prospective partner
as an ordinary human being
and not to contrast him with the bad former partner
or glorify him as the good new partner.

The dreamer thought this goose dream was funny.
He was playing with his goose
rather than taking it seriously.
It didn't seem to mean anything sexual
although you can read anything into it.

The need to be admired by the new lawyer
and his banker friend
suggested he had too much need for admiration of others
which was distorting and interfering with things.
The dreamer concluded that he would make up his own mind
about the decision and expect
an outcome neither great nor grim.
The banker represents the dreamer's sensation function
and his positive shadow who keeps his symbolic gold.

One could read into such a dream a raft of things:
associations to banking, to the banker seen as
the father who guarded the treasure and knew the answer,
to goosing and stroking the goose
while he lay on his back, as though it was a penis.
But all these ideas, however tangentially relevant,
are of no practical help.
An interpretation of Oedipal or homosexual conflicts,
of masturbation or castration anxiety
seems to me to be destructive.
Anyone can be a fool.
Even a brilliant one can be a goose now and then.*

The following three dreams occurred in one night,
separated by awakenings.
The dreamer is a gifted individual
depressed and disheartened in her job.
She is searching for a new job.
She refused antidepressant medication.
Her depression is not just downhearted, low spirits
but the deep darkness of black, hopeless despondency.

---

* A foolish or ignorant person is called a goose because of the alleged stupidity of the bird. "His geese are swans" is a saying apropos the dreamer's prospective partner. Of course, the positive side is inherent in the story of the goose that laid the golden egg and was killed by its foolish and avaricious owner. The goose is an important bird in mythology; see Funk and Wagnall's *Standard Dictionary of Folklore, Mythology and Legend*, pp. 459–460.

Dream 1: *There is a young black woman in a full length pink satin evening dress. Its hem is too long. Her mother is standing by her. I say, "I'll fix it. It won't take but a minute."*

Dream 2: *There is a rare historic pottery dish on display in a museum; it has recently shattered. Strangers and friends of mine are taking pieces as souvenirs. They make me promise I'll take some for them. Then I think it is wrong, and I decide not to oblige them. I notice that the large, intact center part of the dish is in the case along with some fragments. It is a Mayan dish in brown with black and white lines, dots, and designs. I love pottery dishes. The remaining center piece is valuable even though the dish as a whole has diminished value because it has been broken.*

Dream 3: *I am preparing for a party. The guests arrive. I see an attractive woman staring at an empty glass in her hand. I am momentarily confused because I thought that the guests had agreed to bring their own champagne. I search through several refrigerators but can only find two frozen cans of soft drink. I offer them to the guests thinking that this will have to do until I can give them champagne.*

The patient comments:

"I found these dreams helpful despite my gloom. They seem to me to be strongly connected. In each dream I am taking on more than I should do. There was no reason why I had to sew up the hem. Her mother could have done it. I wanted to please them because they were black. I extended myself so that I would be liked.

"I feel like the broken dish in the pottery dream. I've been doing too much for people and promising to be too helpful. I can't fulfill all I offer to do.

"In the third dream I am holding myself responsible for something that I am not responsible for because there had been no agreement. I allow myself to be in intimidated.

"Why don't I just sit down and enjoy myself? The three dreams illustrate variations on the same theme."

- Helping prepare the party dress persona of a shadow figure—
- the near compliance with the shadow tricksters who would steal symbolic parts of an ancient treasure—
- helping her positive party shadow self at a social celebration—

—her dreams suggest an emerging resolution of her depression, illumination of her darkness.

EXAMPLES: The Numinous Dream

A woman who had been highly successful in her academic career,
was considering the offer of a distinguished professorship
at great university.
The position would seem to fulfill a dream of glory,
but on the other hand, she felt honored and contented where she was.
She had almost total freedom
and was highly productive in her life and work.

Dream: I am a visiting professor at a public meeting in a huge hall. I am supposed to give the main address, and there is a large expectant crowd. I walk down the aisle wearing my white lab coat. In the very front of the hall, seated on the stage is a clown wearing a very tall, floppy red hat. I move forward as if pulled by his presence. As I approach him, he is suddenly transformed into a glowing sphere which is either the sun or the moon. He says, "Where are you coming from?" I say, "From another world." It is a glorious moment and I wake up reassured and gratified by the dream. I wanted to go back into the dream and experience that vision of the sun and moon again.

The transformation of the trickster into a celestial body
is the numinous symbol.
The dream did not say to take the big job or turn it down;
it merely showed her as a visiting professor
in an ordinary lab coat drawn by a powerful vision.
The inner achievement which is collective,
is not of this material world.
She later turned the job down without regret.

EXAMPLES: Nightmares

Dream: I am trapped in a deep valley, surrounded by mountains somewhere in Vietnam. I am wading in deep greenish water full of shit and urine. I find a small boat and keep trying to paddle out of the valley. There is only one way out and that is ahead where a river flows into a large lake. But I know the Vietcong are waiting for me at the river. I have to turn back because there are three or four NVA (North Vietnamese regulars) about a hundred yards ahead of me on the shore firing at me. I have a machine gun and I shoot at them. Then I am hiding and going under water to hide from the shooting.

This typical combat nightmare was told to me by a Vietnam combat veteran
suffering from post-traumatic stress disorder.
It portrays a real situation of the mire of war with no way out.
Although the war was long since over, it continued
to be fought in his nightmares several times a week
for twelve years before I saw him.

The patient interprets his dream:

> "I wake up several times during the dream and go right back to sleep and it picks up at almost the same spot. I want to go back to finish the dream. I want to go back to kill the VC and NVA in the dream. I want victory. I knew the gooks were winning the war. They were out there but I couldn't see them. I had a flash in the dream of my escape route. It was about twenty feet across and led through a pass. But I couldn't get to it.
>
> Why has my life been so miserable for the past twelve years? Why do I carry a gun and why do I have to sleep with a gun? Why is the only time when I am happy when I am drunk? I just drink myself into a stupor."

Another Vietnam veteran who had been a medic told me this dream:

Dream: *It is very hot. I am laying on my stomach in a grass field. I can smell pollen. I hear a guy crying, "Doc! Doc! Doc". I crawl through the grass until I come to the edge of the road. I have to get up and go get him. I'm afraid. I get enough guts to go across the road to him. As I do I get shot. It seems like I am shot 50 times or so, but I don't feel any pain. I just feel the thudding of whatever is hitting me. There's blood all over the place, but I don't feel any pain. When I get over to where the guy is, I see that it's a buddy of mine named Cobb. Actually he's been dead for a long time. Cobb was one of the first guys I worked on in Nam. He died. In the dream he looks up at me, and his face is all bloody, and he says, "Welcome home!" and I wake up.*

He said to me:

> "One of the fears I always had in Vietnam was that I would be afraid to go and get those guys who were wounded. But that is something that never really happened. I always did my job. I never punked out on going to get anybody. They gave me a couple of Bronze Stars for doing that. When I got shot in the leg I couldn't feel any pain. But I knew I had been shot and was afraid I had lost my leg. Vietnam nightmares don't stop."

RULE OF THUMB: Nightmares, i

When a child comes to you in the night
terrified by a nightmare,
do not say, "It's only a dream. Go back to sleep."
It may be only a dream to you,
but it is a reality to the child.
You may think you are being reassuring because
the child will probably go back to bed but
the child will think that you don't understand,
and you don't.

RULE OF THUMB: Nightmares, ii

Say to the child,
"Tell me about the nightmare."
And listen.
Listen without interrupting.
If you don't know what to say, read on.

RULE OF THUMB: Nightmares, iii

Say to the child some variation of,
"It sure sounds (or seems) scary.
I am not surprised that you are frightened,"
(This will bolster his ego)
"but the dream is over now."
Some "tough" parents say, "We don't get frightened, do we?"
or "Big boys and girls don't get scared, do they?"
They have forgotten what it was like to be little.
I'm not suggesting sentimental mollycoddling,
just the straight truth.

RULE OF THUMB: Nightmares, iv

If the child is still distressed by the dream
in the morning, ask him to tell it to you again.
It will lose its umph and crunch power
in his telling and your listening.

Guidelines for Working with Dreams

- Clarify each detail of the dream elements and their relationship with one another.
- If the dream is extremely long, this may be impossible. If there are lots of dreams, handle only what you can. Do not try to cover the waterfront. You are only a mortal in a rowboat.
- Try to identify the motif or theme. If it isn't clear to you, try to figure it out, but don't push.
- Identify the affect of the dream and the dreamer. What is the relationship of affect to content?
- Find out what happened the day before the dream to see what the dream may be a reaction to. If this doesn't yield any clue, then find out what is anticipated the next day. Find out the significance of the dream in relationship to actual life experiences at the time of the dream.

- Stick to the manifest content of the dream. There is no latent dream disguised by a dream censor. Stick to the dream facts, images, and story.
- Remember that the dream is to be understood in the context of the dreamer's total life story, but especially the here and now life. Think of the dream as trying to help the dreamer resolve, live through, transcend or understand a life episode.
- Have the patient expand on each dream element. This directed association is called amplification, not free association.
- Is there a continuity and relationship with previous dreams? Follow themes and developments from dream to dream over time. A dream is more difficult to interpret by itself than in relationship to previous dreams. If you can't remember dreams, write what you do remember immediately.
- Make your interpretations few and brief. Keep your personal associations out of it unless they clarify the patient's associations. Use explicit metaphors and images from the dream itself in your explanations and interpretations.
- Avoid jargon, canned speeches, rote commentaries, and the brilliant, ingenious comments you so love.
- To be attentive and appreciative of the dream may be enough. If you are really attentive, you are appreciative. You have done your basic job.
- Your respect for the dream will convey to the dreamer the need to honor dreams.
- Stick to the simple whenever possible.
- Do not fly off into reductive analysis, reducing everything to its atomic particles and particular *nothing but* meanings.
- Do not fly off into archetypal interpretations at the drop of a hat. Don't get hooked on mythology and the bizarre, and forget the ordinary. Jung thought that if one glided from archetype to archetype then everything means everything, and one has reduced the whole process to absurdity.
- A subjective approach begins by assuming that all the people in the dream represent parts of the dreamer with the exception of individuals who are involved in the dreamer's present life.
- Do not, repeat, do not project yourself into every figure in the dream who represents qualities which the patient might attribute to you. You are not that important. They are elements of himself which he sees in you when his unconscious projects them. You are seeing the patient on "this side of projection." When the unconscious intends to make specific observations about you, it will do so in an unmistakable, undisguised fashion.

- Look for the factor of compensation, the self-regulating feedback system of the psyche. If some process goes too far in one direction it calls forth compensation. Compensation dreams are like gyroscopes balancing the ship of psychic adjustment.

- If you have a wrong conscious viewpoint, the opposite will come to you in a dream if you are willing to see it. This helps us when we have unrealistic ideas. If we think too lowly or too highly of ourselves, or others, the dreams will let us know.

- The unconscious has a rare sense of humor. It makes delightful, ingenious puns, jokes, and comical improvisations. We are all creative geniuses in our sleep.

- The phenomenon of dreaming, which is a state of mind, can only be partially recovered and remembered when awake. The capacity to narratize enhances both the therapist's and the patient's ability to envision dream motifs, to get the picture. Many dreams are like extraordinary good fiction.

- Dreams are not to be taken literally. A dream of failing at an examination that is coming up, for which one has studied, and prepared, is called a matriculation dream and invariably means the opposite: the dreamer will succeed at the test or performance. Experience bears this out. The dream shakes overconfidence and presents a sober face to the pessimist. Celebrate when you have a matriculation dream.*

- Dreams about death may mean that a part of the dreamer must die so another part may live. Dreams of serious illness may be saying nothing about the physical disease but may indicate some dis-ease of another sort. Dreams about an atomic explosion may indicate the end of an illness. Dreams of other people dying or dead may have nothing at all to say about their actual death.

- Every doctor or therapist in the dream is not you. He has an inner doctor and therapist that is himself.

Ego consciousness on the day prior to the dream is transformed into the dream ego in the unconscious state of sleep.

Awake, in the post-dream state, conscious ego recreates the dream.

---

* *Cf., Standard Edition of the Complete Psychological Works of Sigmund Freud.* Vol. 4. *The Interpretation of Dreams*, pp. 273–76.

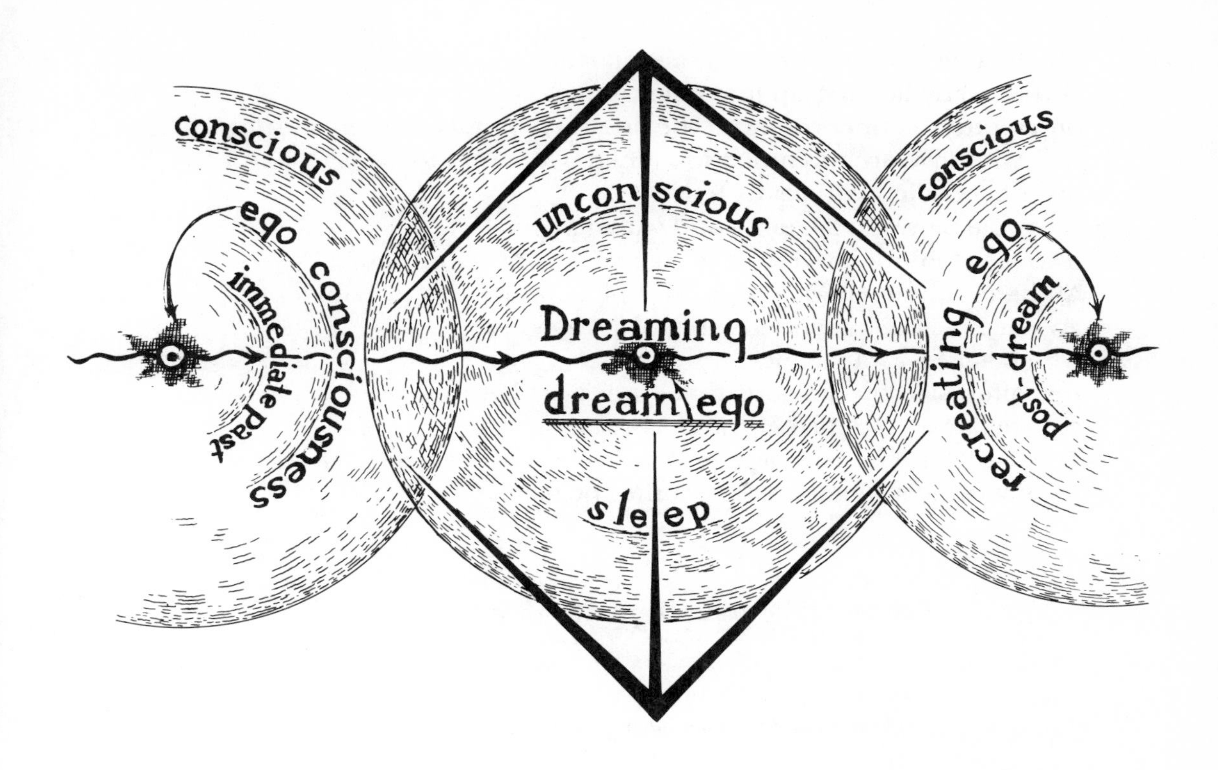

Compensation

The unconscious is the unknown at any given moment, so it is not surprising that dreams add to the conscious psychological situation of the moment all those aspects which are essential for a totally different point of view. It is evident that this function of dreams amounts to a psychological adjustment, a compensation absolutely necessary for properly balanced action. In a conscious process of reflection it is essential that, so far as possible, we should realize all aspects and consequences of a problem in order to find the right solution. This process is continued automatically in the more or less unconscious state of sleep, where, as experience seems to show, all those aspects occur to the dreamer (at least by way of allusion) that during the day were insufficiently appreciated or even totally ignored—in other words, were comparatively unconscious.

(Jung, CW 8:469)

The following illustration of compensation
shows a line flowing up into consciousness and
down into the unconscious. The line is rhythmical, demonstrating
that when we are too much identified with consciousness,
our unconscious draws us to it.
We cycle between sleeping and waking.
If we are too unconscious, we swing into consciousness.
At the moment when conscious problems are most conspicuous
an unconscious reaction is stirred in response,
which serves as a balance.
It is often said by Jungians that outer world events
constellate a response in the unconscious.
The use of the metaphor *constellation* is adroit, since
people project metaphorically onto the stars.

Compensatory function of dreams
the question is - not 'why' but 'what for'

Compensatory relationship between
the conscious and the unconscious

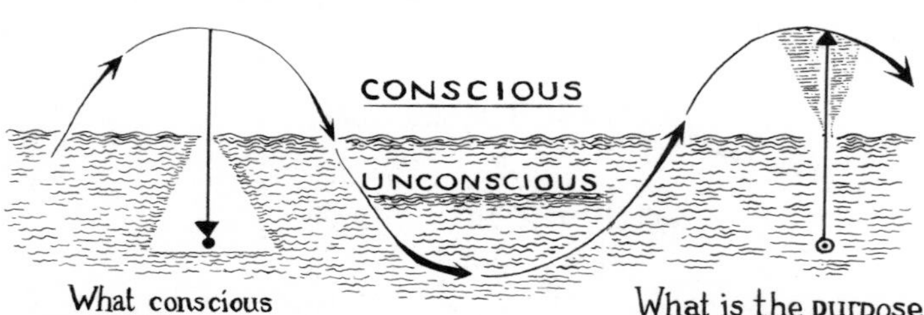

What conscious
attitude is the
unconscious compensating?

What is the purpose
of the dream? How does
it help conscious life?

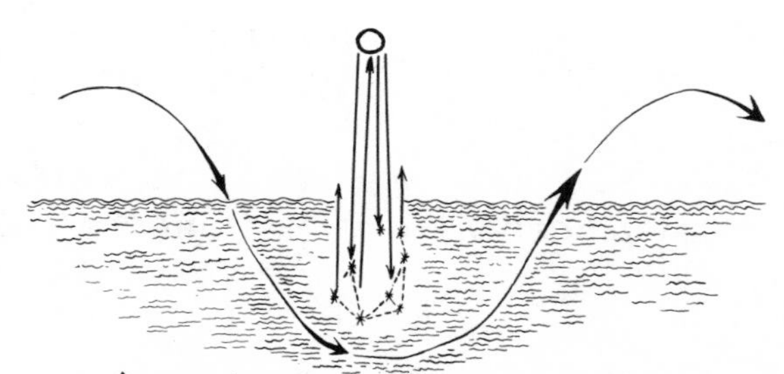

An event in consciousness constellates
symbolic images in the unconscious
which influence consciousness

Listening to a Dream

The quality of listening determines what you hear.
The skills of the professional listener are sharp
and keen. The dream listener has learned how to
tune into another human language.
There are two basic patterns of listening:
linear and configurational.

In linear thinking attention moves from point.

Linear listening to a dream is not a straight line
but it follows a basic path.

There is a certain virtue in linear listening, following a basic
path point to point.
Sometimes this is self-evident in dreams but in others
it is imposed by the listener.
Sensation and thinking types are more apt
to fall into this natural mode of listening.

Other types of people
follow configurational listening patterns.
Configurational listening has the richness
of a fireworks display or the theme and variations
of a symphony.

The configurationally tuned-in listener follows
a story line *but also* its sidetracks, nuances, detours,
and complexities, moving in and out of the trees but
never losing sight of the forest.
It is a complex of interlocking hearing and seeing.

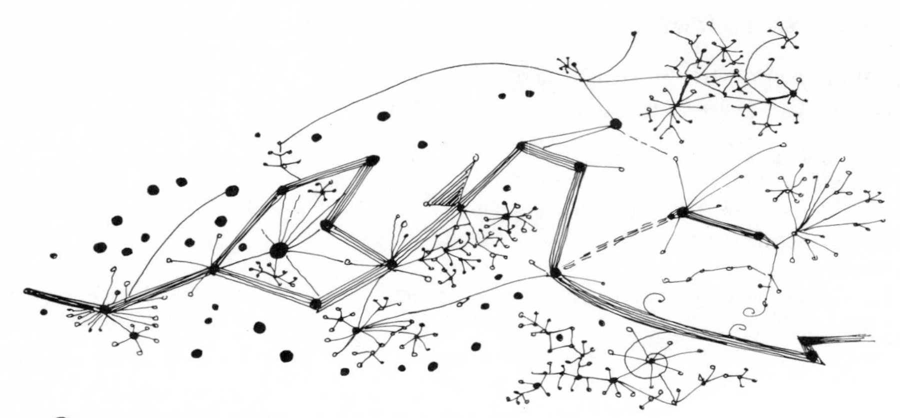

Configurational listening to a dream.

Telling the Dream

The dream we recall and tell someone is never
the whole dream.
The dream recalled is not the same as the dreamed dream.
We reconstitute it from memory for a purpose:
to narrate, to understand, to clarify, to reveal, to deny.
The arrow below that penetrates the dream
symbolizes the point at which we enter a night of dreaming,
much as an explorer views a hitherto uncharted territory.

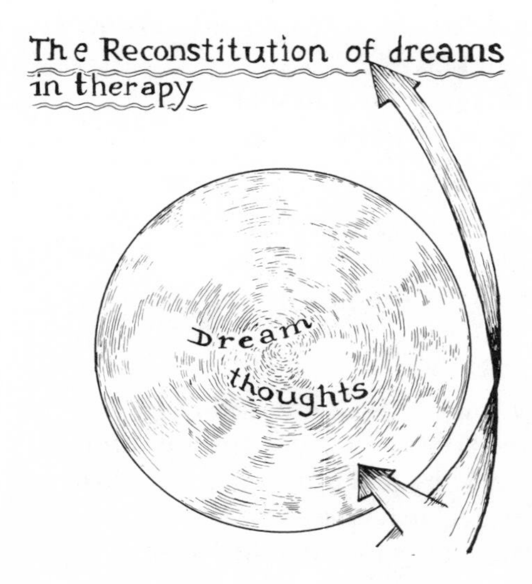

The dream we remember is never remembered fully.
Bits and pieces here and there come back to us.
Writing down a dream helps us
to recall details later; opening the dream world
sets into movement a recall process.

Obviously we can never accurately analyze
the parts of the dream that are not remembered,
or the dreams forgotten totally.
We can be students of only the dreams which
human nature yields to us.

MYTHS & DREAMS

Ancient Greeks surmised that the stories about the gods were old and exaggerated traditions of ancient kings & their deeds
They assumed that these myths did not mean what they said because they were so improbable

Therefore, they tried to reduce the myths to generally understandable yarns.

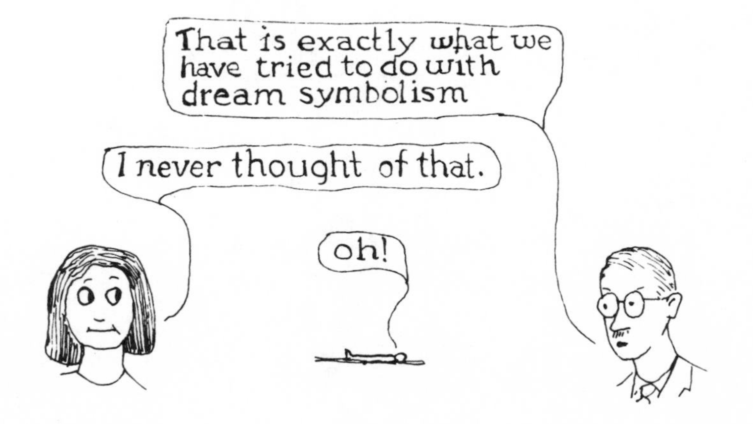

That is exactly what we have tried to do with dream symbolism
I never thought of that.
oh!

There is such a thing as projection compliance
in which Freudian patients dream Freudian dreams
and Jungian patients dream Jungian dreams.
On the other hand, there are enough dreams
to test out the hypotheses which any school puts forth.
Jungian work allows the dreamer
to understand the mythical nature of the psyche
and reach back into the phylogenetic psyche.

How far back does a dream message reach?
Certainly it is possible to see childhood memories
and forces in many dreams.
We do not outlive the child within us.
This inner child lives on in adult life
in an inner world that also reaches back
to the prehistoric psyche of the collective unconscious.
We listen to adult dreams with selective filters
in accordance with our biases.
In the following pictures of recalling and retelling
there are filters which eliminate either infantile memories
or prehistoric psyche symbols.

The dream

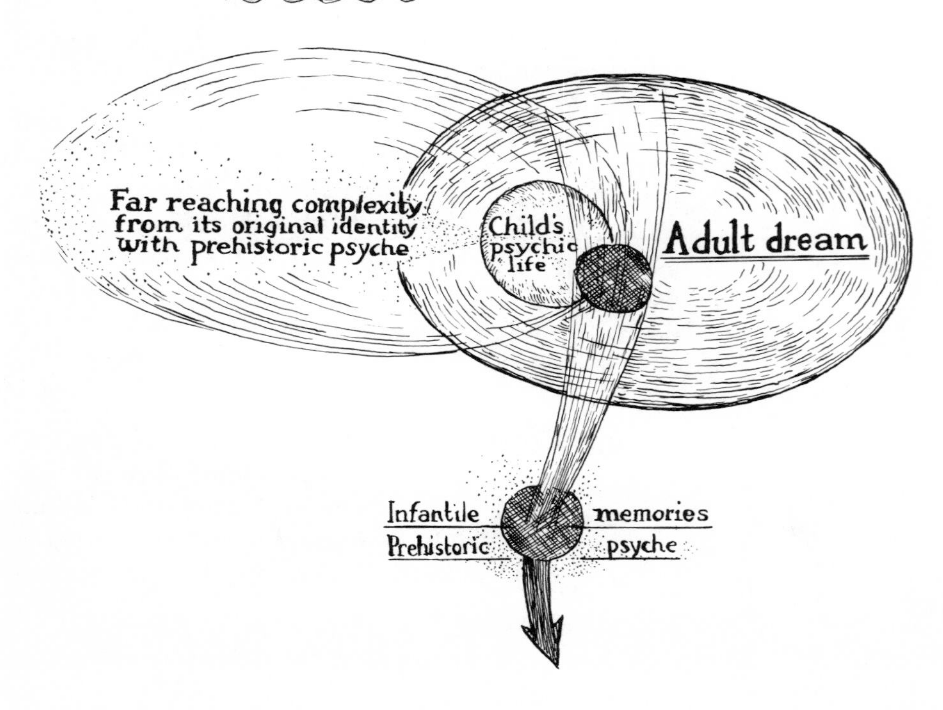

Dream Interpretation

the risk with symbolic interpretation is getting carried away - high in the sky; the risk with reductive interpretation is sinking to "nothing but."....

...the risk also is "either or," when it's "both and"

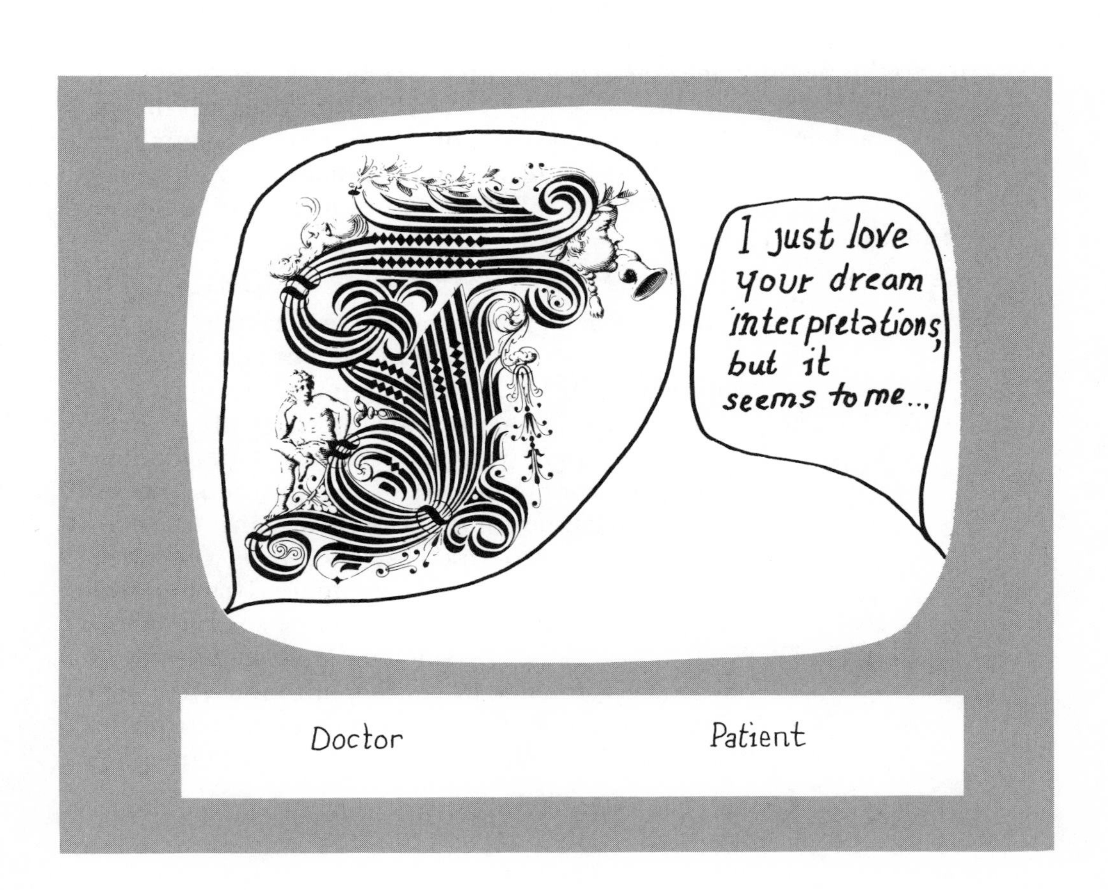

I just love your dream interpretations, but it seems to me...
Doctor
Patient

Jung thought that one of his most important contributions
was the concept of the *reality of the psyche.*
As a separate reality
it is just as real as outer reality.
When we are in it that is how it feels.

If there is an outer world and an inner world, which is the real world?
Both, but are they separate realities or parts of the same reality with a different history?

The Jungian approach amplifies dreams by using
associations, analogous parallel images,
symbols, legends, myths, and archetypes.
We stick to the dream images and words, and look it over
by a process called circumambulation.
The following drawing illustrates amplification
from each dream element and its context (or relatedness)
and the circumambulation in our movement around
and containing the dream.
This approach always keeps the dream images
central.

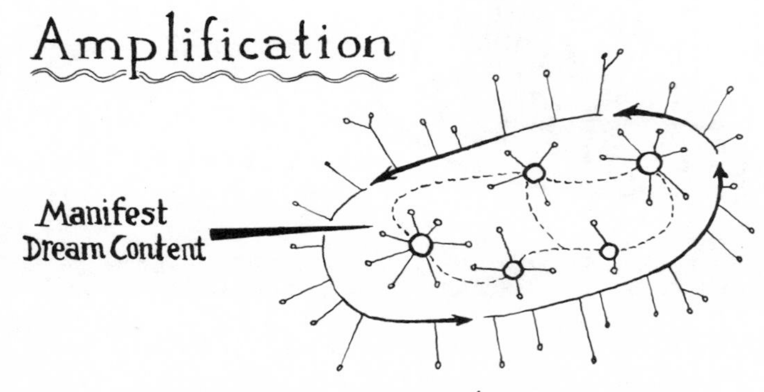

Associations with dream images,
context, and circumambulation

Freud said that the dream was the
royal road to the unconscious.
It is equally valid to say that
the dream is the pedestrian path
to an unconscious city of ordinary life.
Freud's discovery of repression and the
unconscious grew out of hypnosis and free association.
Free association is a form of reductive analysis in which
the dreamer follows his associations wherever they lead.
It is possible through free association to start
from anywhere at all to reach the same place.
In classic Freudian psychoanalysis the analysand
is told not to write down his dreams
because the remembered dream is not the important dream.

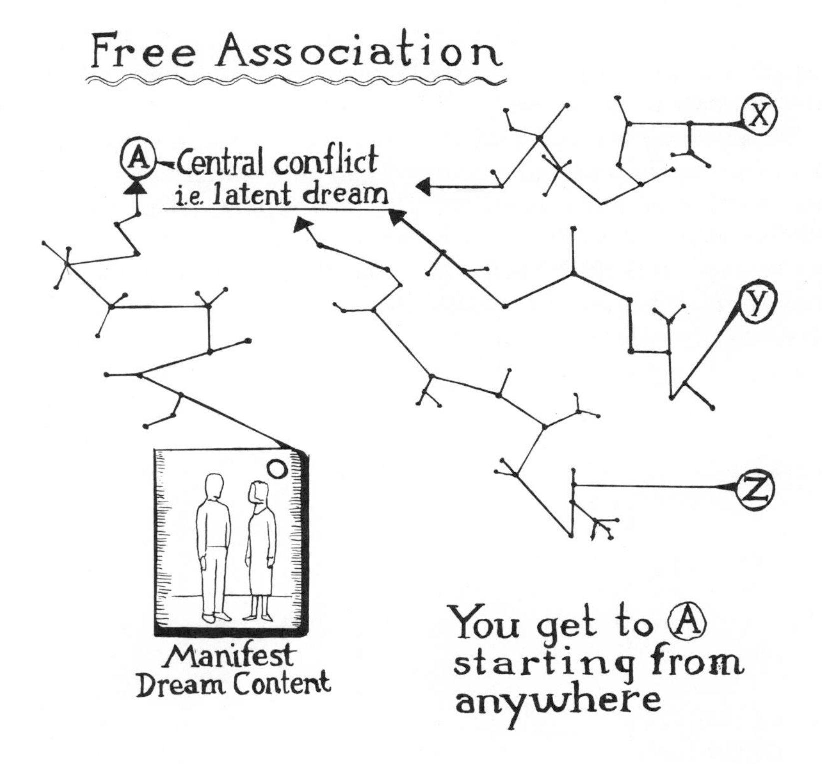

The remembered dream was a façade,
and the method of free association was a
reductio in primum figurum given
a particular bias because of the theory of
infantile sexuality which permeated all Freudian thought.

I want to emphasize that it is not safe to interpret a dream without going into careful detail as to the context. Never apply any theory, but always ask the patient how he *feels about his dream-images. For dreams are always about a particular problem of the individual about which he has a wrong conscious judgement. The dreams are the reaction to our conscious attitude in the same way that the body reacts when we overeat or do not eat enough or when we ill treat it in some other way.* Dreams are the natural reaction of the self-regulating psychic system. *This formulation is the nearest I can get to a theory about the structure and function of dreams.*

(Jung, CW 18:248)

The art of interpreting dreams cannot be learned from books. Methods and rules are good only when we can get along without them. Only the man who can do it anyway has real skill, only the man of understanding really understands. No one who does not know himself can know others. And in each of us there is another whom we do not know. He speaks to us in dreams and tells us how differently he sees us from the way we see ourselves. When, therefore, we find ourselves in a difficult situation to which there is no solution, he can sometimes kindle a light that radically alters our attitude—the very attitude that led us into the difficult situation.

(Jung, CW 10:325)

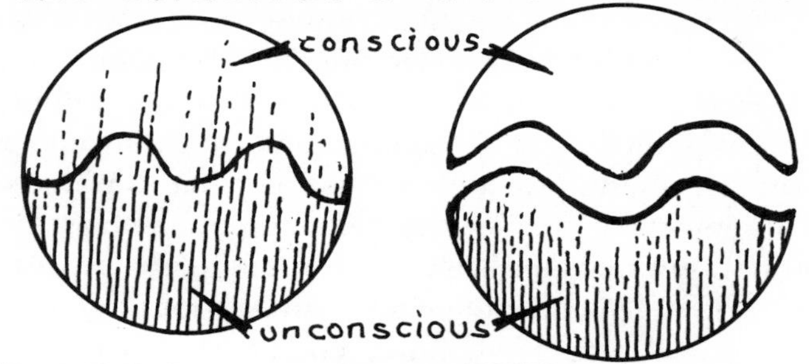

The necessary balance between the conscious and the unconscious
conscious
unconscious
Conscious and unconscious do not make a whole when one of them is suppressed and injured by the other. If they must contend let it at least be a fair fight with equal rights on both sides. Both are aspects of life. Consciousness should defend its reason, and the chaotic life of the unconscious should be given the chance of having its way - as much as we can stand.
JUNG
My God! That means open conflict and collaboration at the same time. I guess that is the way human life should be - the old game of hammer and anvil - between them is individuation.

Symbol of the Dream as a Balance and Wholeness

The word *symbol* is derived from the Greek word *sym*
which means together or with. *Bolon* means
that which has been thrown. The basic meaning is
that which has been thrown together.
In the original Greek usage, *symbol* referred to
the two halves of a coin or stick which
two parties broke between themselves as a pledge
or to prove the identity of the presenter of one part
to the holder of the other.
It was a union of opposites.
The symbol was a tally referring to a missing part
which, when restored, created wholeness,
once broken and forever sought.

So difficult it is to understand a dream that for a long time I have made it a rule, when someone tells me a dream and asks for my opinion, to say first of all to myself: 'I have no idea what this dream means.' After that I can begin to examine the dream.

(Jung, CW 8:533)

Symbol : rock tower above rough sea—unshakable and unyielding strength
Swedish seal c.1700

The ascertainment of the meaning is, I need hardly point out, an entirely arbitrary affair, and this is where the hazards begin. Narrower or wider limits will be set to the meaning, according to one's experience, temperament, and taste. Some people will be satisfied with little, for others much is still not enough. Also the meaning of the dream, or our interpretation of it, is largely dependent on the intentions of the interpreter, on which he expects the meaning to be or requires it to do. In eliciting the meaning he will involuntarily be guided by certain presuppositions, and it depends very much on the scrupulousness and honesty of the investigator whether he gains something by his interpretation or perhaps only becomes still more deeply entangled in his mistakes.

(Jung, CW 10:320)

First Dreams

The first dream reported in psychotherapy, and
particularly the dream which precedes the first appointment,
should be very carefully noted and remembered.

RULE OF THUMB: Initial Dream

Examine an initial dream for evidence of

- the whole ball of wax—
  a capsule symbolic story of the psyche's problem,
- expectations of the treatment and outcome,
- expectations of relationship with the therapist.

In other words, diagnosis, treatment, and prognosis may all be there.

EXAMPLE: An Initial Therapy Dream

A middle-aged professional woman suffered from a major depression.
Her life seemed meaningless and without direction.
Her marriage and her work had become dull and deadened.
She withdrew from friends and sank into isolation.
She decided that what she needed was change—
a change in her job or marriage.
She was offered exactly the kind of job
that she thought she wanted, but she could not take it.
It was as if she was paralyzed, and she
decided to seek my help.
The night before her appointment with me she had a dream.

Dream: It is night and I am crossing a long narrow bridge suspended high over a deep valley. It is only wide enough for one person. I could see that the bridge ahead is unfinished. It came to an abrupt end midway across the valley. I stand looking ahead. Then I hear a buzzing sound from the right side. I look down and note a sound coming from an electrical wire strung along the bridge ending in a light bulb which is not turned on. Beside the light bulb is a switch box. I know that inside the box is a switch and if I turn the switch one way the light will go on, and if I turn it the other way some force will expand the bridge to the other side. While I wonder what I should do, a wind begins to blow. It grows stronger and the bridge sways dangerously. I know that I will have to open the box and make my decision as to which way to turn the switch. I open the box and to my amazement there is a beautiful jewel inside it. I wake up feeling cheerful.

She said that the dream meant hope for her life.
The image of either completing the crossing by a turn of the switch
or illuminating where she was if she turned
it the other way was an encouraging prospect.
Even though she hung suspended, swaying in the wind,
she could see an end.
Energy was in place.
The switch box was at her right side—
the side of consciousness and reality discrimination.
But the extraordinary discovery was
the jewel within.
This was her feminine nature.

The dream encouraged her.
In time she decided neither to change job
nor husband.
Her spirit lit up,
her energy was extended, and the prognosis
of the dream was fulfilled.
The psychological purpose of the depression seemed to have been
to prevent her from making any impetuous life change
and to force her to self-examination
and analysis.

Although I prescribed antidepressant medication for her,
it would have been a cop-out to have called her trouble
"chemical imbalance."
She used her mind, her wits, her chemistry,
and her personality strength to come to
a new understanding of the meaning of her life.

"There is no pill called Salvation"
(said Howard Rome, M.D. of the Mayo Clinic).
But there is salvation
and salvage.

The Final Dream of Therapy

You are not allowed to travel at night,
but you must arrive before daybreak.
(Zen teaching)

Just as the initial dream has unusual significance
so does the final dream in therapy.
It is usually told during the last session.
If treatment has been successful, the dream will be
an obvious gift to the psychotherapist.

If treatment has been helpful but less than expected,
the dream will suggest
what has been learned and what may possibly happen.
If treatment was sham success and the therapist
has deluded himself and misguided the patient,
the dream will lay it all out on the table.
The final dream is likely to be a farewell gift.

EXAMPLE: A Final Dream

Dream: *I am staying at Buckingham Palace in London. After speaking with the Queen I realize that I have been there for a whole month, and it is now time to leave. A soldier stands nearby. He is very handsome and seductive. He hands me his card; it is from the Central Casting Office which he heads.*

It was a grand comic review of her accomplishments.
She dramatized her mother's haughty queenly manner.
She was amused that the man within her,
whom she had previously projected contemptuously on men,
turned out not to be a real soldier hero, guardian of the queen,
but an actor capable of playing many roles as her animus.
Indeed, he was head of his own casting company.
She was now ready to leave the great mother archetype
and go out into the real world of other ordinary people.
Buckingham Palace was to her a
stifling old place.

A dream is nothing but a lucky idea that comes to us from the dark, all-unifying world of the psyche. What would be more natural, when we have lost ourselves amid the endless particulars and isolated details of the world's surface, than to knock at the door of dreams and inquire of them the bearings which would bring us closer to the basic facts of human existence?

(Jung, CW 10:305)

If one believes that the unconscious always knows best, one can easily be betrayed into leaving the dreams to take the necessary decisions, and is then disappointed when the dreams become more and more trivial and meaningless. Experience has shown me that a slight knowledge of dream psychology is apt to lead to an overrating of the unconscious which impairs the power of conscious decision.

(Jung, CW 8:568)

Admonition on Precision

Dream work is hard work.
It is not everyone's cup of tea.
A widespread distrust of dream analysis
is not without some basis in fact.
Not only is its misuse by untrained people
apt to be detrimental,
but, unfortunately, even some trained therapists and analysts
can botch things up.
Bad dream analysis is iatrogenic
of illness,
that is, it is caused by the healer.
But before you point the First Finger Singular at the dream analyst,
remember there may be an unconscious collusion in your wish to harm.
No matter, the therapist should know better.
But even the dream skeptic without any analyst
may find profound meaning from his dreams.

The long journey
is our life quest.
It cannot be comprehended only in terms of the human life span in
the outer world.
Jung wrote:

> Together the patient and I addressed ourselves to the 2,000,000-year-old-man that is in all of us. In the last analysis, most of our difficulties come from losing contact with our instincts, with the age-old unforgotten wisdom stored up in us. And where do we make contact with this old man in us? In our dreams. ("Roosevelt 'Great' in Jung Analysis," *New York Times*, Oct. 4, 1936)

The anthropologist Loren Eiseley in his book, *The Immense Journey,* writes about the evolution of man (pp. 120–121):

> He was becoming something the world had never seen before—a dream

animal—living partially within a secret universe of his own creation and sharing that secret universe in his head with other, similar heads. Symbolic communication had begun. Man had escaped out of the eternal present of the animal world into a knowledge of past and future. The unseen gods, the powers behind the world of phenomenal appearance, began to stalk through his dreams.

Nature, one might say, through the powers of this mind, grossly superstitious though it might be in its naïve examination of wind and water, was beginning to reach out into the dark behind itself. Nature was beginning to evade its own limitations in the shape of this strange, dreaming and observant brain.

Parenthetical Dialogue on the Journey

Question (*patient*): How long does the pilgrimage take?
Answer (*doctor*): It depends on which way you go, and your average speed.
Question: If I go the shortest route?
Answer: Much longer.
Question: Why is that?
Answer: Because pilgrims on that route try to make it faster.
Question: What is the proper time it takes?
Answer: It is not proper to speak of proper, and instead of time perhaps you could speak of perambulation.
Question: You must be kidding—perambulation?
Answer: Would you settle for circumambulation?
Question: I don't know. I never thought of a journey as circumabulation. Sounds like you end up where you started.
Answer: Well? What word would you use?
Question: Words. You mean, use words to find the way like one navigates by the stars, and saunters, shuffles, traipses, staggers, marches, walks, creeps, and crawls, depending on the nature of the way.
Answer: You're shuffling now, aren't you?
Question: Or waddling, swaggering, going hippity-hop, but in the end don't we all go at our own pace?
Answer: And getting there is not so important as the journey.
Question: Do you remember the pilgrim dream I told you last week?
Answer: No. I forgot it. Will you remind me?
Question: I set out for some oriental land like Tibet, and. . . .
Answer: Oh yes. Now I recall. I thought searching to the ends of the world, to the remote mountains had to do with your reaching for a new creative spark within you. In a sense the journey, or pilgrimage, and creativity are the same thing, the ultimate goal we never fully reach.
Question: Can you explain what you are talking about?

PART

VII

Symbolism and Creativity

Symbolism and Creativity

A flower comes from the seed from which the flower comes.
The weed comes from the seed from which the weed comes.

What is the flower and what is the weed
depends upon the subjective inner sense of the beholder.
And where does that come from?
It comes from reflection
and the interrelationship between humans and nature.
It has some basic connections with Chinese yin-yang principle,
from the close of one phase
a new phase begins.
Thus, its culmination, yang goes over into yin,
and what has been positive becomes negative.
Enantiodromia again.

Yin literally means the "dark side"
and *yang* the "sunny side" of the hill,
referring to the light as opposed to the shady side.
In the fourth century B.C. these words were used
philosophically to mean feminine and masculine.
Yin is the dark feminine.
Yang is the light masculine.
The philosophers were *not* implying a triumph
of light over darkness,
but the attainment of a perfect balance
between two interdependent and complementary principles.

And what is creativity?
It is the intuitive reflection of things
apperceived in symbolic expression.

A Chinese verse from the eighth century A.D.
may enlighten us on the nature of reflection:
The wild geese fly across the long sky above.
Their image is reflected upon the chilly water below.
The geese do not mean to cast their images on the water;
Nor does the water mean to hold the image of the geese.
(Chang Chung-yuan, *Creativity and Taoism*, p. 57)

This little poem is a metaphor
of the idea of a reflection as creativity
in an instant of beauty most purely reflected.

In this instant reflection
time is space and space is time,
reflecting the here and now of creation.
This creation can be understood by private reflection.

A person all alone cannot reflect.
A person all alone is empty, devoid of meaning, alienated,
but a person by himself is not alone, but by himself.
A person by herself is beside herself
until she senses in inner reflection
that the nature without is the nature within.

Nature is indeed he or she,
and that individual is humanity and humanity is animal and even
plant and stone and flower and weed and stars.
Alone in sleep we create,
and out of the darkness of sleep we are created.
In the unconscious of day or night
we dream in images that are symbols.
Now and then a voice speaks in metaphor.

In our dreams, symbols arise from the dark depth
of the unconscious and beckon us to search and wonder.
Somewhere from out of this darkness of the mind
our visions come in ceaseless pictures,
weaving stories in the universal language of images
capable of unending interpretations by the ego.
But they fly in the face of reason,
which brands them vague, shadowy, and meaningless,
and are clear and mean something.

In the cosmic in-between,
at the interface of consciousness and unconscious,
of the night of the mind and the day of the head,
symbols spin their cryptic stories.
Dreams play out memories, fantasies, and images
from ages past.

Symbols are stirred by the recollections of the day
connecting past, present, and future
in one panoply.
The ego is here and now.
The dream is then and there,
forming and reforming, changing and yet changeless.

The ancient Chinese said
that there is a point when
the head of a flying arrow neither moves nor stops.
And the Buddhists say "Though things move,
they are forever motionless.
Though things are motionless
they do not cease moving." (Chang Chung-yuan, p. 72)
To comprehend the process of creation
we have to understand, as well, the concept
of the changeless within the ever-changing.

The reflection of creativity
arouses other reflections to be reflected upon
that in turn stimulate ideas, thoughts, and metaphors,
which constellate unconscious symbols
as an echo in the silent deep.
When a powerful thought, memory, or image
grasps our waking mind,
our ego spins round and round to examine it
as if it were a strange sea shell
thrown up on the shore of an island
where we are standing alone.
In the sea of the collective unconscious,
deep below the personal unconscious,
stir tumultuous and momentous archetypal powers.

The impression which the reflecting mind makes
is an act of creation,
a connection of multiplicities.
It is a clue and also a key to questions
that can never be completely answered.
The more powerful the affect image,
the more wondrous the potential act of creation;
when grasped it reverberates in cybernetic cycles.

The ordinary person,
although no one single individual is ever
ordinary in the sense of being an average person,
lets such awareness slip by.
The creative personality is held in the thrall
of the symbols playing in his mind until
within it, he sees visions, myths, fairy tales.
Thus the unconscious messages of Delphic ambiguity,
with the aid of our conscious mind in waking times,

are balancing, correcting, and offering the wisdom of the unconscious
to consciousness.
There is a healing force in the unconscious, autonomous psyche.
In conscious interplay we suddenly discover
we are in possession of a metaphor, an idea, a concept,
a percept, a wisp of a windfall of artistic creation.

In this state we are in the thrall of a
supernatural force.
On the other hand, the insensitive person
takes this experience as something middling,
something ordinary, something to be plucked
from a smorgasbord, strange, and disturbing with
no counterpart in the world of external reality.

In the creative artist's mind this experience sparks
a flame into an act of creation,
into an act of living-art.
It becomes a conscious symbol which guides the artist
through the turmoil of objective life,
gives genuine meaning to pleasure
and unique meaning to the suffering
attendant upon creation and birth.
It has a quality of demonic power.

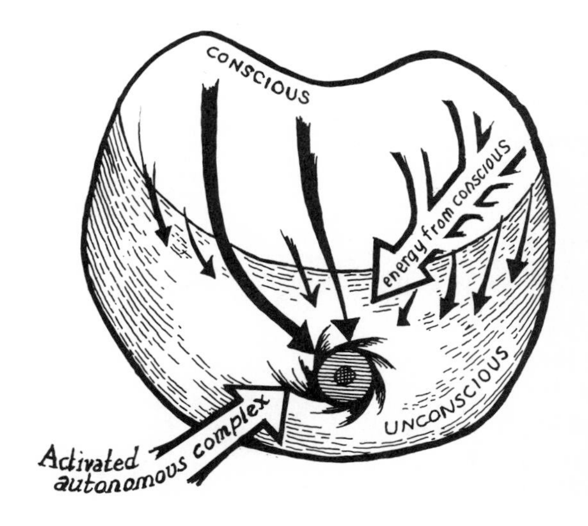

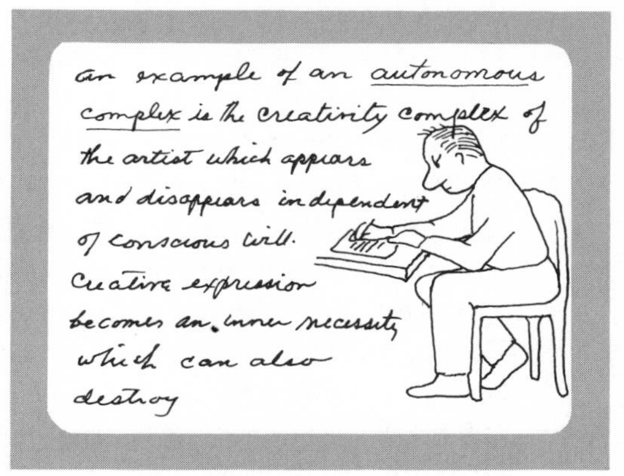

---

26 January 1959

Dear Herr N.,
Best thanks for telling me about the progress of your opus *[N. had illustrated "his individuation process with about 400 pictures" and said that it "needed the constitution of an elephant"]. It does indeed, as you say, make considerable demands on our constitution. It goes to the very limit, but no further. Most people cannot reach their destinies anyway without a streak of craziness, and so long as they haven't it is better not to exorcize their demons. For if one did succeed in doing so it would merely be a successful amputation. . . .*
Wishing you continued good luck and a stout constitution,

Yours sincerely,
C. G. Jung

(Jung, *Collected Letters*, Vol. 2, pp. 479-480)

This symbol, this creativity, this inner subjectivity,
this paradox, this irreconcilable process
is neither crazy nor sane: It just is just as all being is.

In the grasp of genius
this is inspiration for great works—
often born after ponderous doubt and
seeming chaos, and after the mind has overcome
the archetypes of darkness, such as
the trickster who would destroy or paralyze
the artist-creator.

When the spontaneity of the inner child is free from
endless rote, dogma, and the miasma
of neurotic obsessions,
discovery evokes unity and creation or birth
with all the pain and ecstasy that great works conjure
and the depression too.

In the glowing reflection of the marvelous
interconnections of a symbolic life,
one creates what one must, not what one chooses.
Force compels us to move through dark places
speaking the universal language of
the silent voice of humanity
and the metaphors of the collective soul.

Attention to genuine creative persons, geniuses,
those enamored of being creative,
the normal creative child within each of us,
and the muse that says siren-like, "maybe you!".
Attention to you all!
It is often said that the creative person
has nothing to fear from psychotherapy and
from psychoanalysis.

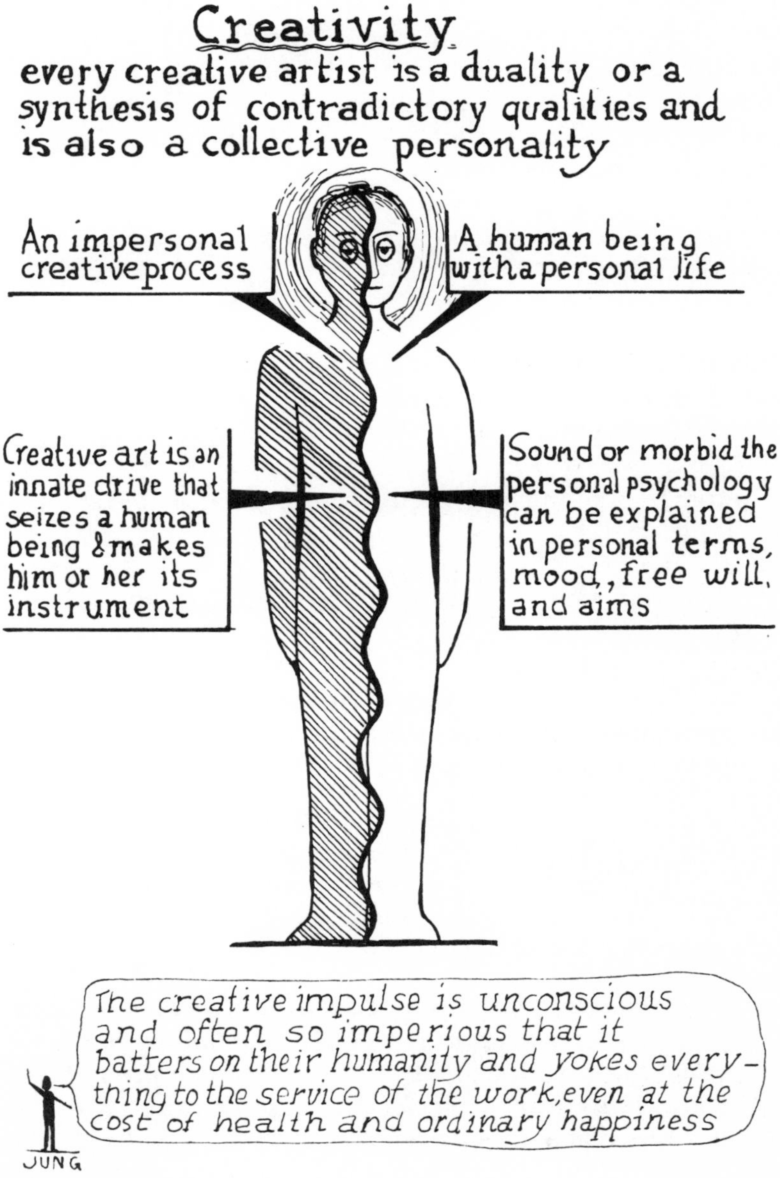

Creativity
every creative artist is a duality or a synthesis of contradictory qualities and is also a collective personality

An impersonal creative process

A human being with a personal life

Creative art is an innate drive that seizes a human being & makes him or her its instrument

Sound or morbid the personal psychology can be explained in personal terms, mood, free will, and aims

The creative impulse is unconscious and often so imperious that it batters on their humanity and yokes everything to the service of the work, even at the cost of health and ordinary happiness

JUNG

Ringing insights, interpretations solemnly intoned,
psychohistoriographing, psychochoreographing,
the finding of meanings behind and hidden behind behind
put the creator in a therapeutic bind.
It is said that creative people need not fear
the analyst's anomalous third ear.
But I tell you, and I tell you clear,
it all depends on whose ear is near to hear.

An Adlerian psychotherapist, who was planning a book
based on the psychoanalysis of important people,
wrote Albert Einstein in Berlin (January 17, 1927)
asking if he would submit to psychoanalysis.
In Einstein's papers a copy of this letter was found,
and in his handwriting he replied,
I regret that I cannot accede to your request, because I should like very much to remain in the darkness of not having been psychoanalyzed.
(Dukas and Hoffman, p.35)

We can describe the creative process.

- This is what happened.
- This is how it was done.
- This is the creation.
- There is the creative person.

But, the actual happening and the inner mysterious catalyst,
what was that?
There is no way of actually knowing.
We cannot recreate a creative event in a laboratory.
Perhaps some model will evolve
through artificial intelligence,
but the spark that created the model, what was that?
The final explanation will always elude us.

Jung and Freud were both convinced beyond doubt that
there was no way the psychologist would find out
what creativity actually is in the creative genius.
Nonetheless, the creative spark, real and would-be,
will blow the Promethean fire of explanations.

Whatever the psychologist has to say about art will be confined to the process of artistic creation and has nothing to do with its innermost essence. He can no more explain this than the intellect can describe or even understand the nature of feeling. Indeed, art and science would not exist as separate entities at all if the fundamental difference between them had not long since forced itself on the mind.

(Jung, CW 15:99)

If a work of art is explained in the same way as a neurosis, then either the work of art is a neurosis or a neurosis is a work of art. This explanation is all very well as a play on words, but common sense rebels against putting a work of art on the same level as a neurosis. An analyst might, in an extreme case, view a neurosis as work of art through the lens of his professional bias, but it would never occur to an intelligent layman to mistake a pathological phenomenon for art, in spite of the undeniable fact that a work of art arises from much the same psychological condition as a neurosis. This is only natural, because certain of these conditions are present in every individual and, owing to the relative constancy of the human environment, are constantly the same, whether in the case of a nervous intellectual, a poet, or a normal human being. All have parents, all have a father- or a mother-complex, all know about sex and therefore have certain common and typical human difficulties.

(Jung, CW 15:100)

There is a whirlwind inside each one of us.
We know it by the storm it brews,
by the misty column of white energy
that rises in the open-minded skies.
The whirlwind eddies in dreams and visions,
in brainstorms, and brilliant flashing thoughts.
It comes out of the blue.
Farsighted world-changing discoveries have been made
by scientists who found the answer in dreams.
Writers, poets, artists, composers know
the power of the muse.
And they have also paid the price in torment
and divine discontent of the creative instinct.
Misery, darkness, and evil lurk in the depth of each one of us,
but in the garrets of creativity
there is inevitable suffering.
There is no glorious goodness that is creativity.

The personality of the creative person is merely
an epiphenomenon, an accidental element
in the great creative spirits.
No amount of psychoanalysis of the unconscious of artists
has revealed what creativity is.
To say that it is a mystery,
that it is an ultimate expression of the self or the Godhead,
is only marginally helpful.

The life history of the artist is fascinating material
for analysts, biographers, historians, and philosophers.

But there is a pedestrian banality
within these expositions.
There is left the truth of the "wings of the wind,"*
and an Eastern mystical view which says,

> *Just as the pure and fragrant lotus flower grows out of the mud of a swamp rather than out of the clean loam of an upland field, so from the muck of worldly passions springs the pure Enlightenment.*
>
> (*The Teachings of Buddha*, p. 124)

We are all born from mothers.
The great mother archetype is a symbol of creativity.
The devouring mother archetype is a symbol of destruction.
What creates can kill.
What poisons can heal.
The therapist is a midwife to birth and rebirth
and partakes of some of the pain of this occasion,
even though he does not know,
and this not knowing is his great wisdom.

---

*"He was seen upon the wings of the wind." 2 Samuel 22:11.
"He did fly upon the wings of the wind." Psalms 18:10.

I look out my window and say, "Where is the sun?"
I know, of course, where it is.
It is where it always is, out there in the sky.
What I am saying is,
"I see only clouds hiding the sun."
But I know it is there; I can feel its warmth.
And the clouds are bright.
I close my eyes to see.
It is a good thing to do now and then
except when crossing streets and/or dogmatic people.

Creation of the It

The creative juices flow with conception.
The inner process grows with gestation.
Barring miscarriage and abortion,
the labor comes at its own sweet, prescribed time,
and the delivery is miraculous with
each creator's creation.
But even when it sees the light of day,
it must be nourished and helped to grow
until it is on its own
and completes the cycle.

But, of course, the creative person can be whole, balanced, and lead a quite satisfactory life. The creative process itself being the healing factor.
Jung said that the secret of creativeness is a transcendental problem we cannot answer, but can only describe, and that the creative personality is a riddle we cannot answer.

The artist's creativity is an innate instinct which
takes hold of him and monopolizes all of his energy.
There isn't much left over for life.
Conscious personality is dominated by the unconscious
and splits the artist into a duality,
so that he is at odds with himself;
his passion for creation and his longing
for ordinary rewards of life are irreconcilable.

The psychology of the artist cannot be understood
through the psychology of his art.
The work is the unique product of a unique individual,
but the secret of the creative process
cannot be revealed through the psychoanalysis of
his life or his art or both taken together,
countless books to the contrary.

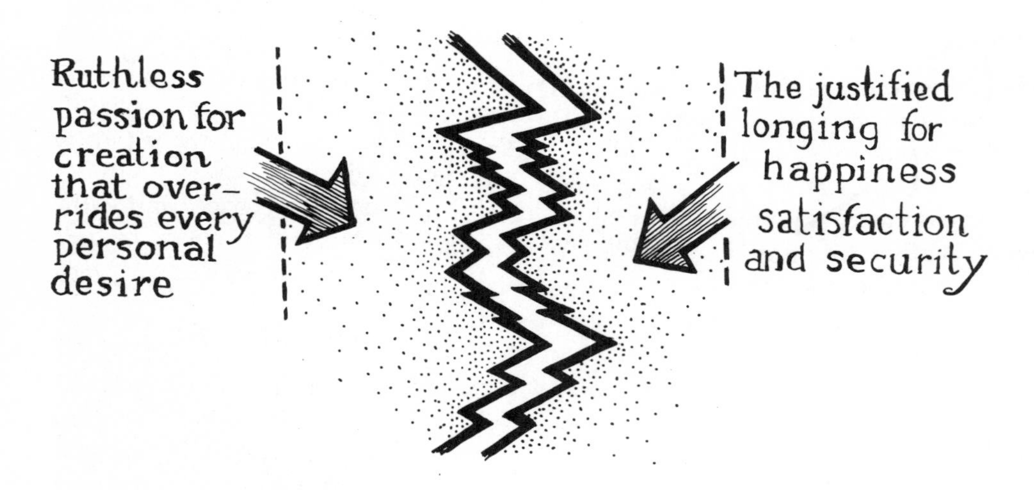

(The special peculiarity of great works of art
is that they are beyond the personal psyche.)
Creativity, what is that anyway?
Originality, that too?
Discovery of patterns previously unseen, that also?
Are not we all creative, at least in our dreams?
Is it possible to divide creativity into
the great and the not-great?
Are these not judgments of history,
and history changes?
Lots of questions, really that's the point.
Is it?

Physiognomic Lightning

Watercolor painting by Paul Klee, 1927:
"'The middle realm is actively struck.' Two heterogeneous elements enter into relation with one another; the tension between them brings out the movement, in contrast to the 'adaptation by evasion.' On the form of lightning Klee notes, around 1927: 'The wonderful thing about lightning is the broken form in the atmospheric medium.'"

(Klee, "The Thinking Eye," p. 330)

Creativity seems so automatic, almost dark, helpless, like "Let the unconscious do it!"-- maybe out of darkness comes light.
You are so right - except that you dont "Let the unconscious do anything. It just does its thing- but why does this happen?
Whenever conscious life becomes one-sided or adopts a false attitude - then archetypal images instinctively rise to the surface in dreams, & in visions of artists and seers to restore the psychic balance of the individual or of the epoch
JUNG

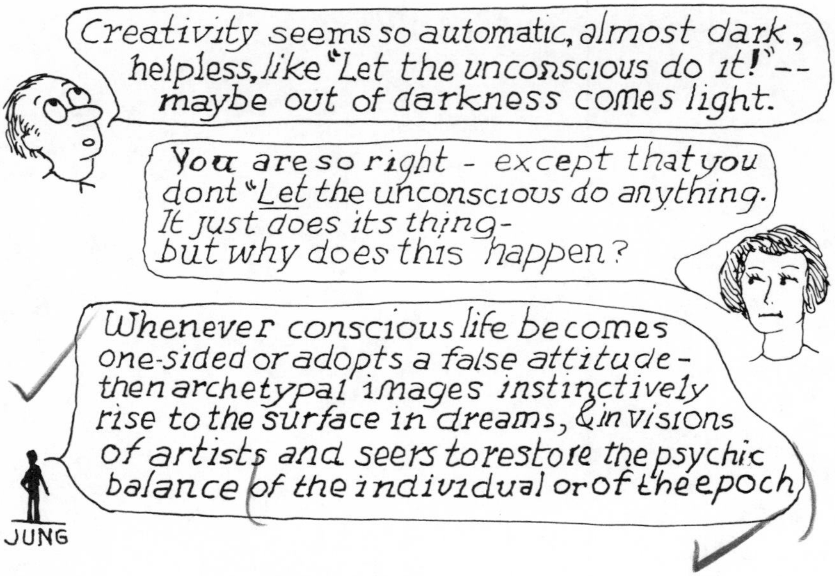

Maybe.
Psychotherapy can help creative people
when their psyche needs attention.
Psychotherapy for creative persons is no different
from the psychotherapy of any other human being.
It can free the individual from destructive unconscious forces
by decreasing neurotic obstruction
to originality and to being one's own person,
following one's own law, and valuing one's own truth.
Psychotherapy for creative people is likely
to reach into the world of archetypes.
The understanding of practical Jung in such cases
will stand you in good stead.

Through geniuses and truly great artists,
poets, musicians, and performers,
we see that
the flower comes from the seed from which the flower comes, and
the weed comes from the seed from which the weed comes.
What is the flower and what is the weed
depends upon the subjective inner sense of the beholder.
And where does that come from?
It comes from reflection,
and the interrelationship between human beings and nature.

CREATIVITY

The creative urge lives and grows in one like a tree in the earth from which it draws its nourishment.

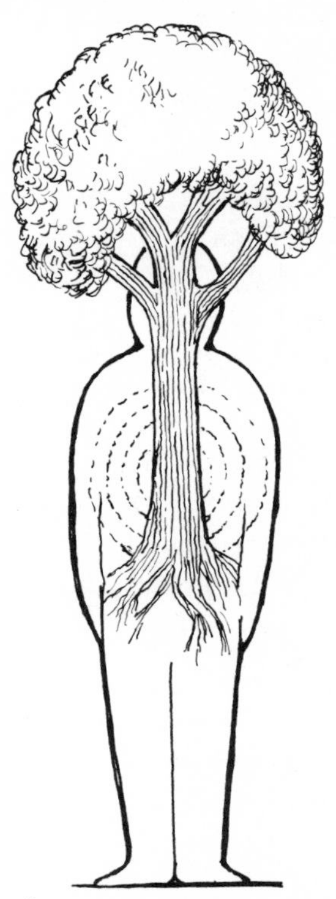

This living thing is an autonomous complex – a split off part of the psyche that leads to its own life outside the hierarchy of consciousness.

Well now I've seen everything!

"We spoke of a work of art as a tree growing out of the nourishing soil, we might equally well have compared it to a child growing in the womb. But all comparisons are lame." (Jung, CW 15:122)

RULE OF THUMB

You cannot ever step in the same
river even once.

Plutarch: *According to Heraclitus one cannot step twice into the same river, nor can one grasp any moral substance in a stable condition, but by the intensity and rapidity of change it scatters and again gathers. Or rather, not again nor later but at the same time it forms and dissolves, and approaches and departs.*

Cratylus, Heraclitus's disciple, denied that you could even step into the river once, since you are changing too.

(Kahn, *The Art and Thought of Heraclitus*, p.168)

If there is such a thing as an animal body, there is also a spiritual body. It is in this sense that Scripture says, "The first man, Adam, became the animate being," whereas the last Adam has become a life-giving spirit. Observe, the spiritual does not come first, the animal body comes first, and then the spiritual. The first man was made "of dust of the earth": the second man is from heaven. The man made of dust is the pattern of all men of dust, and the heavenly man is the pattern of all the heavenly. As we have worn the likeness of the man made of dust, so we shall wear the likeness of the heavenly man.

(1 *Corinthians* 15: 45-50)

"In judging my writings, I can only remark that I have written every book with the utmost responsibility, that I have been honest and that I have pointed out facts which remain valid. I would not want to withdraw any of my publications and I stand by all that I have written." (*Letters* III, February 17, 1961, four months before his death).
C.G. Jung died on June 6, 1961 in Küsnacht.
The gravestone of the family grave in Küsnacht carries the inscription:
PRIMUS HOMO DE TERRA TERRENUS
SECUNDUS HOMO DE CAELO CAELESTIS
(I Corinthians 15:47)

Bibliography

Ackerknecht, E. H. 1966. *The World of Asclepios: A History of Medicine in Objects.* Bern: Verlag Hans Huber.

Auden, W. H., and L. Kronenberger. 1962. *Viking Book of Aphorisms.* New York: Viking.

Bijak of Kabir. 1983. *Parabola: Words of Power.* Vol. VIII, #3. Rev. by J. S. Hawley.

Bryson, B. 1982. *American Way* (Publication of American Airlines). May.

(Buddha). *The Teachings of Buddha.* 1984. Buddhist Promoting Foundation. Tokyo: Kosaido Printing Co., Ltd.

Chamberlin, T. C. 1965. "The Method of Multiple Working Hypotheses." *Science* 148:754-9 (reprint from 1890).

Chang Chung-yuan. 1970. *Creativity and Taoism: A Study of Chinese Philosophy, Arts, and Poetry.* New York: Harper & Row.

Chapman, W. 1965. *Antarctic Conquest: Great Explorers in Their Own Words.* Indianapolis, IN: Bobbs-Merrill Co.

Dalai Lama. 1985. "Fullness of Emptiness." *Parabola* 10:6-19.

Dukas, H., and B. Hoffmann. 1979. *Albert Einstein, the Human Side.* Princeton: Princeton University Press.

Edinger, E. F. 1972. *Ego and Archetype: Individuation and the Religious Function of the Psyche.* New York: G. P. Putnam's Sons.

Eiseley, L. 1957. *The Immense Journey.* New York: Vintage Books.

Eliot, C. W., ed. 1909. *The Meditations of Marcus Aurelius.* Harvard Classics. Vol. 2. New York: P. F. Collier & Son.

Fenichel, O. 1945. *The Psychoanalytic Theory of Neurosis.* New York: W. W. Norton.

Freud, S. 1953. *The Standard Edition of the Complete Psychological Works of Sigmund Freud.* Vol. 4. *The Interpretation of Dreams.* (1900). J. Strachey, ed. in collaboration with A. Freud. London: Hogarth Press.

Fuller, E., ed. 1943. *Thesaurus of Epigrams.* New York: Crown Publishers.

Funk and Wagnall's Standard Dictionary of Folklore, Mythology, and Legend. 1984. M. Leach and J. Fried, eds. New York: Harper & Row.

Guggenbühl-Craig, A. 1971. *Power in the Helping Profession.* New York: Spring.

__________. 1982. *Soul and Money.* Dallas: Spring Publications.

Hannah, B. 1955. "Ego and Shadow." London: Guild of Pastoral Psychology Lecture 85. March (reprinted May 1963).
Hoffer, E. 1955. *The Passionate State of Mind, and Other Aphorisms.* New York: Harper & Row.
__________. 1963 *Ordeal of Change.* New York: Harper & Row.
__________. 1976. in *Family Weekly.* October 17.
__________. 1979. *Before the Sabbath.* New York: Harper & Row.
__________. 1982. *Soul and Money.* Dallas: Spring Publications.

Jung, C. G. *Collected Works of C. G. Jung* [cited *passim* in text as *CW*]. Bollingen Series XX, Vols. 1-18. Princeton: Princeton University Press.
__________. *Letters* [cited *passim* in text as *Collected Letters*]. G. Adler and A. Jaffé, eds. R. F. C. Hull, trans. Bollingen Series XCV, Vol. 1. Princeton: Princeton University Press.
__________. 1939-1941. *Interpretations of Visions—Notes on Seminars in Analytic Psychology Given by C. G. Jung, Autumn 1930–Winter 1934.* Vols. 1-11. Zurich: Multigraphed Typescripts. New Edition, M. Foote, ed.
__________. 1962. *Foreword* to *The Secret of the Golden Flower.* New York: Harcourt, Brace & World, Inc.
__________. 1971. *The Portable Jung.* J. Campbell, ed., R. F. C. Hull, trans. New York: Viking Press.
__________. 1975. *Centenary Brochure.* Zurich: Curatorium of C. G. Jung Institute.
__________. 1984. *Dream Analysis: Notes of the Seminars Given in 1928–1930.* 1984. W. McGuire, ed. Princeton: Princeton University Press.
__________. and W. Pauli. 1955. *The Interpretation of Nature and the Psyche.* New York: Pantheon.

Kahn, C. 1979. *The Art and Thought of Heraclitus.* Cambridge: Cambridge University Press.
Klee, P. 1927. "The Thinking Eye." *Documents of Modern Art* (1964), Vol. 15. J. Spiller, ed. New York: George Wittenborn, Inc.

Main, T. F. "The Ailment." *British Journal of Medical Psychology* 30:129-145.
McGuire, W., ed. 1974. *The Freud/Jung Letters.* Princeton: Princeton University Press.
__________. and R. F. C. Hull, eds. 1977. *C. G. Jung Speaking: Interviews and Encounters.* Bollingen Series XCVII. Princeton: Princeton University Press.
Meier, C. A. 1967. *Ancient Incubation and Modern Psychotherapy.* Evanston, IL: Northwestern University Press.
Mencken, H. L. 1949. *A Mencken Crestomathy.* New York: Alfred A. Knopf.
Mott, M. 1984. *The Seven Mountains of Thomas Merton.* Boston: Houghton Mifflin.

Ortega y Gasset, J. 1963. *Man and People.* New York: W. W. Norton.
Osler, Sir W. 1951. "A Way of Life." *Selected Writings of Sir William Osler.* London: Oxford University Press.
Oxford Classical Dictionary. 1964. London: Oxford University Press.
Oxford English Dictionary. Compact ed. 1984. London: Oxford University Press.

Rank, O. 1964. *The Myth of the Birth of the Hero, and Other Writings.* Ed. P. Freund. New York: Vintage.
Richards, P., and J. J. Banigan. 1942. *How To Abandon Ship.* New York: Cornell Maritime Press.

Schopenhauer, A. 1974. *Parerga and Paralipomena: Short Philosophical Essays.* E. F. J. Payne, trans. Oxford: Clarendon.
Solzhenitsyn, A. I. 1974. *The Gulag Archipelago, 1918–1956.* New York: Harper & Row.
Strunk, W., Jr., and E. B. White. 1979. *The Elements of Style.* New York: Macmillan Publishing Co.
Suzuki, D. T. 1956. *Zen Buddhism.* W. Barret, ed. Garden City, NY: Doubleday Anchor Books.
__________. 1972. *What is Zen?* New York: Harper & Row.

Tabori, P. 1959. *The Natural History of Stupidity.* Philadelphia: Chilton Company Publishers.

Wheelwright, P. 1968. *Metaphor and Reality.* Bloomington, IN: Indiana University Press.
Wilhelm, R., trans. 1962. *The Secret of the Golden Flower: A Chinese Book of Life.* Foreword and Commentary by C. G. Jung. (C. G. Baynes, trans. from German). New York: Harcourt, Brace & World.
Wilmer, H. 1941. *Huber the Tuber: A Story of Tuberculosis.* New York: National Tuberculosis Association.
__________. 1958. *Social Psychiatry in Action.* Springfield, IL: Charles C. Thomas.
__________. 1964. "Odyssey of a Psychotherapist." *Science* 145:903 (Aug.).
__________. 1985. "War Dreams, A Decade After Vietnam." *Vietnam in Remission,* J. Veninga and H. Wilmer, eds. College Station, TX: Texas A & M University Press.
__________. 1986. "Combat Nightmares: Toward a Therapy of Violence." *Spring: An Annual of Archetypal Psychology and Jungian Thought* pp. 120-159.
__________. 1986. "The Healing Nightmare." *Quadrant:47-62.* Spring.
Wilson, R. A. 1982. "Mere Coincidence?" *Science Digest* 90:1, 80-85, 95 (Jan.).

Illustration Credits

Cover and p. 81: Matthews, W. H. *Mazes and Labyrinths: Their History and Development*. Copyright © 1970 Dover Publications, Inc.
Frontispiece: Reprinted with permission from C. G. Jung, *Word and Image*. A. Jaffé, ed. Bollingen Series XCVIII. Vol. 2. Copyright © 1979 by Princeton: Princeton University Press.
Page:
1 © The Roy Export Company Establishment.
4 (*top l.*) UPI/Bettman Newsphotos.
4 (*top r.*) AP/Wide World Photos.
4 (*lwr l.*) with permission from Dover Publications; Isabelle S. Sayers, *Annie Oakley and Buffalo Bill's Wild West*.
5 David Rubinger/Time Magazine.
6 Billy Rose Theatre Collection, The New York Public Library at Lincoln Center; Astor, Lenox and Tilden Foundations. From Universal Pictures, *W. C. Fields and Me*.
7 (*top*) Nikolaus Schwabe, with permission of the Curatorium of the C. G. Jung Institüt, Küsnacht.
7 (*bottom*) © Eric Lindblom from Padma Perera, "Guruji," *Parabola*, August 1984.
8 (*top*) George Tames/NYT Pictures.
8 (*bottom*) AP/Wide World Photos.
10 Reprinted with permission from *Humanities* © The National Endowment for the Humanities, Washington, D. C.
11 (*bottom*) AP/Wide World Photos.
27 (*top l.*) Harter, J., ed. *Women: A Pictorial Archive from Nineteenth Century Sources*. Copyright © 1978 Dover Publications, Inc.
27 (*top r.*) Harter, J., ed. *Men: A Pictorial Archive from Nineteenth Century Sources*. Copyright © 1980 Dover Publications, Inc.
27 (*bottom ctr.*) Photo from advertisement "Kong" by ProForm 1983.
32 Drawing by M. Stevens; © 1983 New York Magazine, Inc.
37 (*top r., lwr. l.*) E. Lehner. *Symbols, Signs, and Signets*. Copyright © 1950 Dover Publications, Inc. (p. 52).
37 (*ctr. r.*) *Dover Pictorial Archive Catalogue*. New York: Dover Publications, Inc.
42 *Pictorial Calligraphy and Ornamentation*, selected by E. V. Gillon. Copyright © 1972 Dover Publications, Inc.
44 "Beatrice" by Gustave Doré, reprinted from *Doré: Illustrations for Dante's Divine Comedy*. New York: Dover Publications, Inc.
48 Drawing by Stevenson; © 1983 The New Yorker Magazine, Inc.
50 Reprinted by permission of the artist, © 1983 Clarence Brown, from the *Saturday Review*.
51 Drawing by Lorenz; © 1973 The New Yorker Magazine, Inc.
55 Reprinted with permission from *Humanities* © The National Endowment for the Humanities, Washington, D. C.
65 Lehner, E. *Symbols, Signs, and Signets*. Copyright © 1950 Dover Publications, Inc.
68 With permission from the Minnesota Historical Society.
82 and 83 *Dover Pictorial Archive Catalogue*. New York: Dover Publications, Inc.
86 (*t. and b.*) Thompson, Sir D'Arcy. 1942. *On Growth and Form*. Reprinted with permission from Cambridge University Press.
87 (*left*) *Dover Pictorial Archive Catalogue*. New York: Dover Publications, Inc.
87 (*right*) Foto Musei Capitolini (Barbara Malter), Rome.
88 C. G. Jung. CW 12:126.
91 C. G. Jung. CW 12:82.
92 *Dover Pictorial Archive Catalogue*. New York: Dover Publications, Inc.
135, 144 *Pictorial Calligraphy and Ornamentation*, selected by E. V. Gillon. Copyright © 1972 Dover Publications, Inc.
146 Illustration by Knight, Naval Medical Research Center, 1957, Bethesda, MD. Negative NH-6-(1) 3857:12 U.S. Navy.
150 *Dover Pictorial Archive Catalogue*. New York: Dover Publications, Inc.
173 Thompson, Sir D'Arcy. 1942. *On Growth and Form*. Reprinted with permission from Cambridge University Press.
187 Copyright © by Universal City Studios, Inc. Courtesy of MCA Publishing Rights, a Division of MCA Inc.
188 Logo, C. G. Jung Institute of San Francisco; designed by Joseph Henderson, M. D.

209 With permission from *Harter's Picture Archive for Collage and Illustration*, J. Harter, ed. Copyright © 1978 Dover Publications, Inc.
211 Drawing by S. Gross; © 1984 The New Yorker Magazine, Inc.
214 From the *Wall Street Journal*. Permission, Cartoon Features Syndicate.
241 *Pictorial Calligraphy and Ornamentation*, selected by E. V. Gillon. 1972. © New York: Dover Publications, Inc.
265 Permission of Mr. and Mrs. Daniel Saidenberg, New York City.
269 Nikolaus Schwabe, with permission of the Curatorium of the C. G. Jung Institüt, Küsnacht.

Index